EVOLUTIONARY PSYCHOLOGY

Alan Clamp

EVOLUTIONARY PSYCHOLOGY

Alan Clamp

Hodder & Stoughton

A MEMBER OF THE HODDER HEADLINE GROUP

ACKNOWLEDGEMENTS

I would like to thank Russell Hill and Emma Creighton for their helpful comments on the manuscript. I would also like to thank Tim Gregson-Williams and Greig Aitken for their patience, help and guidance.

British Library Cataloguing in Publication Data
A catalogue record for this title is available from The British Library

ISBN 0 340 72072 7

First published 2001
Impression number 10 9 8 7 6 5 4 3 2 1
Year 2005 2004 2003 2002 2001

Typeset by Dorchester Typesetting Group Ltd, Dorchester, Dorset.
Printed in Great Britain for Hodder & Stoughton Educational, a division of Hodder Headline Plc, 338 Euston Road, London NW1 3BH
by The Bath Press Ltd.

DEDICATION

To 'Algy'. Have a wonderful life. Love Daddy X.

CONTENTS

Part 4: Cognition

Part 5: Darwinian medicine

PREFACE

The aim of this book is to provide an introduction to the area of evolutionary psychology. In order to do this, I have divided the book into five parts. The first, *The evolutionary approach*, comprises three chapters. In Chapter 1, I consider the application of Darwinian ideas on evolution to human behaviour. Chapter 2 deals with cultural evolution and examines the way in which biological and cultural evolution may have interacted to produce human nature. Chapter 3 looks at issues and debates in evolutionary psychology.

Part 2, *Sexual selection*, consists of three chapters. Chapter 4 discusses mating strategies and social organisation and seeks to explain why different mating strategies exist. Chapter 5 considers the issue of parent-offspring conflict in humans. Chapter 6 is concerned with the nature of sexual selection in humans, examining mate choice, sexuality, and the wide variety of activities that form part of our sexual behaviour.

Part 3, *Prosocial and antisocial behaviour*, comprises three chapters. Chapter 7 deals with the nature of altruism and how it may have evolved. In Chapter 8, I consider the evolutionary psychology view of aggression and examine theories of aggressive behaviour, sex differences in aggression, ritualised aggression and conflict between groups. Chapter 9 examines the evidence for a biological basis to criminal behaviour, and considers evolutionary psychology explanations of two of the most severe crimes: murder and rape.

Part 4, *Cognition*, consists of three chapters. Chapter 10 looks at how evolutionary psychology can improve our understanding of the processes involved in learning. In Chapter 11, I discuss the various theories which seek to account for the evolution of human intelligence. Chapter 12 examines the case for an evolutionary psychology view of language; that humans are born with a 'language instinct'.

Part 5, *Darwinian medicine*, comprises three chapters. Chapter 13 considers the evolution of infectious diseases. In Chapter 14, I look at the nature of anxiety and eating disorders from an evolutionary viewpoint. The final chapter, Chapter 15, examines evolutionary explanations of two further mental disorders: depression and schizophrenia.

I believe that this book covers the major aspects of evolutionary psychology as it would be taught on most courses, including A level and undergraduate courses. For the purposes of revision, I have included detailed summaries of the information that is presented in each chapter. Although I have not included a separate glossary, the Index contains page numbers in **bold** which refer to definitions and main explanations of particular concepts for easy reference.

PART 1
The evolutionary approach

THE DARWINIAN PARADIGM

Introduction and overview

Evolutionary psychology may be defined as the application of Darwinian ideas of evolution to human behaviour. This approach assumes that human nature has been shaped by natural selection and it is a recent development of *sociobiology*, which attempts to explain all social behaviour (in both humans and non-human animals) in terms of evolutionary and other biological principles. However, evolutionary psychology is more flexible than sociobiology as it takes into account the role of the mind in mediating the links between genes and human behaviour. Dennett (1996) describes this approach as a 'marriage of sociobiology and cognitive psychology' (Figure 1.1). Evolutionary psychologists also stress the role of the mind in assessing the prevailing environmental conditions. Variations in these conditions produce variations in behaviour. This is due to the mind's role in weighing up the costs and benefits of the potential range of behaviours in order to select that which is optimal in the circumstances. The strategies used by the mind to assess costs and benefits have evolved through natural selection.

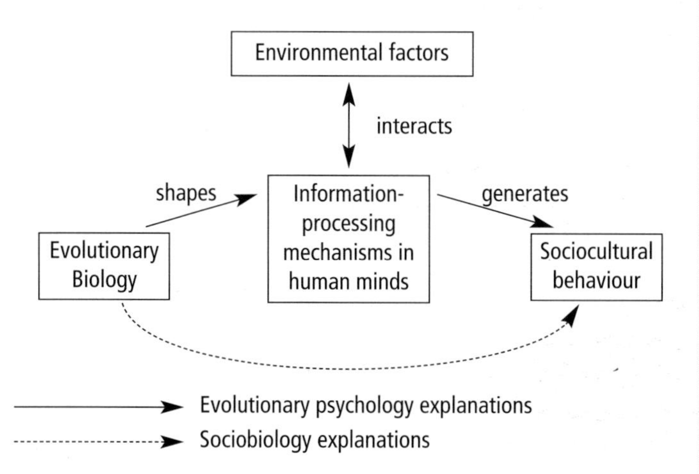

Figure 1.1 Evolutionary psychology: the marriage of sociobiology and cognitive psychology

According to evolutionary psychology, the human mind has been shaped by natural selection to solve problems faced by our ancestors. The evolution of human social behaviour has been adapted for the prehistoric environment in which we lived as hunter-gatherers, known as the *environment of evolutionary adaptedness (EEA)* (Davies, 1995). Despite enormous changes in our lifestyle over the last 100,000 years, we may still possess a Stone Age mind inside a modern skull (Figure 1.2). As a result, the environmental assessment strategies mentioned in the previous paragraph may not be ideally designed for contemporary western culture. In other words, our prehistoric mind may not have the flexibility to cope optimally with modern environments. For example, most of us enjoy the taste of foods which are high in salt, fat and sugars. This trait may have been useful in the Pleistocene era (the geological period equivalent to the EEA), when such foods were in short supply and our cravings drove us to

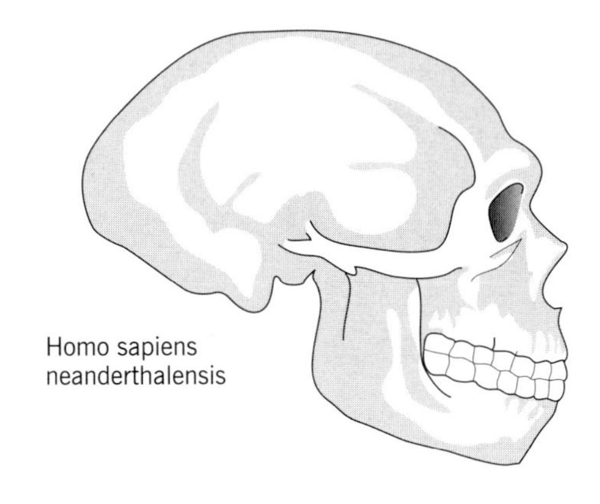

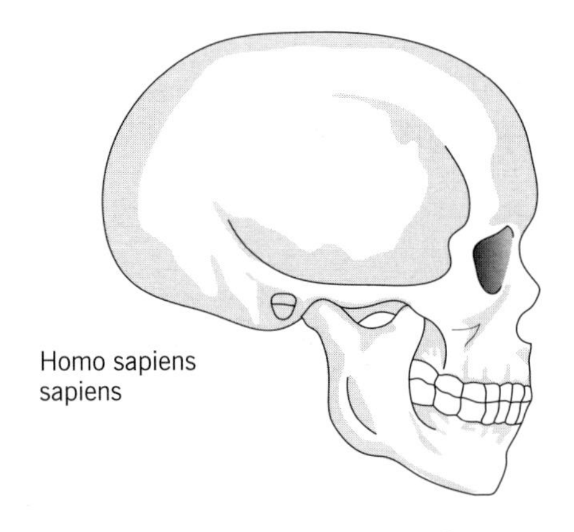

Figure 1.2 The skull of *Homo sapiens* has changed considerably over the last 100,000 years, but has the mind within it?

Copyright: Illustrated London News.

search for more. However, these tastes are now maladaptive in most developed countries, where fast foods high in salt, fat and processed carbohydrates are readily available, with deleterious health consequences, such as coronary heart disease and tooth decay.

Evolutionary psychology uses Darwinian concepts to generate testable hypotheses about human behaviour, based on the assumption that individuals will act in a way that tends to propagate their genes. According to Plotkin (1995), a true and complete understanding of the mind has to include an evolutionary perspective. Chomsky (1975) suggested that our psychological architecture should contain 'mental organs' for the same reason that the rest of the body contains physical organs, and that they evolved in a similar manner. For example, if thre was a reliable correlation over evolutionary time between the movement of human facial muscles and emotional state, we might expect specialised mechanisms to evolve that infer a person's mental state from their facial expression. Recent evidence suggests that we do have mechanisms specialised for 'reading' facial expressions of emotion (Etcoff, 1986). However, not all human behaviour represents an adaptation for survival or reproduction. Furthermore, just because a certain behaviour is considered adaptive, it does not mean that it is developmentally unchangeable or socially desirable (see Chapter 9, on evolutionary explanations of criminal behaviour).

In order to examine the evolutionary approach to psychology, it is necessary to understand Charles Darwin's theory of evolution. The first part of this book (Chapters 1-3) considers Darwinian explanations of evolution, the idea of cultural evolution, and limitations of the evolutionary approach. In these early chapters, although humans remain a central concern, numerous references will be made to the behaviour of non-human animals. Darwin believed that the study of animal behaviour would throw light on human psychology and examples from other species are useful in demonstrating the foundations of evolutionary theory.

Figure 1.3 Charles Darwin in old age. His theory of evolution by natural selection forms the basis of evolutionary psychology

Copyright: Hodder & Stoughton.

Evolution

Evolution in biological terms is the process by which new species arise as the result of gradual changes to the genetic make-up of existing species over long periods of time. The father of evolutionary theory was Charles Darwin (Figure 1.3), and an understanding of his theory of evolution by natural selection is fundamental to the study of evolutionary psychology. Although far-reaching in its effects, this theory is actually quite simple and can be summarised as shown in Box 1.1.

Nature versus nurture

How much of the variability within humans is due to genetic factors and how much depends upon the influence of the environment? This *nature* (inherited characteristics) versus *nurture* (acquired characteristics) debate has been hotly contested in biology and psychology. However, although certain features may fall neatly into one of these two categories, the question of whether learning or evolution underlie any given behaviour is largely meaningless. Any behaviour, however simple or complex, has both an element of inheritance and learning about it (the interaction of which is known as *penetrance*). The only point of debate is over the relative importance of the contributions made to a behaviour by *phylogeny* (inherited, species-specific behaviour patterns) and *ontogeny* (behaviour patterns acquired during the lifetime of the individual, which are not shared with every member of the species). The importance of this, as far as this book is concerned, is that a great deal of human behaviour appears to have some genetic component, and is therefore capable of being influenced by the processes of evolution.

Box 1.1 A summary of Darwin's theory

1 All species tend to produce very many more offspring than can ever survive. For example, Darwin calculated that after 750 years, the descendants of one pair of elephants could number more than 19 million. However, the size of populations tends to remain more-or-less constant, meaning that most of these offspring must die. It also follows that there must be competition for resources such as mates, food and territories. Therefore, there is a 'struggle for existence' among individuals.

2 Individuals within a species differ from one another (**variation**). Much of this variability is inherited (**genetic variation**).

3 Competition for resources, together with variation between individuals, means that certain members of the population are more likely to survive and reproduce than others. These individuals will inherit the characteristics of their parents and evolutionary change takes place through natural selection. Over a long period of time this process may lead to the considerable differences now observed between living organisms. It is important to remember that for natural selection to drive evolutionary change, the environment must select certain individuals *and* the differences between individuals must be (to some extent) inherited. Without these two factors, evolution is not likely to occur.

What causes genetic variation?

One of the major sources of genetic variation is the process of sexual reproduction. In species which reproduce sexually, offspring inherit 50% of their genetic information from the male parent and 50% from the female parent. This genetic information is in the form of discrete units, known as genes. Offspring of the same parents are genetically different from each other, and from their parents, because they all inherit different combinations of genes (unless they happen to be monozygotic or 'identical' twins). This process means that humans have the potential to produce a *minimum* of 70,000,000,000,000 (7×10^{13}) genetically different offspring.

A second source of genetic variation, which could increase the potential number of different offspring indicated above, is *mutation*. A mutation is defined as any sudden change in the genotype (genetic make-up) of an organism. Mutations are relatively rare, occurring at a natural rate of one per 100,000 genes in each generation. However, this rate may be increased by so-called 'mutagens', which include ionising radiation such as X-rays or UV light, or chemicals such as caffeine. Most mutations are disadvantageous, but a few confer a selective advantage on the individual and may spread through populations. Other potential sources of genetic variation include *genetic drift* (random fluctuations in gene frequency which usually only occur in small populations), and *migration* into or out of populations.

The evidence for evolution

Darwin's theory of evolution by natural selection is supported by evidence from 4 main areas. These are shown in Box 1.2.

Box 1.2 The evidence supporting Darwin's theory

1 Palaeontology: fossil records indicate clear evidence for evolution, particularly for the vertebrates (animals with backbones). The most convincing evidence is found in cases where, in successive rock layers from the same locality, a series of fossils exhibit gradual change.
2 Comparative anatomy: when the anatomy of one group of animals is compared with that of another, resemblances are generally more obvious than differences. One example of this is the pentadactyl ('five digit') limb, which is found in various forms in all animals. Comparing the physiology or embryology (development of the embryo) of species also provides evidence for evolution by natural selection.
3 Geographical distribution: places with the same climatic conditions in different regions of the world do not always possess the same animal forms. Elephants, for example, live in India and Africa, but not in South America. This phenomenon is best explained by assuming that existing animals are the descendants of extinct populations which were of a more generalised type. These ancestors were dispersed from their place of origin, became geographically isolated (for example, by sea or mountains), and evolved along different paths, becoming adapted to their new environments.
4 Artificial selection: modern varieties of domesticated animals are very different from their ancestors. They have evolved as a result of humans choosing examples with the most desirable qualities through selective breeding. Artificial selection is essentially the same as natural selection, except that it is very much quicker and the features selected may not be of survival value in natural populations.

Types of selection and other evolutionary forces

NATURAL SELECTION

All animals are subjected to selection according to the environmental conditions that exist at the time (known as the selection pressure). There are three types of natural selection. *Stabilising selection* occurs during periods of minimal environmental change, when most variations from the norm are likely to be harmful. The organisms most likely to reproduce successfully are those which are close to the average, with selection pressure acting against extreme versions. The fossil records of sharks suggest that they have the same structure today as they did tens of millions of years ago, representing a good example of stabilising selection (Figure 1.4 (a)).

Directional selection occurs when environmental change favours a new form (phenotype) of an organism (Figure 1.4 (b)). This has been demonstrated by industrial melanism in populations of the peppered moth. This species exists in two genetically determined forms: a light-coloured peppered form and a melanic (dark) form. The onset of the industrial revolution, in the middle of the nineteenth century, lead to the melanic form being better camouflaged in polluted areas and so less likely to be eaten by birds. In such areas, strong directional selection leads to almost total replacement of the typical mottled form by the melanic variety.

Disruptive selection occurs when selection favours forms which represent the extremes of the range of phenotypic variation (the reverse of stabilising selection). The effect of disruptive selection is to eliminate phenotypes in the middle of the range, producing a bimodal distribution (Figure 1.4 (c)). A good example of disruptive selection is seen in the evolution of specialised gametes (eggs and sperm). In this case, small gametes (sperm) could be produced in large numbers, and large gametes (eggs) would have sufficient energy to survive and nourish the initial growth of the zygote. Both would have advantages over medium-sized gametes, which would be selected against (Baylis, 1981).

SEXUAL SELECTION

Natural selection cannot explain all evolutionary processes. Certain behaviours or anatomical structures

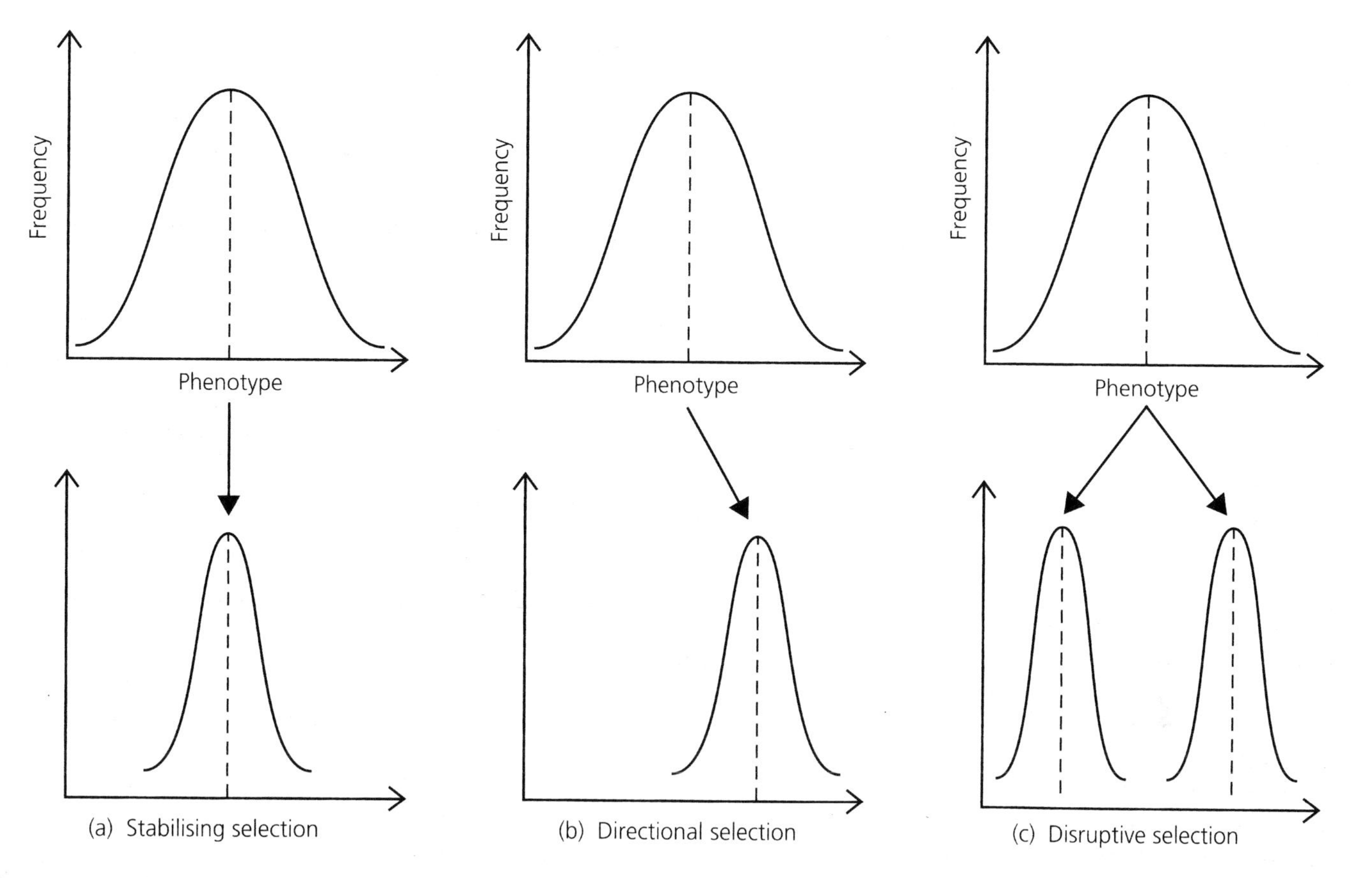

Figure 1.4 The three types of natural selection

appear to *reduce* the probability of survival. The tail of the peacock, for example, appears to have the dual disadvantage of attracting predators and impeding efficient flight, making escape difficult. Such features may be explained by sexual selection. According to Darwin, sexual selection 'depends upon the advantage which certain individuals have over others of the same sex and species solely in respect of reproduction' (Darwin, 1871). In the case of the peacock, female preference for longer tails has outweighed any disadvantages involved in owning such a cumbersome appendage. Evidence suggests that humans are also a sexually selected species (Figure 1.5) and the implications of this for evolutionary psychology are discussed in Part 2 (Chapters 4-6).

ADAPTATION

An adaptation is any feature of an organism that has been shaped by natural selection such that it enhances the chances of survival or reproductive success of the organism. Adaptation can also refer to the process by which the differential survival of genes influences a particular trait such that it now appears to be designed for some survival-related purpose. We should not expect all behaviours to be currently adaptive. Some behaviours may be adaptively 'neutral', in the sense that they no longer serve an essential function in promoting survival. It is also possible for certain behaviours to become maladaptive, particularly following a rapid

Figure 1.5 Humans are an example of a mutually sexually-selected species

change in ecological conditions. The analysis of any behaviour pattern should include some consideration of the function for which it was originally adapted. In times of rapid ecological change, the behaviour repertoire of many animals will consist of a conglomerate of adaptive, neutral and maladaptive patterns (Davies, 1995). The extent to which an individual animal is genetically adapted to its particular environment, therefore surviving and reproducing successfully, is known as the *fitness* of the animal.

Fitness

Darwin's theory of evolution by natural selection has often been summed up by the phrase 'survival of the fittest'. However, this is an oversimplification. Fitness is not a quality that individuals possess, such as size or speed, but is closely linked with evolutionary success and may be defined as a measure of the ability of an individual to leave behind offspring. The relative fitness of the offspring is also important. It is likely that at least some of this fitness is genetic in nature and therefore determined by natural and sexual selection.

More recent examinations of Darwin's work have tended to replace the term fitness with *inclusive fitness* (Dawkins, 1989). Inclusive fitness may be defined as the total number of an animal's genes present in subsequent generations. These genes will be present in direct offspring *and* in the offspring of close relatives, such as brothers and sisters. The concept of inclusive fitness may solve one of the problems of Darwin's theory, that being the existence of *altruistic behaviour* in certain species (see Box 1.3).

Box 1.3 The paradox of altruism

Altruistic behaviour refers to any act which increases the survival potential of others at a potential risk to the altruist's survival (or at least a *cost* to the altruist). Animals sometimes draw a predator's attention to themselves to divert it from their mate, nest or offspring. Army ants, for example, sacrifice their own lives to form bridges across small streams so that others may cross in safety. Such behaviour is difficult to explain by natural selection because it reduces the survival chances of the altruistic individual. On this basis, altruism would be expected to diminish with each successive generation because all individuals displaying this behaviour would be selected against. This is because genes for altruism will *reduce* the survival chances of their owner and so not get passed on to the next generation.

The existence of altruism becomes less of a problem to explain if we think in terms of inclusive fitness. A good example of this can be seen in Florida scrub jays (*Aphelocoma coerulescens*). These birds are communal breeders, in which parents are assisted by up to six non-breeding helpers, 75% of whom are offspring of a previous brood. It has been found that nests with helpers produce more fledglings than nests without (Woolfenden and Fitzpatrick, 1984). These birds often produce no young of their own and this is a significant cost of helping. However, the inclusive fitness of helpers is not zero as they increase the survival rates of close genetic relatives. The helpers also gain by obtaining experience that will help them to become successful parents if they do breed. In addition, they are first in line to occupy the scarce nest sites once their parents die or vacate the nest for some reason (altruistic behaviour in humans is discussed in detail in Chapter 7).

The evolution of human behaviour

BACKGROUND

The aim of this chapter is to consider evolutionary concepts as explanations of the behaviour of humans. With this in mind, evolution may be more specifically defined as the processes by which human behaviour is altered by means of adaptation through natural selection. It is important to remember that natural selection works by differential reproduction. When examining human behaviour, therefore, we should usually ask, 'How does that behaviour enable that individual to produce more offspring?' or 'Why would an individual that performed a different behaviour pattern leave fewer offspring?' Grier and Burk (1992) suggest that nearly all behaviour is influenced by genetic factors to some degree and that behaviour makes important contributions to survival and reproductive success. The behaviour of humans must, therefore, be subject to the forces of evolution in the same way as their anatomy and physiology.

One important question which needs to be addressed is how do *new* behaviours arise? It is important to realise that most behaviour patterns do not suddenly appear as a whole, especially if they are complex. They probably originate as very small modifications of ancestral behaviour, which conferred a slight but significant advantage (perhaps due to a mutation). This behaviour pattern would then spread by natural selection. New behaviour patterns can also arise by combining pre-existing behavioural units (single observable acts) in novel forms.

INSTINCTIVE AND LEARNED BEHAVIOUR

The 'nature' versus 'nurture' debate mentioned on page 3 may also be applied to human behaviour. In this case, nature traditionally represents *instinctive* behaviours and nurture represents *learned* behaviours. As we will see, this is an oversimplification as instincts are not purely genetic and learning is not purely environmental.

Instinctive behaviour evolves gradually and is modified by natural selection in order to adapt animals to fit a fixed and unchanging environment. Such behaviours are advantageous for animals that have short life spans and little or no parental care. These animals have little opportunity or need for learning. Learned behaviour enables animals to discover which responses give the best results in certain circumstances and to modify their actions accordingly. The ability to learn gives animals an adaptive advantage in that it gives them a greater potential for changing their behaviour to meet changing circumstances within their own lifetime. In humans, therefore, we would expect that much behaviour is learned. However, few behaviours can be said to be entirely dominated by either inheritance or learning and an interaction between the two is the norm.

Seligman (1970) has suggested that animals (both non-human and human) are biologically prepared to learn some things more readily than others. Some associations, such as taste avoidance, may be more biologically useful (or have greater survival value) than others and are therefore learned more quickly and are more resistant to *extinction* (the loss of a learned response). Research on language acquisition in humans has demonstrated the importance of both instinct and learning, as shown in Box 1.4.

Box 1.4 The roles of instinct and learning in human language acquisition

Chomsky (1959) suggested that humans are born with an ability to formulate and understand language. The *Language Acquisition Device (LAD)* is an innate, hypothetical brain mechanism, which is pre-programmed with the underlying rules of a universal grammar. This idea is supported by the existence of linguistic universals, such as nouns and verbs, and the rapid speed at which language is acquired. Furthermore, language is species-specific and virtually all children acquire language at about the same age and in the same sequence. However, as a theory it lacks falsifiability and learning must play some role in the acquisition process.

Skinner (1957) believed that language is *learned* through the process of operant conditioning (selective reinforcement, shaping and imitation). This idea was supported by Clarke-Stewart (1973), who found that children whose mothers talk to them a lot have larger vocabularies, which indicates the importance of the learning environment as well as social interaction. The learning theory also explains certain aspects of language acquisition, such as word meaning and accent. However, there seems to be little evidence supporting a connection between correct grammar and positive reinforcement. In addition, deaf children learn language without speaking and being reinforced.

In conclusion, language acquisition in humans is probably best explained by a combination of Chomsky's nativist theory and Skinner's learning theory (see Chapter 12 for a more detailed discussion of language).

EVIDENCE FOR THE EVOLUTION OF BEHAVIOUR

Explanations of the evolution of behaviour are essentially the same as those of the evolution of anatomy and physiology. However, evidence for the evolution of behaviour is not as easily obtained. For example, behaviour is not easily fossilised. However, fossil records may provide evidence of particular anatomical features which *imply* certain behaviours. The role of head ornaments in dinosaurs, such as the horns of *Triceratops*, has been inferred from the behaviour of animals such as deer and certain beetles that have head ornaments today (Molnar, 1977).

By far the best evidence for the evolution of animal behaviour comes from interspecies comparisons (this is the basis of *comparative psychology*). To do this we need a phylogenetic tree (Figure 1.6), which shows the ancestral relations of modern forms based on anatomical and physiological evidence. If we know the evolutionary relationship between a group of species we can infer whether common behaviour patterns are *homologous* (species share a common ancestor) or *analogous* (similar behaviour patterns evolved in unrelated organisms owing to similar environmental pressures). Phylogenetic trees based on behavioural similarities can be constructed and compared to those based on anatomical and physiological evidence. Konrad Lorenz (1958) did this with ducks and geese and found that the grouping of species according to their behaviour is similar to, but not exactly identical with, groupings based on anatomical similarity.

If similar behaviours evolve independently in a number of unrelated species, this is known as *convergent evolution*. The social insects represent a good example of convergent evolution, with termites and the social hymenopterans (ants, bees and wasps) developing this distinctive behaviour independently. If, however, different behaviours are observed among related species, this is known as *divergent evolution*. An example of this is courtship behaviour in ducks, which is typically a distinctive pattern of vocalisations and head and tail movements (Lorenz, 1958). In this case, the behaviour is probably advantageous in ensuring that individuals do not waste time and effort courting members of a different species.

Convergent and divergent evolution form the basis of two approaches to studying comparative psychology. The first considers the function of analogous behaviours among unrelated species and attempts to explain what caused these behaviours by searching for similar environmental factors. The second looks at differences among closely related species to investigate the evolutionary changes undergone by a particular behavioural unit based on phylogenetic relationships. A comparison of closely related species living in different habitats can often reveal those aspects of behaviour which are particularly important in adapting the animal to its environment. For humans, these comparisons are usually made with other primates, particularly the apes (such as chimpanzees and gorillas). It is also possible to combine the convergent and divergent approaches for a detailed study of the evolution of a particular behaviour.

Several experimental studies have shown that differences in behaviour can result from differences in genes. For example, Seymour Benzer (1973) induced genetic mutations that changed behaviour in the fruit fly *Drosophila*. One example of this is the 'amnesiac fly', which learns normally but forgets very rapidly. The physiological basis of these altered behaviour patterns have been investigated and shown to be due to a mutation in a specific gene (Dudai, 1989). Artificial selection experiments have also demonstrated that genetic factors are important in behaviour (Cade, 1981). In humans, however, the situation is more complex and there are probably very few examples of behaviour being influenced by a single gene. A possible exception is discussed in Box 1.5.

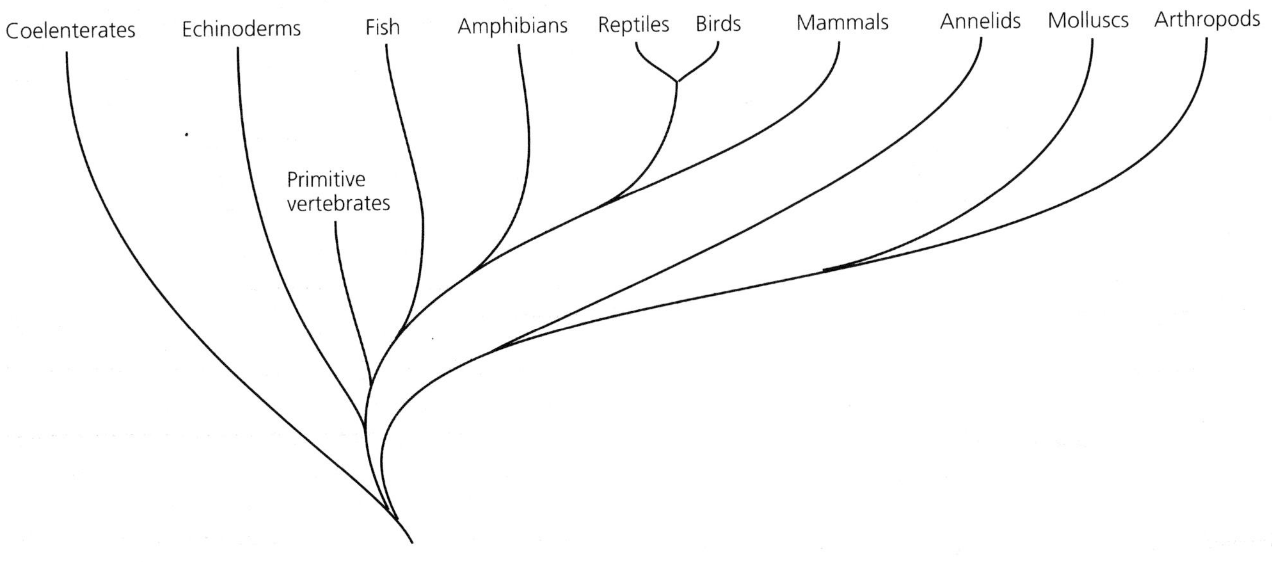

Figure 1.6 A phylogenetic tree

Box 1.5 The genetic basis of 'women's intuition'

Skuse (1997) has suggested the existence on the X chromosome of a single gene (or possibly a small cluster of genes) that plays a major role in normal social skills, such as awareness of other people's feelings and the ability to chat and make friends. Normal human females have two X chromosomes, one from each parent. Males, on the other hand, have only one X chromosome (inherited from their mother) and a Y chromosome (from their father). Skuse found that girls with Turner's syndrome, who have one X chromosome only, differed in their behaviour depending on whether they inherited this chromosome from their mother or their father. Girls who inherit their mother's X chromosome lack social skills, whereas girls who inherit their father's have normal skills. This may explain why normal girls tend to have rather better social skills than their male counterparts. Skuse suggests that girls are genetically pre-programmed to learn to interpret social cues. Boys, however, do not have this advantage and have to work harder to get to the same level of social competence.

When examining the evolution of human behaviour, it is important to consider two main points. First, when we talk about genes for a particular behaviour it does not mean that one gene alone codes for the trait. It is much more likely that several genes are involved. However, a difference in behaviour between two individuals may be due to a difference in a single gene. Second, just because it can be shown that genes influence behaviour this does not imply that genes alone produce the behaviour, or even that the behaviour can be divided up into genetic and environmental components. The way in which behaviour develops is the result of a complex interaction between genes and the environment.

Sociobiology

Sociobiology was introduced by Hamilton (1964) and Wilson (1975). It can be defined as the systematic study of the biological basis of all social behaviour, including altruism, aggression and sexual behaviour. Sociobiology differs from classical studies of animal behaviour (known as *ethology*) in that it generally considers the set of genes, rather than the individual, as the basic unit of evolution. In other words, it is not as important for individuals to survive as for their genes. Sociobiologists have suggested that this may explain the existence of altruism (Dawkins, 1989). What *appears* as an altruistic act is actually selfish at the gene level (see Box 1.3 on page 6). This approach has been named the *selfish gene* theory. It proposes that any behaviour of an organism is specifically 'designed' to maximise the survival of its genes. From the 'gene's point of view', a body is a sort of survival machine created to enhance the gene's chances of continued replication. (For a detailed examination of this idea, refer to *The Selfish Gene* by Richard Dawkins (1989).)

Sociobiology has been criticised for oversimplifying explanations of behaviour and overemphasising the role of genetic factors. It has also been suggested that the extension from non-human animal to human behaviour is doubtful because genetic evolution has been overtaken by cultural evolution (see Chapter 2).

Evolutionarily Stable Strategy (ESS)

An ESS is generally considered as a behaviour pattern (or set of behaviour patterns) which, if most of the population adopt it, cannot be bettered by any other strategy and will therefore tend to become established by natural selection. Individuals must weigh up the fitness costs and benefits of a particular behaviour and identify the optimal strategy to enhance their own fitness at that point in time. An ESS is therefore an optimum strategy dependent on the circumstances in which it is used. This means that an individual cannot successfully behave differently from the others in a population, even if it appears that there would be a short-term gain by doing so. A good example of this is described in Box 1.6.

Box 1.6 An evolutionarily stable strategy (ESS)

Consider a species in which *both* parents are usually required to raise the young. If a male of this species had a mutant gene which made it take no part in parenting, it would be able to mate with a great number of females. The short-term gain, in evolutionary terms, is that he would produce many offspring and, therefore, many copies of his own genes. However, the success of his strategy depends upon the solitary females being able to raise the young alone. If this is not possible, none of the offspring will survive. The male would not benefit from breaking away from the ESS (parental care by *both* sexes) and his mutant gene would not survive to change the behaviour of later generations.

It should be noted that this ESS is also dependent on *environmental* conditions. If conditions change, either sex can alter its previous stable strategy to further increase its fitness. For example, the male dunnock (a small sparrow-like bird) will desert his mate and their fledglings if he estimates that this particular season provides an abundance of food. In this case, his mate should be able to successfully complete the task of raising their joint offspring on her own. The male is then free to mate with another female, raise another brood and thus increase his fitness (the *quantity* of his offspring). Similarly, female dunnocks are known to mate with more than one male during the breeding season and to indulge in covert behaviour to accomplish extra-pair matings (to improve the *quality* of her offspring). Although this is a relatively simple example, it serves to illustrate the idea that the evolutionary success of one behavioural strategy depends on the other strategies present in the environment.

Using a concept known as *game theory*, mathematicians such as David Wise (personal communication) have calculated the outcomes of various different strategies and determined theoretical ESSs. These have then been compared with the actual behaviour observed in the animals concerned, and this idea is discussed further in Box 1.7.

Box 1.7 The Prisoner's Dilemma

The Prisoner's Dilemma is a game which many biologists, economists, psychologists and politicians believe represents simple decision-making in humans. The rules are simple. Suppose that there are two men, Wilf and Nobby, who are in jail, suspected of collaborating in a crime. Each prisoner, in his separate cell, has to choose whether to *defect* (betray his colleague) or *co-operate* (remain silent). There are four possible outcomes, summarised below (written from the point of view of Wilf).

		Nobby	
		Defect	*Co-operate*
Wilf	*Defect*	10 years	Freedom
	Co-operate	25 years	5 years

Wilf should think about the game as follows. If Nobby plays *defect*, the best thing Wilf can do is *defect* (10 years in prison is better than 25 years). If Nobby plays *co-operate*, Wilf should *defect* (and go free). Therefore, Wilf should always defect, whatever Nobby does. However, Nobby will also work this out, meaning that the most likely outcome is for them both to defect, each receiving 10 years in prison. But if they had both decided to cooperate, they would have both received the lighter sentence of 5 years. Hence the dilemma. If the game is played over several rounds, it becomes more interesting. Opportunities arise to build up trust or mistrust, to reciprocate or placate, forgive or avenge. Generally, over a long period of time, the best strategy for all concerned is mutual co-operation or, as Richard Dawkins (1989) puts it, 'nice guys finish first'.

Conclusions

In general, evolutionary psychologists use a Darwinian approach to explain the behaviour of humans. They ask questions about how particular behaviour patterns contribute to an individual's chances of survival and their reproductive success. The appeal of the evolutionary approach is that it is based on a logical concept (the Darwinian paradigm) and produces plausible hypotheses, many of which can be tested. There is a wide range of evidence for the evolution of human behaviour, based on both comparative and experimental studies. However, this approach takes no account of the influence of *cultural evolution* and this will be addressed in the next chapter.

SUMMARY

- **Evolutionary psychology** may be defined as the application of Darwinian ideas of evolution to human behaviour, based on the assumption that individuals will act in a way that tends to propagate their genes. This approach takes the view that human nature has been shaped by natural selection and it is a recent development of **sociobiology**.
- **Evolution** in biological terms is the process by which new species arise as the result of gradual changes to the genetic make-up of existing species over long periods of time. Evolution results from **superior genetic variants** having an advantage in the **struggle for existence**. These individuals are more likely to **survive** and **reproduce**, resulting in a change in the **gene frequency** of a population. This process may gradually lead to the considerable differences now observed between living organisms.
- There is considerable debate as to how much of the variability within a species is due to genetic factors (**nature**) and how much depends on the influence of the environment (**nurture**). However, all behaviour has both an element of inheritance *and* learning about it, the interaction of which is known as **penetrance**.
- Genetic variation arises as a result of **sexual reproduction**, **mutation**, **genetic drift**, **non-random mating** and **migration** into or out of populations.
- Darwin's theory of evolution by natural selection is supported by evidence from **palaeontology**, **comparative anatomy**, **geographical distribution** and **artificial selection**.
- There are three types of natural selection: **stabilising selection**; **directional selection**; and **disruptive selection**.
- **Sexual selection** depends on the advantage which certain individuals have over others of the same sex and species solely in respect of **reproduction**. It is a specialised form of natural selection, used to explain the existence of behaviours or anatomical structures which do not enhance the probability of survival, such as the tail of the peacock. Evidence suggests that humans are also a sexually-selected species.
- An **adaptation** is any feature of an organism that has been shaped by natural selection such that it enhances the chances of survival or reproductive success of the organism. In times of rapid ecological change, the behaviour repertoire of many animals will consist of a conglomerate of adaptive, neutral and maladaptive patterns. The extent to which an individual animal is genetically adapted to its environment, therefore surviving and reproducing successfully, is known as the **fitness** of the animal.
- Fitness is a measure of the ability of an individual to **leave behind offspring**. This term has generally been replaced by **inclusive fitness**, which may be defined as **the total number of an animal's genes present in subsequent generations**. These genes will be present in direct offspring *and* in the offspring of close relatives. The concept of inclusive fitness may solve one of the problems of Darwin's theory, that being the existence of **altruistic behaviour** in certain species.
- It appears that nearly **all** human behaviour is influenced by genetic factors to some degree and that behaviour makes important contributions to survival and reproductive success. The behaviour of humans must, therefore, be subject to the forces of evolution in the same way as their anatomy and physiology.
- Behaviour may be divided into **instinctive** (predominantly genetic) and **learned** (predominantly environmental). Few behaviours can be said to be entirely dominated by either inheritance or learning and an interaction between the two is the norm. Research suggests that animals (both human and non-human) are **biologically prepared** to learn some things more readily than others. These associations may have survival value and are therefore learned more quickly and are more resistant to extinction. Research on language acquisition in humans has demonstrated the importance of both instinct and learning.
- The best evidence for the evolution of animal behaviour comes from **interspecies comparisons**. Phylogenetic trees based on behavioural similarities are generally similar to those based on anatomical and physiological evidence. In addition, several experimental studies have shown that **differences in behaviour can result from differences in genes**.
- **Sociobiology** is the systematic study of the biological basis of all social behaviour. It differs from classical ethology in that it generally considers the set of genes, rather than the individual, as the

basic unit of evolution. Sociobiology has been criticised for oversimplifying explanations of behaviour and overemphasising the role of genetic factors. It has also been suggested that the extension from non-human animal to human behaviour is doubtful because genetic evolution has been overtaken by cultural evolution.

- An **evolutionarily stable strategy (ESS)** is a behaviour pattern which, if most of the population adopt it, cannot be bettered by any other strategy and will, therefore, tend to become established by natural selection.
- Evolutionary psychologists use a Darwinian approach to explain the behaviour of humans. The appeal of the evolutionary approach is that it is based on a logical concept and produces plausible hypotheses, many of which can be tested. There is a wide range of evidence for the evolution of human behaviour, based on both comparative and experimental studies.

2

CULTURAL EVOLUTION

Introduction and overview

Culture may be defined simply as 'shared knowledge'. Organisms capable of sharing their knowledge with others, and acquiring knowledge from others, are capable of entering into culture. For humans, culture is the part of the environment that is made by ourselves and, in turn, influences our behaviour. The function of culture seems to be the possibility for much more rapid adaptation than genetic evolution allows. A potential problem for evolutionary psychology is that behaviour can also be acquired through these cultural influences, which can be transmitted from generation to generation in a way that owes nothing to natural selection. However, if culture itself can be shaped by evolution, this may cease to be an issue (see page 16).

Cultural evolution is the social transmission from one generation to the next, via teaching and imitation, of knowledge, values and other factors that influence behaviour (Maynard-Smith, 1993). In many ways, the evolution of culture may be seen as analogous to the process of genetic evolution (see Chapter 1). This chapter considers cultural evolution and examines the way in which biological and cultural evolution may have interacted to produce human nature.

Cultural versus genetic evolution

Cultural behaviour is that which is passed on from one generation to the next, leading to a process of evolutionary change. Those behaviours which are successful, or adaptive, will be imitated (*selected*) and passed on to future generations (*inherited*). The non-genetic process of cultural evolution often mimics the results of Darwinian adaptation. In non-human species, it is probable that good behavioural design has been shaped by natural selection. Humans, however, may devise good solutions and pass these on to others by cultural means (Gould, 1990). At any point in time, therefore, our behaviour may be influenced by genetic and cultural factors, in addition to our immediate environment (Figure 2.1). Cultural transmission is generally considered to be faster and more flexible than its genetic equivalent (Brown, 1986). For example, little or none of the change in average human height over the last 200 years is genetic in nature. Rather, it is due to improvements in health care and living conditions, which are cultural phenomena. Rapid cultural change can therefore alter selection pressures considerably, although it cannot exert an influence beyond that made possible by genetically encoded flexibility (Dennett, 1996). For example, however strong the cultural pressures, we could not override our genetically encoded need for sleep.

Human cultural evolution is not truly Darwinian in nature. The useful discoveries of one generation are

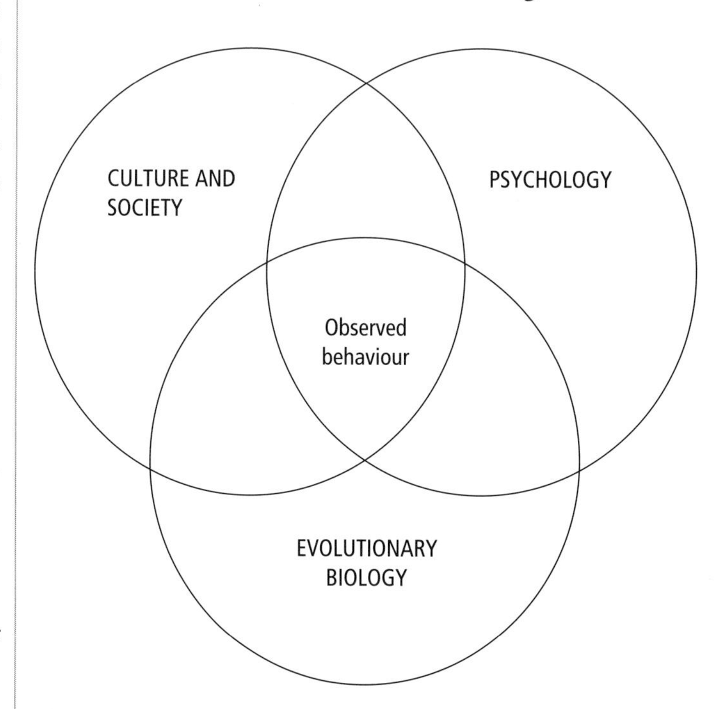

Figure 2.1 Human behaviour is influenced by several interacting factors

passed directly to offspring by writing, teaching and so forth. Culture is not only passed on via parents, but also from other family members, friends, teachers and the media. Furthermore, cultural evolution works by amalgamation and coalescence across lineages, something not permitted by the Darwinian paradigm (Gould, 1990). Many models of human cultural evolution have shown that it is possible for some cultural traits, such as celibacy, to spread even at the expense of direct genetic benefits to their carriers (Sperber, 1994). Cultural evolution has its own dynamics, constrained but not fully determined by human evolutionary adaptations. In view of these differences, we may need a separate set of laws for cultural evolution. However, it may be difficult to apply *any* evolutionary perspective to human culture as much of post-Pleistocene society is very different to what came before (Barkow, 1992).

Cultural evolution: a comparative approach

Although examples of cultural evolution are most readily available for humans, examples of non-human animal culture also occur. Byrne (1995) reported a study of Japanese macaques (*Macaca fuscata,* a species of monkey) where he left sweet potatoes on the beach for the monkeys, one of whom (Imo) 'invented' the idea of washing the sand off the potatoes in the sea. Soon other monkeys imitated her (Ridley, 1986). Another example of non-human animal culture involves the removal of foil tops of milk bottles, and drinking of the milk, by blue tits (Sherry and Galef, 1984) (Figure 2.2). Chimpanzees also appear to be able to acquire information from one another (Clamp and Russell, 1998), and are therefore capable of entering into culture (see Box 2.1). However, some psychologists prefer to view these examples as forms of social learning, rather than true cultural transmission.

Figure 2.2 Blue tits opening milk bottle tops and drinking the milk. This behaviour appears to be influenced by both environmental and genetic factors, and represents an example of cultural evolution

Box 2.1 Cultural behaviour in chimpanzees

Chimps share 99% of our genes, use tools to gather food, and show a wide variation in behaviour between separate populations. This looks like a strong case for cultural behaviour in a non-human species.

McGrew (1992) claims that all known behaviour exhibited by our hominid ancestors is within the cognitive capacity of chimps. For example, chimps 'fish' for termites with thin twigs specially shaped for the purpose, biting the probes to different lengths according to the circumstances. Likewise, it seems that even the most complex hominid tools may be produced by trial and error. However, chimps do not appear to use tools to create tools. This may present a problem for equating chimp and hominid cognition. Furthermore, chimps do not seem to imitate one another, an observation which has led some psychologists to reject the idea that their behaviour is cultural. Nevertheless, there are many human cultural practices that require only observation for their dissemination. We must be careful of falling into the trap of describing similar behaviours observed in human and ape populations as cultural and genetic respectively. It would appear that chimpanzees do possess culture, but in a much more limited fashion than found in humans. This is probably because chimps tend to live in relatively stable ecological and social environments and the need for rapid adaptation is limited. McGrew (1992) believes that if we wish to reconstruct the prehistoric origins of human behaviour, we need to study those creatures with whom we last shared a common ancestor.

According to Ridley (1996), the study of non-human animals has profound implications for our understanding of the human mind. Human society is derived from the society of *Homo erectus*, which is derived from the society of *Australopithecus*, and so on back through primates to the original mammals. Although examples of cultural transmission have been observed in non-human animals, it is still genetic factors which play by far the largest role in determining behaviour. In humans, however, much of our behaviour is due to cultural rather than genetic determinants. It is for this reason that many psychologists are hesitant to apply the same insights to humans as to non-human animals.

There are several features of the human capacity for learning from others that make human culture different from that of any other animals (Tomasello *et al.*, 1993). The major differences are that every member of the social group shares in knowledge, and that knowledge is of many different things. By contrast, in chimpanzees only a limited number of individuals will share a small number of isolated behaviours. It is possible that culture evolved as a way of exploiting the long-term dependency of human offspring. This may have helped us to solve the problems of detecting and mastering short-term stabilities in the world, by vicarious experience and the sharing of knowledge (Plotkin, 1993). A second unique feature of human culture is cumulative modification of knowledge over generations (Plotkin, 1996), which requires that individuals have a 'theory of mind' (Box 2.2). Furthermore, humans are probably the only species to possess *language*, the primary medium for cultural transmission. Therefore, if one is looking for insights and understanding of human culture, comparisons with other living species may be of little use.

Box 2.2 Theory of mind

Recent studies have suggested that humans possess an evolved ability to assign beliefs or desires to the actions of others. This ability appears to be generated by a domain-specific cognitive system that is sometimes called a 'theory of mind' module (Leslie, 1987). This module allows us to represent the idea that another person can have thoughts about certain objects or situations, that is, we can attribute minds to others. For example, we may explain why Peter is looking in the fridge by assuming that he has a *desire* for food and he *believes* that food can be found in the fridge. This ability is not present at birth, but develops between the ages of three and five in a characteristic pattern that appears to be universal. A theory of mind may have initially evolved to allow individuals to better predict the behaviour of other members of their social group. Once it had evolved for that reason it could be elaborated, because it allowed cumulative cultural evolution (Boyd and Richerson, 1985).

Occasionally, the neurological basis of the theory of mind module can be selectively damaged. Such damage is thought to be the basis of autism in many children, who do not appear to distinguish between living and non-living entities. In other words, autistic children are 'mind-blind' (Pinker, 1997).

Memes and culturgens

A *meme* is the smallest element of culture that can replicate itself with reliability and fecundity (Dennett, 1996). This idea of a meme as a unit of cultural transmission, passed on by imitation, was first proposed by Dawkins (1976). Dawkins observed that language seems to 'evolve' by non-genetic means, and at a rate which is orders of magnitude faster than genetic evolution. One example of a meme could be a tune or, more accurately, the physical structure in the brain which represents the tune. In this case, the whistled tune would represent the phenotypic expression of the meme. Memes propagate themselves (as do 'catchy' tunes) by passing from brain to brain via a process of communication. The success of a particular meme will depend upon how many people hold a representation of the meme and/or its durability. (Box 2.3 describes an example of jokes as memes.) Over a period of time, we would expect memes to 'evolve' phenotypic effects that favour their own replication. For example, consider a meme for free speech. The phenotypic expression of such a meme would make its own replication more likely.

According to Dawkins, if memes are truly analogous to genes they must be self-replicating brain structures. In other words, the actual patterns of neuronal connections must reconstitute themselves in one brain after another. Darwinian evolution depends on very high-fidelity copying. It seems that there is a much higher rate of (usually non-random) mutation and recombination in cultural evolution. This may be because memes

Box 2.3 Why *did* the chicken cross the road?

Jokes are good examples of memes. A topical joke will probably be very successful (many people will hold a representation of the meme), but short-lived. In contrast, a joke which dates less rapidly may have a slower rate of transmission, but succeed due to its durability. Jokes which are not funny are less likely to be transmitted (like a disadvantageous mutation) and will eventually become 'extinct'.

It is not clear where new jokes come from. The most likely explanation is that the jokes we hear (and pass on) have *evolved* from earlier stories, picking up revisions and updates as they are transmitted. A joke typically has no one author. It authorship is distributed over hundreds of people, settling for a while in some particularly topical and currently amusing version, before going dormant like the ancestors from which it originated (Dennett, 1996).

can replicate only by generating a phenotypic representation of themselves, whereas genes replicate by a direct template process (Maynard-Smith, 1993). For example, Darwin's theory as I understand it is probably different from the version in the minds of other biologists. However, the *essence* of it is much the same, and it is this essence which is the meme.

Like genes, memes also compete with each other, for entry into human minds. Benign or harmless memes will tend to flourish, other things being equal. Memes that tend to be fatal to those whose minds carry them, such as a meme for suicide, can only be successful if they have some way of publicising themselves before they 'go down with the ship' (Dennett, 1996). The idea of evolutionarily stable strategies outlined in Chapter 1 (page 9) also applies to memes. The success of a particular meme depends upon what other memes are present in the population at that time. For example, the meme for education is a meme that reinforces the very process of meme implantation.

The meme concept is probably only applicable to humans. *Homo sapiens* is the only species with brains that can provide shelter, and habits of communication that can provide transmission media, for memes. What makes humans 'special' is that we can rise above the imperatives of our genes, thanks to memes. Furthermore, we can also rise above, if necessary, the 'selfish memes' of our indoctrination (Dawkins, 1989).

A *culturgen* is a hypothetical cultural trait, such as a particular tool or form of grammar, which selects for genes that allow its carriers to employ the culturgen most effectively (Wills, 1993). For example, the wheel could be considered as a culturgen, which would select for genes that allowed their carriers to exploit this invention in an efficient manner. In other words, culturgens are capable of influencing the genetic composition of a population. Culturgens represent a selective force upon the genes involved in the production of complex and powerful human brains. In turn, these brains then produce more culturgens (such as the wheelbarrow or bicycle). This 'co-evolutionary circuit' may be the basis for many of the differences observed between humans and other species (Lumsden and Wilson, 1981). An analysis of cultural evolution considers the spread of each culturgen, considered independently, via the adaptive force of natural selection (Gould, 1990).

It should be noted that there is little supporting evidence for the existence of culturgens. In particular, it is not clear whether the necessary genes will always be available for novel culturgens to act upon. Furthermore, there is no direct connection between culturgens and genes: it is not simply a case of 'one culturgen – one gene'. The culturgen approach is also reductionist in nature, and therefore subject to the same criticisms as reductionism in general (see Chapter 3, page 23). Nevertheless, the concept of culturgens may be useful when trying to unravel gene-culture coevolution (see below).

Genetics and culture: a case of coevolution?

The case for genetic evolution of human behaviour was outlined in Chapter 1. However, there is no evidence that our Stone Age ancestors were biologically very different from modern humans. Most of the vast transformations that have taken place over the last 100,000 years appear to have been the outcome of cultural evolution, which is socially rather than genetically transmitted (Jahoda, 1978). Similarly, the large variety that can be observed in human behaviour suggests that it is determined mainly by culture, not by genes (Dawkins,

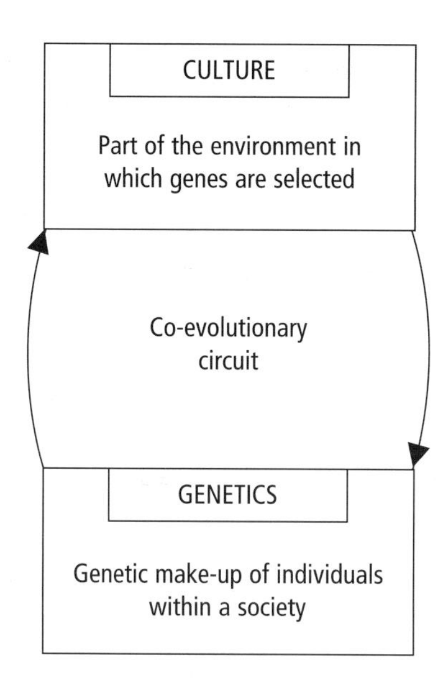

Figure 2.3 The co-evolution of genetics and culture

1989). However, this view may be oversimplified and, in reality, human nature is the product of the coevolution of genetics and culture (Figure 2.3). Human genes affect the way that the mind is formed. In turn, this generally causes individuals to adopt cultural choices that enable them to survive and reproduce more successfully (celibacy among monks would be an exception to this rule and some cultural practices are clearly fitness-neutral or even maladaptive). Our behaviour is influenced by what we learn from others and even if this ability to learn is a product of genes, what we do learn is culture (Cartwright, 2000). Therefore, culture affects genetic evolution, and genes affect cultural evolution. An example of the interweaving of culture and biology is described in Box 2.4.

Cavalli-Sforza and Feldman (1981) suggested a 'transmission rule' for gene-culture interaction, which combines the effects of other members of society (such as parents or teachers) with any bias causing people to more readily accept some traits rather than others. Some of this bias could have a genetic basis, and several evolutionary psychologists have claimed that a great deal of human culture is genetically determined. Natural selection does not act on genetic variation alone, but on a combination of genes and culture. Organisms select and transform environments by learning new practices and creating new cultures. Rose and Rose (2000) point out that even an amoeba changes the water in which it lives, as it consumes nutrients and emits waste products. As a result, the amoeba will then interact with a slightly different environment to that it encountered previously. This may generate new selection pressures that speed-up the selection of genes. Alternatively, it may reduce evolutionary pressures that would normally have an impact on genetic make-up, slowing down the pace of evolution.

Many social scientists claim that, during human evolution, natural selection has removed 'genetically determined' systems of behaviour and replaced them with general-purpose learning mechanisms (or content-independent cognitive processes). It was thought that these would be favoured by evolution because they did not constrain human behaviour to be maladaptively inflexible (Tooby and Cosmides, 1995). The standard social science viewpoint is that evolved aspects of human behaviour are negligible, having been superseded by the capacity for culture. However, it is unlikely that a general-purpose mechanism could successfully solve the adaptive problems encountered during human evolution, such as the acquisition of language (see Chapter 12). Rather, a range of more specialised content-dependent cognitive mechanisms

Box 2.4 Lactose tolerance: an example of cultural and biological interaction

Approximately two-thirds of all people in the world have varying degrees of difficulty in digesting lactose, a sugar found in mammalian milk. During the suckling period, the enzyme that allows lactose absorption (*lactase*) is present in the digestive system of all people. At weaning, lactase levels decline in most people (they become *lactose intolerant*) and such people are prone to sickness and diarrhoea if they drink milk. Most people from Africa and south and east Asia are lactose intolerant, whereas 95% of Scandinavians are *lactose tolerant*. These differences are probably due to dietary habits in these areas. In those human populations where cows' milk has been drunk for more than 300 generations, the vast majority of people produce lactase. In groups which do not have a history of dairy farming, four out of five people carry a different (mutant) version of the gene for this enzyme and are lactose-intolerant. The important point about this example is that the force driving this evolutionary event was not the mutant lactase gene but part of the agricultural revolution, a cultural phenomenon (Durham, 1991).

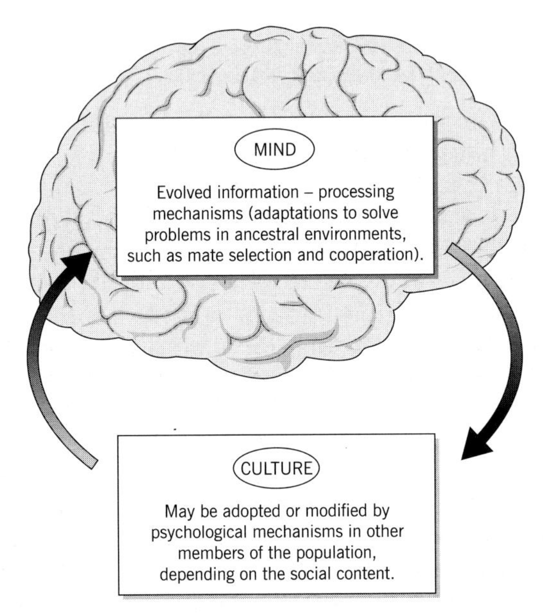

Figure 2.4 The interaction of the human mind and culture

Box 2.5 The evolutionary psychology of gossip (Barkow, 1992)

Gossip has to do with the exchange of information about other people. But which 'other people' and what kinds of information have we been selected to attend to? The evolutionary psychology answer to these questions would be: those people most likely to have affected the inclusive fitness of our Pleistocene ancestors (such as relatives, rivals, mates, offspring and the very high-ranking); and the kinds of information that would have had the most bearing on fitness (such as health, control over resources, sexual activities, births and deaths). In general, these are exactly the things we tend to gossip about.

Gossip is an invaluable source of information, but it is also unreliable. The evolutionary psychology explanation for this is that selection would have favoured our disseminating information in the interests of our own success in social competition (Barkow, 1989). Therefore, we tend to derogate rivals and mask our own weaknesses (Buss and Dedden, 1990).

One problem with evolutionary psychology explanations of gossip is that they cannot explain our fascination with (and subsequent gossip about) strangers and fictitious characters, neither of whom are likely to influence our fitness. However, the mass media (a phenomenon unknown in the Pleistocene era) may have tapped into evolved psychological mechanisms designed for the acquisition of social information. Because popular media stars did not exist in our earlier environments, there was never selection pressure in favour of our distinguishing between genuine members of our community and the images, voices and words that bombard us via television, radio and newspapers. According to Barkow (1992), media stars represent 'an evolutionarily unanticipated phenomenon'.

may be needed. If we extend this idea further, psychology may have to come full circle back to William James (1892), who proposed that the reason why humans are capable of solving a vast range of problems is that we have *more* 'instincts' (content-specific cognitive processes) than other species, not less. Evolutionary psychologists regard culture as the product of these evolved psychological mechanisms (Figure 2.4). An example of this, the evolutionary psychology of gossip, is described in Box 2.5.

Conclusions

Culture is an important part of the environment that influences human behaviour. The evolution of culture may be seen as analogous to the process of genetic evolution, involving memes instead of genes as the units of inheritance. However, cultural evolution is not truly Darwinian in nature. It seems likely that most aspects of human nature, particularly our large and complex brains, are the result of gene-culture coevolution. Evolutionary psychologists regard culture as the product of evolved information-processing mechanisms in the brain.

SUMMARY

- **Culture** may be defined simply as **'shared knowledge'**. For humans, culture represents an important part of the environment that influences our behaviour.
- **Cultural evolution** is the social transmission from one generation to the next, via teaching and imitation, of knowledge, values and other factors that influence behaviour. In many ways, **the evolution of culture may be seen as analogous to the process of genetic evolution**.
- The non-genetic process of cultural evolution often mimics the results of genetic adaptation. However, **human cultural evolution is not truly Darwinian in nature**. Cultural transmission is generally considered to be faster and more flexible than its genetic equivalent.
- Although examples of cultural evolution are most readily available for humans, instances of non-human animal culture also occur (although these may be seen as forms of **social learning**). However, it is still genetic factors which play by far the greatest role in determining behaviour in other species. In humans, a greater emphasis is placed on cultural determinants. Furthermore, there are several features of the human capacity for learning from others that make human culture different from that of any other animals. It is for these reasons that many psychologists are reluctant to apply the same insights to humans as to non-human animals.
- A **meme** is a unit of cultural transmission. Memes propagate themselves by passing from brain to brain via a process of **communication**. The success of a particular meme will depend upon how many people hold a representation of the meme and/or its durability. Over a period of time, we would expect memes to evolve phenotypic effects that favour their own replication. For example, a meme for free speech is more likely to be successful than a meme for suicide.
- A **culturgen** is a hypothetical cultural trait that selects for genes which allow its carriers to employ the culturgen most effectively. Culturgens and genes may form a **co-evolutionary circuit**, which may be the basis for many of the differences observed between humans and other species (particularly our complex and powerful brains). However, the culturgen approach has been criticised for its vagueness, a lack of supporting evidence, and its reductionist nature.
- **Human nature** represents the product of the **coevolution** of genes and culture. The human mind is a **product** of genes and culture and, in turn, is a **source** of culture. Therefore, **culture affects genetic evolution and genes affect cultural evolution**.
- Many social scientists claim that, during human evolution, natural selection has removed 'genetically determined' systems of behaviour and replaced them with **content-independent cognitive processes**. However, it is unlikely that such general-purpose mechanisms could successfully solve the adaptive problems encountered during human evolution, which require a range of **content-specific cognitive processes**. Evolutionary psychologists regard culture as the product of these evolved psychological mechanisms.

3

ISSUES IN EVOLUTIONARY PSYCHOLOGY

Introduction and overview

In Chapter 1, we looked at the nature of the evolutionary approach to psychology. This approach is potentially very useful when seeking explanations of human behaviour, but it cannot account for all aspects of the diverse behavioural repertoires seen in our species. One of the main limitations of the evolutionary approach is that behaviour is also culturally transmitted, particularly in humans (see Chapter 2).

This chapter considers some of the major issues in evolutionary psychology, examining:
- the role of the environment
- the influence of cultural evolution
- objections that the approach is both deterministic and reductionist in nature
- the limited evidence for evolutionary explanations of behaviour
- ethical concerns about the approach.

It should be noted that most of these limitations are valid for sociobiology but not evolutionary psychology, which arose as a response to these sorts of criticisms. Nevertheless, these are included early in this book because there is often confusion over the differences between the two disciplines. This should also serve two further purposes: to explain how evolutionary psychology improves on sociobiology; and to enable free discussion of the applications of evolutionary psychology in Chapters 4-15 without recourse to reviewing these criticisms in each chapter.

The role of the environment

Behaviour is always an interaction between genes and the environment, never purely genetic. According to Hayes (1994), genetic factors may be sources of variation in animal and human behaviour, but this is not enough to provide a basis for an entire theory of behaviour. However, this is actually a criticism of sociobiology, *not* evolutionary psychology, which is a much more flexible approach as it takes into account the role of the mind in assessing environmental conditions and mediating the links between genes and behaviour.

The genetic/environmental debate is subject to the same misunderstandings as the nature/nurture debate outlined in Chapter 1 (page 3). To say that a certain behaviour is *innate* does not mean that it will develop in a fixed way, regardless of the environment. It means that we acquire some characteristics very readily and others only with great difficulty (Maynard-Smith, 1993). Furthermore, we should not ask whether *characteristics* are genetically determined (as clearly both genes and an environment are required), but whether *differences* are genetically determined. It is differences that matter in the competitive struggle to survive, and it is genetically-controlled differences that matter in evolution (Dawkins, 1989). Rather than talking about there being 'a gene A *for* behaviour X', we should better discuss 'the *influence* of gene A on behaviour X'. This influence may be modified by environmental events, both internal (e.g. diet) and external (e.g. education). Furthermore, other genes in the body may modify the influence of gene A and of the environment (Figure 3.1). This is an important point, because although I (and other authors) will occasionally talk about 'genes for . . .', evolutionary psychology deals primarily with 'adaptive strategies of behaviour'. Evolutionary psychology proposes that genes build brains (and bodies) that readily process environmental information to elicit adaptive behaviour that promotes the survival and reproduction of the individual in that environment.

Another problem for evolutionary psychology is that some critics suggest there are very few *human universals* (behaviour patterns common to all members of the species) and the approach cannot account for the differences among us, which are mainly due to culture

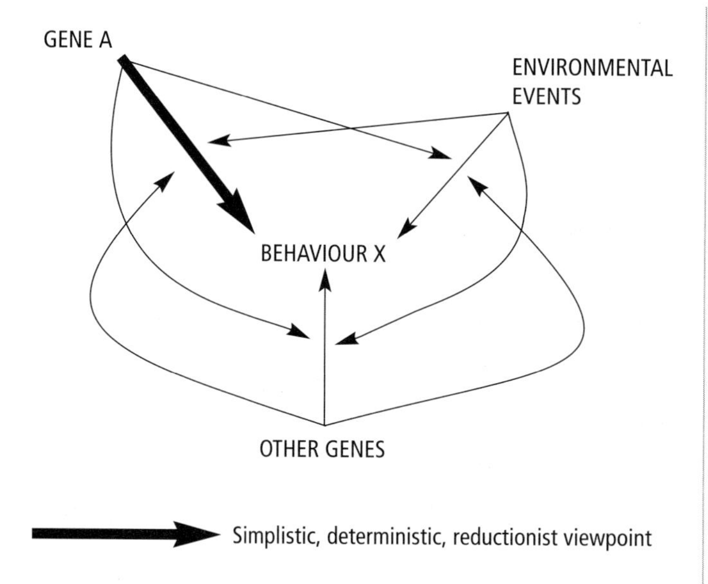

Figure 3.1 The influence of gene A on behaviour X

(see Chapter 2). Therefore, at a simple level, it seems that evolutionary psychology may be limited in its ability to explain human nature. In order to resolve this problem, we need to address the question of whether there is such a thing as *universal human nature*.

Box 3.1 Human sex differences: fact or fiction? (Gould, 1990)

Many evolutionary biologists believe that humans demonstrate genetically adaptive differences between the psychology of the sexes. However, the evidence for this assertion is far from conclusive. One of the main problems may be the failure to report null results (an example of biased reporting). Null results represent the failure of a researcher to find any effect in any direction. In rare cases where these are reported, they are unlikely to be cited in secondary literature or acknowledged in the scientific press. This results in large scale under-reporting of studies which fail to demonstrate differences between the sexes in humans. Coupled with the prominent publishing of measured gender differences (often with much press attention), this may result in a significant exaggeration of human sex differences. For example, the suggestion that women have less lateralised brains (less specialisation between the two cerebral hemispheres), is a currently popular theory. However, most experiments have detected no measurable difference in lateralisation. The effect of such non-reporting may be amplified by our subjective preference for the idea that the human sexes are significantly different in terms of their psychology. Most of us would rather be seen as distinctly male or female and therefore prefer to exaggerate the differences between the sexes, whether or not they are actually true.

Is there a universal human nature?

According to Wilson (1978), universal human nature is a collection of behavioural traits shared by all human societies. These behaviours are the expression of specific genetic structures and are the result of evolutionary adaptation through natural selection (see Chapter 1, page 6). For example, one of the most common claims for universal behaviour is that of genetically adaptive differences between the sexes (see Chapter 6). However, this claim has been criticised by Gould (1990), as described in Box 3.1. Other critics of Wilson suggest that he depicts only western capitalist society, and that many other societies do not fit this mould. Wilson has responded to this challenge by claiming that any exceptions to universal human nature are 'temporary' adaptations or deviations. However, in general, rigid sociobiological explanations of a universal human nature are unconvincing and Wilson's ideas on human nature have generally been rejected.

The evolutionary psychology approach is that there *is* a universal human nature, but that this universality exists primarily at the level of evolved psychological mechanisms, not of expressed cultural behaviours (see Box 3.2). Nevertheless, it may also be possible to talk about a 'general culture' because being human imposes all kinds of restrictions across and within cultures, as do the common features of the environments we inhabit. It is within these common elements of culture that we would expect to see the effects of evolutionary psychology.

Tooby and Cosmides (1995) suggested a thought experiment to illustrate that, despite appearances to the contrary, humans do share a universal nature. Consider each human as a jukebox, equipped with thousands of songs. Each jukebox is identical and selects what song

Box 3.2 The evolutionary psychology model of universal human nature (Cosmides and Tooby, 1992)

According to evolutionary psychology, universal human nature consists of evolved psychological mechanisms (mental adaptations) to solve common problems. These mechanisms respond differently to a wide range of environmental inputs, producing the great variability observed in human culture. In other words, most human behaviour is a product of the interaction of a large number of environmental inputs with a myriad of psychological mechanisms designed by natural selection. This may be considered similar to a chess-playing computer. The programme is consistent, but the games played are enormously variable, depending on the inputs. The sole aim of the chess programme is to win the game. Likewise, although human behaviour is flexible, the basic goals that motivate our behaviour are inflexible, specific and universal. In general, complex adaptations in humans are genetically invariant. Most genetic variability in our species is confined to the periphery, and is probably mainly concerned with protection against contagious disease (see Chapter 13). Therefore, despite criticism to the contrary from social scientists, the evolutionary approach actually *minimises* genetic differences between individuals.

it will play on the basis of its location, the time, and the date. This situation would result in the same kind of pattern of within-group similarities and between-group differences observable among humans. In New York, every jukebox would be playing the same song, which would be different from the song that every jukebox would be playing in Bombay, and so on, around the world. Each jukebox's behaviour would change over time and with changes in location, appearing to adopt local 'behaviour'. Nevertheless, the generation of this distinctive, culture-like pattern involves no social learning or transmission. This pattern is brought about because, like humans, the jukeboxes share a universal architecture that is designed to respond to inputs from the local situation (although this is a highly simplified situation, and in humans there are many more inputs than simple date, time and location).

Cultural evolution

According to Maynard-Smith (1993), human societies change far too rapidly for the differences between them to be accounted for by genetic differences between their members. This has prompted critics to suggest that most human behaviour is a product of human culture. This could make it difficult to find evolutionary explanations. However, there may be fundamental human characteristics that underpin our culture and an evolutionary approach *may* be useful in explaining these particular characteristics. Furthermore, I argued in Chapter 2 that the effects of genes and culture on generating observed behaviour are virtually indistinguishable. Rather than reiterate the ideas examined in Chapter 2, I will examine only one aspect of the influence of cultural evolution – the difference in the relative importance of cultural evolution in humans and non-human animals.

It is widely accepted that culture has played a much greater part in the evolution of human behaviour than in other species. This has led to the idea that differences between non-human animals and humans are qualitative, rather than quantitative, and the degree to which investigations of non-human animal behaviour are applicable to humans has been questioned. According to Hinde (1982), there are four sources of difficulty for those attempting to draw inferences from behavioural ecology (the study of non-human animal behaviour in the natural environment) to human social behaviour. These are summarised in Box 3.3.

Box 3.3 Problems in using behavioural ecology to explain human social behaviour

- The differences in cognitive ability between non-human animals and humans.
- The unique human capacity for language and culture.
- The extremely large diversity of behaviours observed in non-human animal species.
- The requirement to examine human behaviour at a number of levels of analysis – focusing on one level and drawing parallels is insufficient.

Genetic determinism

Determinism is the idea that all behaviour is caused (determined) by external or internal events. People are seen as passive responders and so are not free to decide their own actions. Determinists argue that all human behaviour could potentially be explained as resulting from some definite cause or causes, and we are thus under the control of our heredity (genes) and our environment. Within this framework, there appear to be different schools of thought as to the most important determinants of our behaviour. Burrhus Skinner, for example, was considered to be an *environmental* determinist, believing that internal processes have very little influence on the way we behave. In contrast, Edward Wilson is considered by many to be a *genetic* (or *biological*) determinist, assuming that most of our behaviour is directed by the need to survive and reproduce.

Philosophically opposed to the idea of determinism are those who believe in the notion of *free will.* According to this doctrine, we are free to make whatever decisions we want in life. In other words, we are the cause of our own actions. This is an appealing concept and fits in with the idea that we are at least in partial control of our behaviour. However, it could be argued that free will implies that our behaviour is uncaused or random. Furthermore, most successful sciences are based on the assumption of determinism. In terms of the present chapter, we need to address the criticism that the evolutionary approach is a 'biologically determinist explanation of human existence' (Rose and Rose, 2000) and that evolutionary psychology is simply a 'biological version of Calvinism' (Honeybourne, personal communication). (Calvinism is the idea that our fate is predestined, based on the teachings of the theologian John Calvin.)

It should be pointed out that evolutionary psychologists do *not* make a claim for genes *determining* behaviour. Rather, they talk about the *influence* of genes on behaviour. One reason why this confusion may arise is that, when examining the influence of gene A on behaviour X, we may talk about a gene (A) *for* behaviour X. What this actually means is that there is genetic variation in the population for a trait X and, other things being equal, a person with gene A is *more likely* to produce behaviour X than a person without the gene. However, it should be pointed out that genes do not influence behaviour directly, in the sense of interfering with everyday actions. They only influence behaviour in the sense of *programming* before the behaviour occurs (Dawkins, 1989). (This idea is similar to that of the computer chess example discussed in Box 3.2). Therefore, genes 'determine' behaviour only in a statistical sense, and must exert an influence on any behaviour pattern that evolves by natural selection. However, behaviour is influenced in very complex ways by many factors (Figure 3.2). There is no reason why the influence of genes cannot easily be modified or reversed by other factors.

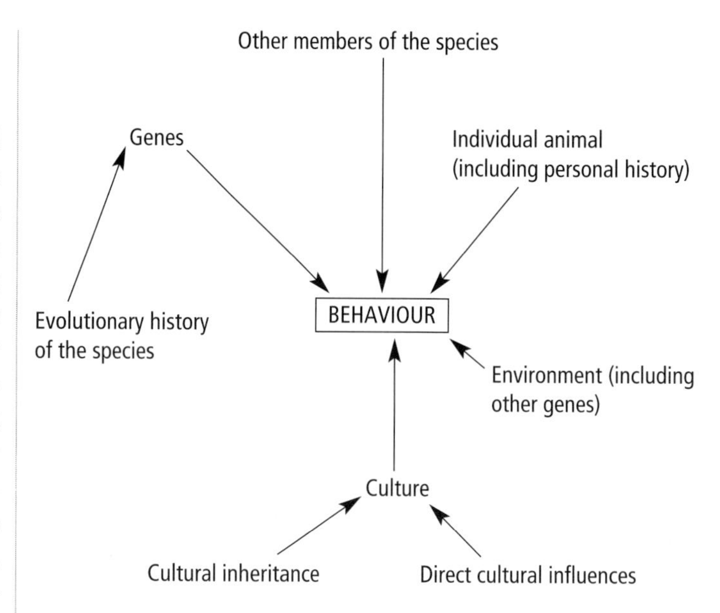

Figure 3.2 Behaviour is influenced in very complex ways by many factors

In conclusion, evolutionary psychologists are *not* biological determinists, although they do believe in a universal human nature. Contrary to the social science viewpoint, behaviour can vary between people and still be biological in nature. To reject biological explanations because they are considered to be synonymous with determinism is to 'throw the baby out with the bath water' and reject a whole level of explanation which is potentially very enlightening.

Reductionism

Reductionism is the analysis of complex things into simple constituents. Biological reductionists believe that all psychology can be explained in terms of biology (physiology and biochemistry) and that these biological explanations are preferable because they are more detailed and 'scientific'. The following quotation by

Crick (1994) is a typical example of biological reductionism:

> You, your joys and your sorrows, your memories and your ambitions, your sense of personality and free will, are in fact no more than the behaviour of a vast assembly of nerve cells and their associated molecules . . .

However, our joys, our memories and our sense of free will are all properties of the brain as a *system*, not properties of individual nerve cells. In other words, the whole is definitely greater than the sum of its parts. Similarly, *psychological* reductionists, such as Skinner, advocate analysis behaviour into simple stimulus-response (S-R) relationships. This is the basis of *behaviourism*, the limitations of which are discussed elsewhere (Clamp and Russell, 1998). Therefore, at this point in time at least, most human behaviour cannot be understood solely in terms of basic neurophysiological or S-R processes, and the usefulness of reductionism is questionable (Eysenck and Keane, 1995).

Genetic 'explanations' of behaviour, such as sociobiology, have been accused of being reductionist in nature. However, evolutionary psychology advocates integration and consistency between fields of knowledge (such as cognitive psychology, anthropology, evolutionary biology and social psychology), not psychological or biological reductionism. In other words, it is better if genetic explanations are used to enhance psychological explanations, not replace them, as seen in the *eclectic* approach (see Box 3.4).

Box 3.4 'Explaining' schizophrenia: the use of the eclectic approach

Evidence suggests that genetic factors are involved in the development of schizophrenia. Other studies have pointed out that schizophrenics tend to be unduly sensitive to the neurotransmitter dopamine (see Chapter 15). Therefore, reductionists might be tempted to produce a genetic and/or biochemical theory of schizophrenia. However, such an approach would ignore environmental factors, such as poor social relationships and adverse life events, which also play a role in producing schizophrenia (Davison and Neale, 1990).

According to the eclectic approach, a full understanding of schizophrenia will necessitate considering all the relevant factors and the ways in which they combine together. Similarly, evolutionary psychology advocates integration between fields of knowledge, such as cognitive psychology and evolutionary biology. However, one problem with the eclectic approach is that it is often very difficult to integrate information from different disciplines into a single theory. Nevertheless, a full understanding of psychological phenomena will often require knowledge from other subject areas.

In summary, to rely solely on the evolutionary approach is an example of reductionism and, as such, limits our understanding of human behaviour. Evolutionary psychology, while pointing out the importance of evolved psychological mechanisms, also emphasises the need for a collective approach to the analysis of human nature.

Evidence for the evolutionary approach: the adaptationist debate

Evolutionary explanations of behaviour have been accused of over-emphasising the adaptationist approach (Gould and Lewontin, 1979). Critics of this approach claim that humans are afflicted with the worst excesses of 'pop sociobiology' (speculative, storytelling adaptationism) because we have so little data about a slow-breeding species that cannot be manipulated for experimental purposes. Furthermore, the issue is further complicated by cultural evolution minimising the effects of Darwinian adaptation (Gould, 1990).

An adaptation is any characteristic that has been shaped by natural selection. Williams (1966) suggested three criteria that should be employed to ascertain whether a feature is truly an adaptation, these being: reliability, economy and efficiency. A feature is reliable if it regularly develops in all members of the species under normal environmental conditions. It is economical if it solves an adaptive problem without a huge cost to the future success of the organism. Finally, the feature must also be an efficient solution to the adaptive problem. If all three criteria are satisfied, it is unlikely that the feature could have arisen by chance alone (Cartwright, 2000).

Evolutionary psychologists recognise that not all human behaviour represents an adaptation for survival or reproduction. A behaviour may currently raise the inclusive fitness of an individual, or it may be currently maladaptive, but did promote fitness in the past in different environments. Alternatively, the behaviour in question may never have been adaptive, simply representing a by-product of some other feature of the species. Furthermore, just because a certain behaviour is considered adaptive, it does not mean that it is developmentally unchangeable or socially desirable (see page 5).

Hayes (1994) suggests that the evolutionary approach has a methodological weakness in that it tends to look only for confirmatory instances of human and animal behaviour, and to ignore those examples that do not seem to support the approach. Gould (1990) believes this bias is symptomatic of a major problem in science, the reluctance to publish null results. Hayes (1994) also claims that evolutionary arguments are 'strikingly lacking' in supporting evidence. For example, genetic arguments suggest that step-parents tend to be hostile to step-children, but Hayes claims there is no evidence to support this assertion. As it happens, this does not appear to be the case, and such evidence does exist (Pinker, 1997). Nevertheless, there is no doubt that it is difficult to identify the genes responsible for a particular human behaviour, and there is currently little scientific evidence to support the theoretical arguments. However, this assumes a simple relationship between genes and behaviour, which is probably not the case, and a lack of scientific evidence in favour of an approach is not the same as evidence against the approach. Moreover, it is entirely possible to test evolutionary hypotheses about the adaptive nature of certain human characteristics without knowing the details about the genetic basis of these characteristics (Alcock, 1993).

Ethical concerns

The evolutionary approach has been criticised for apparently supporting anti-social behaviours such as aggression and *eugenics* (the improvement of human society through selective breeding, see Box 3.5). There is also an ethical concern that the approach may be seen to support gender stereotypes, such as expecting males to be promiscuous or considering rape to be an 'adaptive' male trait (see Chapter 6, page 53).

Box 3.5 Eugenics: breeding better humans

The term eugenics was first coined by Sir Francis Galton, a cousin of Charles Darwin, and means 'noble in heredity' or 'good in birth'. Galton believed that humans could be improved by artificial selection (see Chapter 1, page 4). Those that were 'genetically gifted' should be encouraged to interbreed, while the 'unworthy' should be prevented from breeding.

From 1900, popular eugenics movements and centres for eugenic study were set up in Britain, America and the Soviet Union. However, the most famous example of a eugenics programme was the disastrous attempt to create a 'master race' in Nazi Germany. After the war, the idea lingered on for several decades in the USA, supported by legislation to sterilise criminals and the 'feebleminded'. Eventually, it became recognised that the scientific basis of these social policies did not actually exist.

Eugenics, in its original sense, is no longer considered a valid method for the improvement of humanity. However, some psychologists believe that the new sciences of genetic testing, embryo manipulation and cloning are merely 'eugenics in disguise'.

Hayes (1994) suggests that evolutionary biologists select only negative aspects of human behaviour, such as aggression and cheating, and portray them as *inevitable* biological consequences of human nature. This is shown in the words of the sociobiologist Edward Wilson (1978), when he wrote:

> . . . because these are genetic differences, and because the behaviour is adaptive, we can show that it will be difficult to modify the behaviour by altering the social environment.

However, the criticisms of Hayes (1994) are invalid in two important respects. First, evolutionary biologists do use examples of pro-social behaviour, such as co-operation (see Chapter 7). Second, very few advocates of the evolutionary approach believe that any behaviour is inevitable.

The use of evolutionary theory in a social or political context is known as 'Social Darwinism'. In this case, the 'survival of the fittest' is seen as the survival of those individuals who are the most ruthless, and this concept is applied to the social system. For example, unregulated capitalism may be seen as good for the economy. Therefore, any social welfare programmes would interfere with the 'survival of the fittest' and hence the progress of society. It is important to realise that unchecked capitalism would brings costs to the winners as well as the losers, such as increases in crime. Social Darwinism is not true Darwinism, and it is really only an argument used to justify exploitation.

In summary, many ethical concerns have been expressed about the nature of sociobiology. However, few of these concerns apply to evolutionary psychology. Moreover, it is important to remember that evolutionary psychology is a discipline that attempts to *explain* human behaviour; it does not attempt to *justify* the behaviour.

Conclusions

The evolutionary approach is potentially very useful when seeking explanations of human behaviour, but it cannot account for all aspects of the diverse behavioural repertoires seen in our species. The approach is limited by the fact that behaviour is also influenced by the environment, and can be culturally transmitted. In addition, evolutionary theory has been accused of being both deterministic and reductive in nature. Furthermore, there is currently limited evidence for evolutionary explanations of behaviour and ethical concerns have been expressed. Nevertheless, these arguments apply almost exclusively to sociobiology *not* evolutionary psychology, which represents a unique and invaluable perspective for understanding human behaviour.

SUMMARY

- There are several potential limitations of the evolutionary approach. These include: **the role of the environment; the influence of cultural evolution; the deterministic and reductive nature of the approach; limited supporting evidence;** and **ethical concerns**. However, these limitations apply mainly to sociobiology and **not** to evolutionary psychology.
- **Behaviour is always an interaction between genes and the environment, never purely genetic**. The influence of a gene may be modified by environmental events, both internal (e.g. other genes or diet) and external (e.g. education).
- **Sociobiologists** believe that **universal human nature** is a collection of behavioural traits shared by all human societies. These behaviours are the expression of specific genetic structures and are the result of **evolutionary adaptation through natural selection**. However, this approach has been criticised and is far from convincing. In contrast, **evolutionary psychologists** believe that universal human nature exists primarily at the level of **evolved psychological mechanisms**, not of expressed cultural behaviours.
- Human societies change far too rapidly for the differences between them to be accounted for by genetic differences between their members, and critics have suggested that **most human behaviour is a product of human culture**. The influence of culture on human evolution questions the validity of using the comparative approach to investigate the behaviour of our species.
- Sociobiology has been accused of being a **biologically determinist explanation of human existence**. However, genes determine behaviour only in a statistical sense, and must exert an influence on any behaviour pattern that evolves by natural selection. There is no reason why the influence of genes cannot easily be modified or reversed by other factors.
- Sociobiology has also been criticised as **reductionist**. However, evolutionary psychology advocates integration and consistency between fields of knowledge, not biological reductionism. It is better if genetic explanations are used to enhance psychological explanations, not replace them, as seen in the **eclectic** approach.
- Evolutionary explanations of behaviour have been accused of over-emphasising the **adaptationist** approach. However, evolutionary psychologists recognise that not all human behaviour represents an adaptation for survival or reproduction. Furthermore, just because a certain behaviour is considered adaptive, it does not mean that it is **developmentally unchangeable**.

- It has been suggested that the evolutionary approach has a methodological weakness in that it tends to look only for confirmatory instances of human and animal behaviour, and to ignore those examples that do not seem to support the approach. Critics have also claimed that **evolutionary arguments lack supporting evidence**. However, this assumes a simple relationship between genes and behaviour, which is probably not the case. Moreover, it is entirely possible to test evolutionary hypotheses about the adaptive nature of certain human characteristics without knowing the details about the genetic basis of these characteristics.
- Many **ethical concerns** have been expressed about the nature of sociobiology, including its apparent support for **anti-social behaviour** and **gender stereotypes**. However, few of these concerns apply to evolutionary psychology. It is important to remember that evolutionary psychology is a discipline that attempts to **explain** human behaviour, it does not attempt to **justify** the behaviour.

PART 2
Sexual selection

MATING BEHAVIOUR AND SOCIAL ORGANISATION

Introduction and overview

The second part of this book (Chapters 4-6) looks at evolutionary explanations of reproductive behaviour in humans. It examines mating behaviour and social organisation, parent–offspring conflict and human sexual behaviour. This chapter considers the nature and consequences of human mating behaviour, including the influence of such behaviour on social organisation.

Human mating behaviour has traditionally been considered as a number of possible *systems*, where each system is defined by the typical number of mates possessed by a person. This chapter starts with a review of this classification, together with a consideration of the advantages and disadvantages of each system for males and females. I will then attempt to explain why evolutionary psychologists consider the notion of systems to be outdated and too inflexible, replacing them with mating *strategies* (behavioural plans that individuals use to raise fitness through the successful pursuit of a mate). This approach focuses on the strategies of individuals rather than the behaviour of whole groups, showing us that sex is as much about conflict as cooperation, each sex employing tactics that best serve its own interests (Cartwright, 2000).

Mating systems

I shall define mating systems by the number of partners each sex maintains. A male could have one mate or many. Similarly, a female could have one mate or many. Thus, there are four basic mating systems, as shown in Box 4.1. *Monogamy* is where one male and one female form a pair which is exclusive of others: this may be annual (a new pair bond formed each year) or perennial (a pair bond formed for life). All other mating systems are *polygamous* – that is, they involve more than one member of one or both sexes. In *polygyny*, one male mates with many females (females mate with only one male), whilst in *polyandry* one female mates with many males (males mate with only one female). Where both sexes have multiple partners, the strategy is called *polygynandry*. For example, a pride of lions typically consists of a stable group of two males and 4-10 females. Furthermore, both polygyny and polyandry may be either *simultaneous* (bonding with several members of the opposite sex at the same time) or *successive* (bonding with several members of the opposite sex, but one at a time).

The term *promiscuity* has been used to describe mating systems where both sexes have multiple partners at one time. However, this makes it difficult to distinguish promiscuity from serial monogamy or polygamy. It is also a poor choice of term for a mating system where

Box 4.1 Possible mating systems

		Number of males in partnership 1	2+
Number of females in partnership	1	Monogamy	Polyandry
	2+	Polygyny	Polygynandry

Mono: = one; poly: = many; andry: = male; gyny: = female.

both males and females have multiple partners, suggesting that mate choice may be indiscriminate (which it rarely is) and that it is not a stable system. Many mammals have stable multi-male, multi-female mating systems and so the term polygynandry may be more appropriate than promiscuity, which should only be used to refer to males and females seeking extra matings outside a monogamous pairing.

Males and females: vive la différence

Males and females need not be physically or behaviourally different, as is the case in humans (who are *sexually dimorphic*). They are simply required to produce gametes of different sizes (*anisogamy*). 'Males' produce small mobile gametes called *sperm*, and that is what makes them male. 'Females' produce large immobile gametes called *eggs*, which have a store of energy which serves to assist the embryo in its development (Figure 4.1). Sperm are produced in very large numbers, each individual sperm having the capacity to fertilise an egg, although very few will do so. Eggs are more costly to produce, so females make fewer in a lifetime and release them in significantly smaller numbers than males produce sperm. Overall, males and females put the same amount of energy into making gametes, they simply spread that energy out differently.

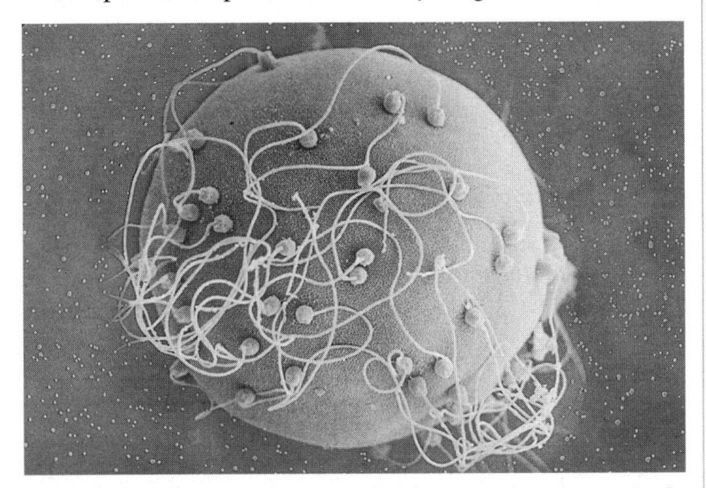

Figure 4.1 For any species, each gamete (sperm or egg) contains the same amount of genetic information. Eggs, however, are much bigger so require greater investment, hence females can afford to produce fewer gametes than males Copyright: Science Photo Library © D Phillips.

A human female is able to produce fertile gametes for only a short proportion of her lifespan, and during this time she is only *fertile* (carrying an egg which can be fertilised) for about two days every month. Once the egg is fertilised, the woman will then be pregnant for nine months, during which time she will release no further eggs. A woman who became pregnant at every opportunity would only be fertile for about 900 days in total. Men, by contrast, are fertile for decades. Therefore, females bearing fertile eggs are a scarce resource, but fertile males are common. It is this key biological difference that underpins human sexual behaviour: men will seek to increase the *quantity* of their offspring, whilst females are more interested in ensuring the *quality* of their offspring. The mating strategies of males and females will often not coincide and a compromise is required.

The difference between male and female reproductive capacity, which underlies the belief that they should favour different mating systems, is supported by several studies on humans. For example, the largest number of children fathered by one man is 888, whereas the largest number of children for a woman is a mere 69 (and was only that high as a consequence of an unusual rate of triplets). Alcock (1993) makes several predictions, based on the difference in restraint on genetic success for males and females, which are shown in Box 4.2. This suggests that males will prefer polygyny, but that females will prefer monogamy. However, it is not quite that simple, as the rest of this chapter will attempt to explain.

Box 4.2 Differences in the sexual behaviour of human males and females (Alcock, 1993)

Trait	*Male*	*Female*
Threshold for sexual arousal	Low	High
Desire for sexual variety	High	Lower
Adultery	More frequent	Less frequent
Rape	Occasional	Almost never
Concern for mate's sexual fidelity	Very high	Moderate

Monogamy

As noted above, monogamy is a mating system in which each male and female pair is exclusive. The pair may bond for life (*perennial monogamy*), or individuals may have several mates during a lifetime, one after the other (*serial monogamy*). Monogamy is the norm in species where parental care is labour intensive, so it is not surprising that this is the most common mating system in humans.

Monogamy is not without its problems. Males have the potential to fertilise many females and may benefit from *cheating* (Figure 4.2) Therefore females cannot be sure that they are the single mate of any male, or that he will stay to care for the young. Males, by contrast, risk *cuckoldry* (being duped by the female into raising young which they did not father). As males do not give birth, they are less sure than females as to which offspring are theirs. In other words, males have *low paternity certainty*. Nevertheless, this is unlikely to prevent the evolution of parental care in males, as investing in just a few of their own offspring would accrue sufficient genetic benefit for selection pressure to favour such care. In species where offspring require some parental investment by the male in order to survive, parental care is a better strategy than promiscuity. Fewer offspring may be conceived, but a much greater proportion of them will survive to reproduce themselves – there is no point in fathering large numbers of offspring if none of them survive to reproductive age.

Figure 4.2

The two main issues facing males are the net gain from an individual helping its own progeny, and the cost of raising the fitness of others by caring for young that are not the individual's own. Male tactics for avoiding cuckoldry include controlling resources, 'guarding' the female (related to the intense sexual jealousy associated with males) and sperm competition. Females also employ tactics to ensure the fidelity of their mates, including demanding a vast commitment of time and effort during courtship, and concealed ovulation (maintaining constant male interest, as the timing of fertile periods is unknown). These issues are discussed further in Chapter 6.

It should be noted that while humans are generally 'socially monogamous', *adultery* is fairly common. The reasons for this are examined in Box 4.3. Extra-pair

Box 4.3 Adultery

Adultery may have had a big part to play in shaping human society, because there have often been advantages to both sexes from within a monogamous marriage in seeking alternative sexual partners. This conclusion is based on studies of human society, both modern and tribal, and on comparisons with apes and birds.

The main advantage of adultery to males is relatively clear-cut, in that each extra mating is likely to improve reproductive success (see main text). However, women appear to prefer monogamous marriage and do not seek sexual variety *per se*. Nevertheless, women are sometimes unfaithful. Though she may rarely or never be interested in casual sex with a male prostitute or stranger, a woman is perfectly capable of engaging in an affair with a male acquaintance. Ridley (1993) suggests that there are three possible explanations for this paradoxical behaviour.

1 *Dangerous Liaisons*: adultery is the fault of men, who persuade or coerce women into affairs.
2 *Dallas*: modern society is to blame for female adultery. The frustrations and complexities of modern life, and of unhappy marriages, have introduced this 'unnatural' habit into women.
3 *Emma Bovary*: there is some valid biological reason for seeking sex outside marriage without abandoning the marriage. Adultery may serve to procure high-quality genes from a healthy, attractive and successful lover, whilst maintaining the care and support provided by an attentive husband.

copulation (EPC) is superficially most beneficial to males, as their minimal parental investment in each breeding attempt prescribes no limit to the number of offspring they could father. Consider a foraging man with one wife, who could typically expect two to five children with her. A premarital or extramarital liaison that conceives a child would increase his reproductive output by twenty to fifty percent (assuming the child survives). The optimal situation is probably a liaison with a married woman whose cuckolded husband would help bring up the child, but sex with an unmarried partner could also increase reproductive success. Therefore, we would expect men to seek a variety of sexual partners and to be relatively promiscuous. However, the same logic does not apply to women, because there is no direct relationship between the quantity of matings and number of offspring, as there is for males (Box 4.4 describes recent studies on attitudes to sex that appear to support these ideas). Nevertheless, there *are* benefits to females of engaging in extra-pair copulations, as described on pages 32-33.

Box 4.4 Post-modern sexual attitudes

Are the ideas proposed by evolutionary psychology out-dated following the feminist revolution and the emergence of the 'new man'? Two recent studies suggests that this is not the case.

Research by Buss (1999) used confidential questionnaires to investigate male and female attitudes to sex. Some of the findings are outlined below.

Question	*Male*	*Female*
"How strongly are you seeking a one-night stand?"	Pretty strongly	Not very strongly
"How many sexual partners would you like to have in your lifetime?"	Eighteen	Four or five
"Would you consider having sex with a desirable partner that you had known for a week?"	Probably yes	Definitely not

The second study used a field experiment to investigate sexual attitudes. Attractive men and women were hired to approach strangers of the opposite sex on a university campus, introduce themselves and ask one of three questions. The questions, and their responses, are shown below.

Question	*Male*	*Female*
"Would you go out with me tonight?"	50% said yes	50% said yes
"Would you come over to my apartment tonight?"	69% said yes	6% said yes
"Would you go to bed with me tonight?"	75% said yes	None said yes

An awakening of male sexual desire by a new partner is known as the *Coolidge effect,* following a visit by President Coolidge and his wife to a government farm. When Mrs Coolidge was told that the rooster copulated dozens of times each day, she asked for the president to be told. When the president was told about the rooster, he asked, "Same hen every time?" "Oh no, Mr President, a different one each time." The president said, "Tell that to Mrs Coolidge!" This effect shows that male desire is not undiscriminating. According to Pinker (1997), males may not care *what kind of* female they mate with, but they are very sensitive to *which* female they mate with.

Sexual behaviour, of course, also depends on the desirability of the individuals, not just the average desires of the sexes. People "pay" for sex (in cash, commitment or favours) when the partner is more desirable than they are. Since women are more discriminating than men, the average man has to pay for sex with the average woman. If we assume that a marriage commitment is a kind of payment, the average man could attract a higher-quality wife than casual sex partner. However, the average woman could attract a higher-quality casual sex partner (who would pay nothing) than her husband (Pinker, 1997). The highest quality men, in theory, should have a large number of women willing to have sex with them. Nevertheless, a desire for variety does not always lead to promiscuous behaviour. A man's sexual tastes can be controlled by a number of factors, including his attractiveness, the availability of partners, and his assessment of the costs of a dalliance. These costs include the risk of sexually transmitted diseases, aggression from competing males, reduction of sperm reserves (and so a lower capacity for sperm competition [see below]) and leaving the primary mate unguarded, increasing the risk of cuckoldry.

Extra-pair copulation (EPC) also has several advantages for females. One of these is *superior genes*; females may cuckold investing males when other males appear to offer better genes. A second possible advantage of having several consecutive mates for females could be *sperm competition*, a kind of internal race in which the most fit sperm wins, the consequences of which are described in Box 4.5. A third reason for females to engage in EPC is simply the material benefit of whatever aspiring males can offer (Symons, 1979). Kaplan and Hill (1985) found that the better hunters in a foraging society outreproduced poorer ones, partly because their children survived better, but also in part because hunting prowess gained men extramarital affairs with fertile women. A fourth potential benefit of female adultery is that uncertainty over paternity may sometimes increase the total investment by potential fathers, or at least reduce the possibility that those males will damage the young at a later date (Hrdy, 1981). Other potential advantages of EPC include status enhancement, greater genetic diversity among offspring, and the avoidance of aggression from ardent males.

Box 4.5 Mating systems and sperm competition

Sperm competition provides the female with a simple and effective strategy for deciding which male is the best. She simply mates with several males and lets their gametes fight it out! Of course, gamete viability is not necessarily related to the vigour or success of adults, but even so, for sons inheriting the capacity to produce fit sperm, it is still an advantage in its own right.

Anatomical evidence for a history of extrapair mating by females can be seen in the testis size of males (Short, 1976). Men's testes are significantly larger, relative to body size, than those of gorillas, a species in which females mate monogamously (although the males are polygynous) so that sperm competition is absent. This suggests that men evolved in an environment where sperm competition was more extreme than in gorillas (as men have relatively larger sperm counts and ejaculate volumes). By contrast, female chimpanzees live in large polygynandrous groups, leading to intense sperm competition. Male chimpanzees have a relative testis size much greater than our own, implying that human sperm competition is less vigorous than that in chimpanzees. This suggests that humans are adapted to an ancestral mating system in which females were not so polygamous as chimpanzees, but were certainly not monogamous like the gorilla. (A further discussion of sperm competition is provided in Chapter 6.)

There are several potential costs to extrapair mating in females, including wasted time in acquiring superfluous gametes and risk of disease transmission (Daly and Wilson, 1978). Males may use violence to deter infidelity if it seems likely to occur, and it is also possible that paternal investment may be reduced or withdrawn should the male mate discover that he has been cuckolded. In general, females would be expected to weigh up the costs and benefits of each mating system, and act accordingly (see 'from systems to strategies' on page 35). However, one factor influencing their behaviour will be the strategies of males, and game theory analysis is often useful (see Chapter 1, page 10).

Polygyny

Polygamous mating systems involve multiple pairings. As noted earlier, in *polygyny*, one male mates with several females. This may arise as a series of separate meetings (*serial polygyny*), or relatively permanent groups of females may stay with a male (*simultaneous polygyny*). It is interesting to note that sex differences are more pronounced in polygamous than monogamous species and the exaggeration of male traits is related to competition for resources, mates, or both (Low, 1979). Since males appear to be mainly concerned with the quantity of mates, and females with the quality of mates, we might expect men to favour polygyny and women to prefer monogamy. Which of these two systems have been generally employed by our species? According to Ridley (1993), there are five ways to answer this question, leading to five different conclusions:

1. *Study modern people directly:* monogamous marriage is the norm.
2. *Examine historical mating strategies:* rich and powerful men kept many females in large harems, poor men remained celibate.
3. *Look at people living in simple societies in the present day:* less polygamous than early civilisations, less monogamous than modern society.
4. *Compare ourselves with our closest non-human relatives:* we appear to be somewhere between the monogamy of gibbons, the harem polygyny of the gorilla, and the polygynandry distinctive of chimpanzees.
5. *Compare ourselves with other animals that share our highly social habits:* studies of colonial birds, monkeys and dolphins suggest that we are designed for a system of monogamy plagued by adultery.

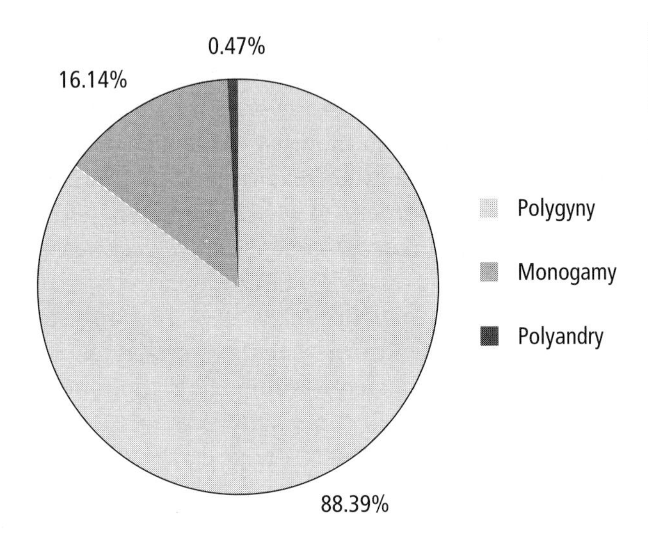

Figure 4.3 Human mating systems in traditional cultures prior to western influence (from Smith, 1984)

Most people live in monogamous societies, but this may be due to the influence of western culture, not human nature (Figure 4.3). Although the most populous societies are monogamous (perhaps in name only, see Box 4.3), about three-quarters of all tribal cultures are polygamous. Polygyny is eight times more common than monogamy in pre-industrial societies with a strong bias towards inheritance through males, but less than half as common where there is no such bias (Mace and Pagel, 1997). (However, monogamy and polygyny in this context refers to the marriage system, not the actual mating system. This is because patriarchal inheritance concentrates wealth in the hands of a small number of males, encouraging a polygynous system). Throughout history, powerful men have usually had more than one mate each, even if they have had only one legitimate wife (see Box 4.6). However, even in openly polygamous societies, most men have only one wife and virtually all women have only one husband. It seems that humans are both polygamous and monogamous, adapting their behaviour according to the circumstances. A historical perspective on the monogamy-polygamy debate is provided in Box 4.7.

Box 4.6 Polygyny in ancient civilisations

In the ancient civilisation of the Incas, the Sun-King Atahualpa kept 1500 concubines in 'houses of virgins' throughout his kingdom. They were selected for their beauty, and at a very young age (rarely more than eight years old) to ensure their virginity. Beneath him, each rank of society was granted a harem of a particular size. This ranged from 700 women for Great Lords to three women for chiefs of five men. Of course this meant that the average male Indian had little access to women, and may have been tempted to cuckold his seniors. However, the penalties for this were severe, involving death to the man in question and to his whole family, servants, fellow villagers and llamas!

The accumulation of vast power is often translated into prodigious sexual productivity. The Babylonian king Hammurabi had thousands of slave 'wives', and the Aztec ruler Montezuma enjoyed four thousand concubines. All of these powerful rulers used similar techniques to preserve their reproductive success. They recruited virginal women and kept them in forts, protected by eunuchs. Furthermore, wet nurses were employed and careful records kept of fertile periods to ensure maximum reproductive output. Chinese emperors were taught to conserve their semen so as to keep up their quota of two women a day, and some even complained of their onerous sexual duties! These polygynous systems could hardly have been more carefully designed as breeding machines, dedicated to spreading the genes of powerful men (Betzig, 1986).

Box 4.7 Human mating behaviour: monogamy or polygyny?

Jews practised polygyny until Christian times and outlawed it only in the tenth century. Mormons encouraged it until it was outlawed by the US government in the late nineteenth century, and even today there are thought to be tens of thousands of clandestine polygynous marriages in Utah and other western states. Whenever polygyny is allowed, men seek additional wives and the means to attract them (Pinker, 1997). Are there any patterns in human history that may explain the waxing and waning of polygyny?

In foraging societies, it is difficult to accumulate wealth. A great deal of luck is involved in hunting and only a few particularly good hunters, or skilled leaders, would have the resources required for polygyny. However, with the invention of agriculture, the opportunity for some males to be polygynous arrived with a vengeance. Men could accumulate a surplus of food with which to buy labour, allowing them to increase their resources still further. Wealth brought further wealth, and great differences in resource-holding power (the control over resources) ensued. It is not surprising that nearly all pastoral societies are polygynous.

Today, few modern cultures practise polygyny to any great extent. The reasons for this change are unclear, but may be related to the rise of democracy. It seems likely that extreme polygyny only existed for a short period of evolutionary history, between the end of hunter-gathering and the spread of democracy (Cartwright, 2000). According to Ridley (1993), once monogamous men had a chance to vote against polygamists, their fate was sealed. We are back to the same situation that existed before 'civilisation', in the (relatively) monogamous Pleistocene era.

Polyandry

Polyandry is like polygyny with sex role reversal, because here one female mates with many males. In polyandry, it is the male's parental care which is the scarce resource, as it is this that guarantees the survival of the young. The males are investing more, and are therefore more choosy.

Unsurprisingly, polyandry is rare in all species, including humans. Men occasionally share a wife in harsh environments, such as Tibet (see below), but the arrangement usually collapses when conditions improve. The Inuit occasionally have polyandrous marriages, but the co-husbands are often jealous and one frequently murders the other (Pinker, 1997). One way to reduce this competitive element is for the males to share a genetic interest. This is what sometimes happens among Tibetan farmers, where two brothers marry a woman simultaneously in the hope of putting together a family that can survive in the bleak territory. This arrangement avoids the split of a family landholding by keeping the family unit above a certain minimum size (the tax system is also weighted against the division of property). However, this often remains an unsatisfactory arrangement for the junior brother, who aspires to have a wife of his own (Crook, 1980).

A number of morphological and physiological phenomena in humans appear to reflect a history of selection in which polyandrous mating was frequent enough to be consequential (Wilson and Daly, 1992). However, it seems likely that both males and females had multiple partners, and these issues are best considered under the heading of *polygynandry*.

Polygynandry

Polygynandry refers to a stable multi-male, multi-female mating system. From the point of view of males, this system has the advantage of more mating opportunities, but carries a much greater risk of cuckoldry. This disadvantage is less important if the males in a polygynandrous group are related to each other, as they will all gain (although not necessarily to the same extent) via inclusive fitness. Females gain access to resources, which are often better than they could receive in a monogamous system. However, they lose out in terms of parental investment from males (compared to monogamy), although it is rare to see *no* parental care by males. In human populations, polygynandry is vary rare. One example is seen in the Pahari people of north India, where wives have to be purchased at a substantial price. Brothers may typically pool their resources to buy a wife, resulting in temporary polyandry. When they can afford it, another wife is usually taken. The eventual result is group marriage or polygynandry in which two or more husbands are married to two or more wives. The Pahari are the only human society in which such polygynandry is the norm (Berreman, 1962).

From systems to strategies

On several occasions throughout this chapter, I have referred to individuals changing their mating systems according to the environmental conditions (which includes a consideration of the mating systems employed by the opposite sex) in order to optimise their inclusive fitness. This is why evolutionary psychologists prefer to use the term mating *strategy* (which is flexible) rather than mating *system* (which is fixed). Individuals will change their behaviour according to the conditions, weighing up the costs and benefits of each possible strategy, as shown in Figure 4.4. In other words, it is better to analyse mating behaviour in terms

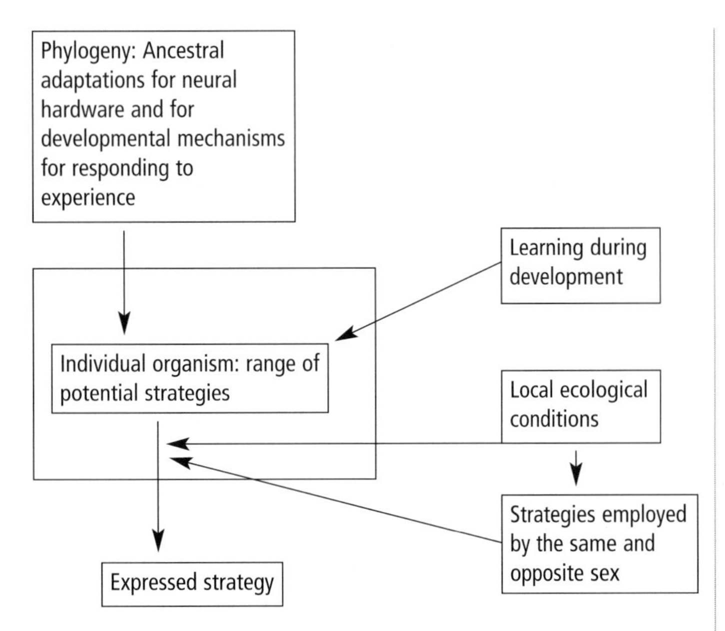

Figure 4.4 Model of factors influencing the mating strategy of an individual (from Cartwright, 2000)

of a compromise between male and female strategies for maximising the number of offspring in certain environmental conditions. This idea is well illustrated by the *polygyny threshold model* (Orians, 1969).

THE POLYGYNY THRESHOLD MODEL

Imagine a population of ancestral humans in which the males were highly polygynous and spared no time to help rear the young. A junior male with no prospect of becoming a harem master may not strive to be polygynous, but may opt to marry one female and help rear their offspring. In this case, the male would not have been as successful as he *could* have been, but would probably have done better than most of his more ambitious contemporaries. Furthermore, it is likely that his offspring would have a greater chance of survival than those of polygynous fathers with no parental care. Females seeking a faithful mate may have superior fitness, and the advantage of being a polygynist would decline. Monogamy would have fitness benefits for both sexes and become established as the norm in society.

This argument also works in reverse. By joining a polygynous male, the female forfeits the chance of paternal help for the offspring. But if he is particularly well-off for resources, it may still pay to choose him. When the advantage of choosing a bigamist for his resources or genes exceeds the advantage of choosing a monogamist for his parental care, polygyny ensues. This is the basis of the *polygyny-threshold model.* This model suggests that, where males possess equal resources, females gain by having a monogamous mate (which would help them care for offspring). However, where males vary in *resource holding potential (RHP)*, females can achieve greater reproductive success by sharing a high RHP male with others. They will therefore enter into polygyny and forego the benefit of male parental assistance with the young (see Figure 4.5). It should be noted that the polygyny-threshold model is based on three assumptions: that female reproductive success is related to male RHP; that polygynous males have greater RHP; and that monogamous males offer more care to the female and/or her young than polygynous males. The model also ignores the possibility that male and female interests may conflict, a situation which may prevent either sex from following their optimal strategy.

There is some evidence that the polygyny-threshold model does apply to humans. Among the Kipsigis of Kenya, rich men have more cattle and more wives. Each wife of a rich man is at least as well off as the single wife of a poor man, a fact clearly recognised by the women. There is generally companionship and a sharing of the burden between co-wives, although it seems that the first wife sometimes resents the arrival of later spouses. Perhaps as a response to this problem, the first wife commonly inherits the greatest proportion of the

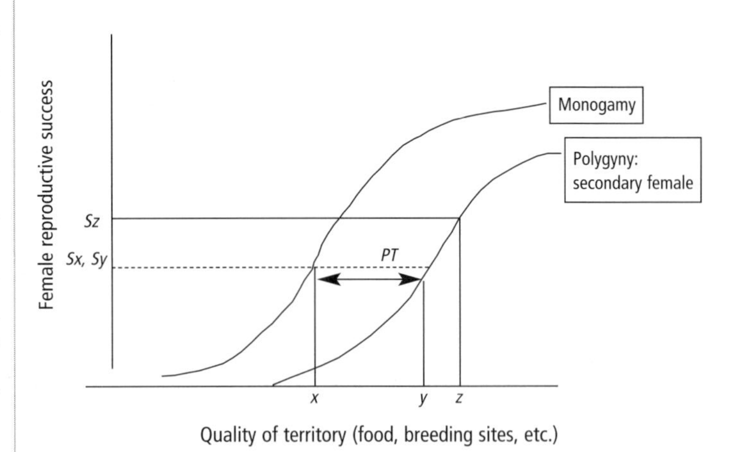

A female mating monogamously on territory of quality *x* would achieve the same success (*Sx* = *Sy*) as a female sharing a male on territory *y*. *PT* is the polygyny threshold. If the female increases the quality of the territory to *z*, her success is greater than with the monogamous mating strategy (*Sz* > *Sx*)

Figure 4.5 The polygyny threshold model (after Orians, 1969)

husband's wealth, and her children often have greater legitimacy than the other offspring.

In general, if females do better by choosing monogamous and faithful males, monogamy will result *unless* men can coerce them into polygyny. If females do no worse by choosing already-mated males, polygyny will result *unless* the first-wives can prevent their males mating again, maintaining monogamy. It is misleading to think that a highly polygynous society represents a victory for men, whereas a monogamous one suggests a victory for women. A polygynous society represents, primarily, a victory for one or a few men over all other men. Furthermore, it is the women who usually determine the prevailing strategy.

Conclusions

Human mating behaviour has traditionally been considered as a number of possible systems, where each system is defined by the typical number of mates possessed by a person. However, people rarely restrict themselves to a single system, but adapt their behaviour according to the prevailing environmental conditions. Therefore, evolutionary psychologists consider the notion of systems to be outdated and too inflexible, replacing them with mating strategies, which are the behavioural plans that individuals use to raise fitness through the successful pursuit of a mate. The strategies employed by males and females have a significant effect upon the social organisation of a population.

SUMMARY

- Human mating behaviour has traditionally been considered as a number of possible **systems**, where each system is defined by the typical number of mates possessed by a person. There are four basic mating systems. **Monogamy** is where one male and one female form a pair that is exclusive of others. In **polygyny**, one male mates with many females, whilst in **polyandry**, one female mates with many males. Where both sexes have multiple partners, the strategy is called **polygynandry**.
- By definition, males and females need not be physically or behaviourally different, as is the case in humans, they are simply required to produce gametes of different sizes (**anisogamy**). 'Males' produce small mobile gametes called **sperm**, and that is what makes them male. 'Females' produce large immobile gametes called **eggs**, which have a store of energy which serves to assist the embryo in its development. Females bearing fertile eggs are a scarce resource, but fertile males are common. It is this key biological difference that underpins human sexual behaviour: men will seek to increase the **quantity** of their offspring, whilst females are more interested in ensuring the **quality** of their offspring. The mating strategies of males and females will often not coincide and a compromise is required.
- **Monogamy** is the norm in species where parental care is labour intensive, so it is not surprising that this is the most common mating strategy in humans. In this system, males may benefit from **cheating**, characterised by extrapair matings and reduced parental care. However, males also risk **cuckoldry** (being duped by the female into raising young which they did not father).
- Females employ tactics to ensure the fidelity of their mates, including demanding **a vast commitment of time and effort during courtship**, and **concealed ovulation** (maintaining constant male interest, as the timing of fertile periods is unknown). Male tactics for avoiding cuckoldry include **controlling resources**, **guarding the female** and **sperm competition**. Despite these strategies, **adultery** is fairly common in socially monogamous humans.
- **Extrapair copulation (EPC)** is superficially most beneficial to males, as their minimal parental investment in each breeding attempt prescribes no limit to the number of offspring they could father. **We would expect men to seek a variety of partners and to attempt to be relatively promiscuous**. 'High quality' men are the most likely candidates to be successful in this quest. There are several potential costs of EPC for males. These costs include the **risk of sexually transmitted diseases, aggression from competing males, reduction of sperm reserves** (and so a lower capacity for sperm competition) **and leaving the primary mate unguarded, increasing the risk of cuckoldry**.
- There are several benefits to EPC for females.

These include **sperm competition**, the acquisition of **superior genes**, **greater investment** from males, and **the avoidance of infanticide**. There are also several potential costs to extrapair mating in females. These include **wasted time**, **the risk of disease transmission**, **aggression** from guarding males, and **withdrawal of investment** should the male mate discover that he has been cuckolded.

- Since males appear to be mainly concerned with the **quantity** of mates, and females with the **quality** of mates, we might expect men to favour polygyny and women to prefer monogamy. Most people live in monogamous societies, but this may be due to cultural pressures, not human nature. Although the most populous societies are monogamous, about three-quarters of all tribal cultures are polygamous. **It seems that humans are both polygamous and monogamous, adapting their behaviour according to the circumstances**.
- **Polyandry** is rare in all species, including humans. Men occasionally share a wife in environments so harsh that a family unit must be of a certain minimum size, but the arrangement usually collapses when conditions improve.
- **Polygynandry** refers to a stable multi-male, multi-female mating system. From the point of view of males, this system has the advantage of more mating opportunities, but carries a much greater risk of cuckoldry. This disadvantage is less important if the males in a polygynandrous group are related to each other, as they will all gain via inclusive fitness. Females gain access to resources, which are often better than they could receive in a monogamous system. However, they lose out in terms of parental investment from males, although it is rare to see *no* parental care by males. In human populations, polygynandry is vary rare.
- Evolutionary psychologists prefer to use the term mating **strategy** (which is flexible) rather than mating **system** (which is fixed). Individuals will change their behaviour according to the conditions, weighing up the costs and benefits of each possible strategy. In other words, it is better to analyse mating behaviour in terms of a **compromise between male and female strategies** for maximising the number of offspring in certain environmental conditions.
- The **polygyny-threshold model** suggests that, where males possess equal resources, females gain by having a monogamous mate. However, where males vary in **resource holding potential (RHP)**, females can achieve greater reproductive success by entering a polygynous relationship. The model is based on three assumptions: **that female reproductive success is related to male RHP; that polygynous males have greater RHP;** and **that monogamous males offer more care to the female and/or her young than polygynous males**. The model also ignores the possibility that male and female interests may conflict, a situation which may prevent females from following their optimal strategy.

5

PARENT–OFFSPRING CONFLICT

Introduction and overview

While there are many common and overlapping interests between parents and offspring, there are also some important points of divergence. The conflict has been analysed from the point of view of the interests of adults and the young. The most common conflict arises when the offspring, in trying to maximise its own interests, attempts to manipulate the feeding parent into providing extra resources. In certain conditions, the offspring may have a negative impact on the long-term fitness of the parent and one extreme manifestation of this conflict is infanticide (the killing of children).

The issues addressed in Chapter 4 suggest that sexual reproduction is as much about conflict as cooperation and the optimal strategy will vary within and between individuals according to environmental and cultural conditions. However, the conflicts discussed have been predominantly between *adults*. This chapter examines evolutionary explanations for *parent–offspring* conflict, and attempts to explain the genetic basis of the tension which exists between the demands of offspring and the future reproductive success of parents.

Background to the conflict

According to Trivers (1974), the basis of parent–offspring conflict is genetic asymmetry. It seems obvious that, since offspring contain the genes of their parents, parents will be bound to look after their genetic investment (Cartwright, 2000). A parent is equally related (50%) to each of its offspring, but an offspring is twice as related to itself (100%) as to its siblings (50%). The conflict is due to the parent (usually the mother) having other potential offspring to raise. He or she will view all the offspring as roughly equal and will best further his or her reproductive success by producing more and sharing the time and energy between them. The parent should transfer investment from an older child to a younger one when the benefit to the younger exceeds the cost to the older. The first infant, however, is more self-centred. It will have some interest in the welfare of its siblings, but will be far more concerned with itself. Offspring therefore tend to favour a longer period of parental investment than the parent is selected to give, and conflict results. This dispute can be seen most clearly in weaning conflict.

Weaning conflict

Weaning conflict occurs in mammals when a lactating mother tries to wean her offspring off milk, while they attempt to prolong the period of suckling (Grier and Burk, 1992). Studies have shown that the period of lactation is enormously demanding physiologically on the female, and she cannot begin setting aside body reserves for further children until she has weaned the current one (Clutton-Brock *et al*, 1989). In industrial

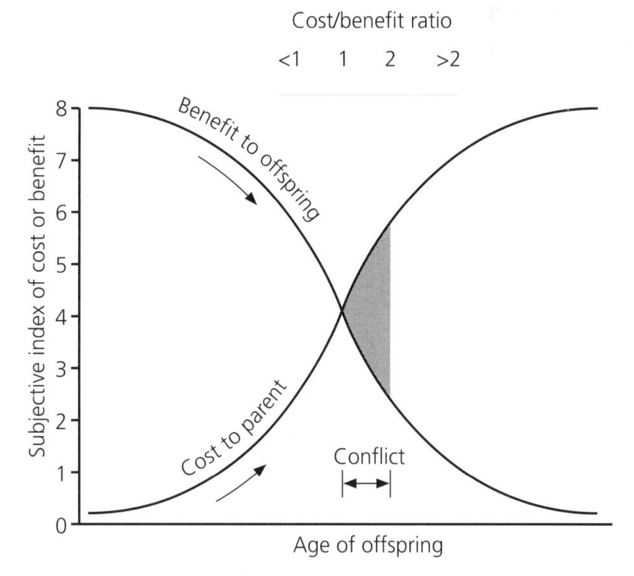

Figure 5.1 Changes in the ratio of cost to parent/benefit to offspring as the age of the offspring increases (Trivers, 1974). Parent-offspring conflict occurs during the time represented by the shaded area, when the parent is expected to attempt weaning and the offspring is expected to resist

Box 5.1 Weaning conflict

When the offspring is very young the benefits of parental care are so large relative to the costs that the parent gains more by feeding the offspring than by ignoring it. As the offspring grows, the cost/benefit (C/B) ratio increases and it will eventually reach a point where it can do as well on its own as it can by receiving parental help. At this point (where the C/B ratio = 1) the parent will have been selected to avoid any further investment in the offspring, since such investment would decrease the total number of offspring surviving. However, because of the genetic asymmetry mentioned above, it is advantageous for the current offspring to become independent only when the C/B ratio has risen to 2. We should not expect any conflict beyond this point as each of the offspring has some genetic investment in its brothers or sisters. Independence becomes desirable for the offspring because its inclusive fitness (gene transmission by the individual *and* by relatives carrying the same genes) is best served by the mother's production of new siblings.

societies, weaning usually occurs some time in the first year, while in hunter-gatherer cultures nursing lasts an average of three to four years. The interval between births is crucial to maximising reproduction. If it is too short, the first infant may still need so much milk and effort that the next infant will not survive. If the mother waits too long, she is wasting her reproductive potential.

Figure 5.1 shows parent–offspring conflict with changes in the ratio of cost to parent/benefit to offspring, as proposed by Trivers (1974). During the time represented by the shaded area, the parent is expected to attempt weaning and the offspring is expected to resist. This is explained further in Box 5.1.

Who wins the conflict?

On theoretical grounds there is no expected winner of parent–offspring conflict, although arguments have been advanced in favour of both parents and young. In their attempts to manipulate each other, we would expect adaptation and counter-adaptation to occur, as seen in predator–prey arms races (Clamp and Russell, 1998). However, in the case of parent–offspring conflict, the competition would be expected to be less severe because they share genes.

OFFSPRING MANIPULATION OF PARENTS

Parents are physically superior to offspring, more experienced and they control the resources at issue. Offspring therefore usually employ *psychological* tactics and attempt to *induce* more investment than the parent is selected to give. Trivers (1974) argued that selection should favour parental attentiveness to signals from offspring because the offspring are best at evaluating their own needs. As adults become increasingly proficient at assessing the needs of their young, Trivers predicted that successive offspring would have to employ more convincing tactics to elicit additional care from their experienced parents. In this situation, the baby may not literally be faking. Since parents should evolve to recognise sham crying, the baby's most effective tactic might be to feel genuinely miserable, even when there is no biological need. (Other aspects of offspring manipulation of parents are described in Box 5.2.)

Generally, adaptations in offspring would be expected to include faking symptoms of hunger/need and suppressing signals indicating satiety. This deception should, in turn, be counteracted by parental evolution of discriminatory powers to detect the *true* state of the offspring. Either or neither participant may achieve outright success.

Box 5.2 Regression and temper tantrums

Offspring typically become less helpless and vulnerable with age, so parents will have been strongly selected to respond negatively to signals emitted by the offspring the older it gets. During

Figure 5.2 Human children may have temper tantrums to elicit care from their parents

parent–offspring conflict, therefore, the offspring may be selected to revert to the gestures and actions of an earlier stage of development in order to induce parental care. In short, it may be tempted to regress when under stress (Trivers, 1985).

Temper tantrums may be used by youngsters to threaten the parent by suggesting that the offspring may actually harm itself. Such tantrums have been observed in a variety of species. Young pelicans, for example, sometimes indulge in convulsions, throwing themselves on the ground and pecking their own wings. This may convince the parents that withholding food will have dire consequences for the health of the chick (Trivers, 1985). Similar temper tantrums have been observed in chimpanzees. It seems likely that tantrums in human children serve a similar function (Figure 5.2).

PARENTAL MANIPULATION OF OFFSPRING

Richard Alexander (1974) disagreed with Trivers's description of conflict between parents and offspring, claiming that parents are heavily favoured to win the contest. His argument was based on the fact that most offspring eventually become parents. An offspring that successfully manipulated its parents when young would lose out when it became a parent because its offspring would inherit the ability to manipulate. Over the long run, therefore, the most successful reproducers would be parents who did not get manipulated. However, it is possible that genes could predispose for the superior tactic of being successfully manipulative offspring when young and successfully manipulative parents when old.

Richard Dawkins (1989) has pointed out that Alexander's argument is flawed because it rests on the assumption of a genetic asymmetry which is not really there. There is no fundamental *genetic* asymmetry between parents and offspring, the relatedness being 50% whichever way round you look at it. Dawkins claims that the argument could just as easily be made with the parent and offspring actions reversed and then the opposite conclusion would be reached. Alexander's prediction of routine parental victory has also not stood up to examination with mathematical models (Parker, 1985). Therefore, it appears that the most likely outcome is a level of investment intermediate between the best situation for parents and offspring.

Finally, parents and offspring may also be in conflict over the behavioural tendencies of the offspring. Parents are selected to influence their offspring to be more altruistic toward relatives than the offspring would normally act on their own (Trivers, 1974). This is because it pays the parents for a child to be altruistic when the benefit to a sibling exceeds the cost to the child, but it pays the *child* to be altruistic only when the benefit exceeds *twice* the cost. Similarly, parents may try to persuade children that other outcomes which are good for the parent (and hence the child's unborn siblings) are in fact good for the child. This may have implications for future behaviour, because the development of conscience and personality may occur partly as a result of parent-offspring conflict.

Timing of the conflict

The nature and extent of parent–offspring conflict is influenced by the age of the parent and that of the offspring. In general, the older a parent, the less will be its future reproductive success and the lower will be the cost of current investment, measured in terms of future offspring (Trivers, 1985). This should result in a longer period of parental investment and reduced conflict with offspring.

PRENATAL CONFLICT

During pregnancy the mother has to share her bodily resources with the foetus and her best interests are served by providing adequate, though not excessive, resources. The mother must consider her own state of health, as well as her future reproductive potential, and retain some resources to safeguard her well-being (Trevathan, 1987). The foetus's interests are also in not damaging the mother's state of health during the pregnancy (or subsequent parental feeding period), but it may still attempt to demand more resources than the mother will be adapted to supply.

It has been argued that there could be no net advantage to a gene that benefits an offspring at a cost to its mother, because its early advantage would be exactly reversed by the later cost. However, a foetus that enjoys an advantage may avoid the cost when it grows up, because its offspring may not carry the gene. Furthermore, it will pay the cost only if it is female.

Therefore, the cost will be paid in a maximum of 50% of pregnancies in the next generation. Conflict would be expected between parent and offspring, even though the ideal contribution from the mother's perspective may be only slightly less than the ideal for the foetus.

It should be noted that paternal genes and maternal genes within the foetus may compete with one another over what is best for the infant. From the paternal perspective, it does not necessarly matter to the male if the female over-invests in the current offspring such that it damages her future reproductive potential, since the male may be able to find another mate. The male will want the current offspring to have as much access as possible to nutritional resources in the womb, so that it grows as large and strong as possible. Therefore, female genes will try to hold the male genes in check, since future reproduction is an issue for the mother.

It has been suggested that 'morning sickness' and food cravings in pregnant women may be due to the foetus attempting to avoid certain food-based toxins and demand certain essential minerals respectively (Profet, 1992). High blood pressure in expectant mothers may also be caused by the foetus in its attempts to garner more blood-borne resources for the placental supply. This is shown in Box 5.3. It has even been suggested that pregnancy-related diabetes is induced by the unborn child in order to receive more glucose (blood concentrations of which are raised as a result of the condition). This extra glucose is probably used to lay down fat as food reserves, increasing the chances of survival after birth.

Box 5.3 High blood pressure in pregnancy as a result of parent–offspring conflict

High blood pressure is a common problem in pregnant women. Occasionally, it may be severe enough to result in kidney damage, a condition known as pre-eclampsia. One explanation of this condition is that it occurs as a result of conflict between the foetus and the mother.

In the early stages of pregnancy, foetal cells destroy the nerves and muscles that adjust blood flow to the placenta. When the foetus perceives that it is receiving inadequate nutrition, it releases substances into the mother's circulation which constrict arteries throughout her body (except in the placenta). This causes her blood pressure to increase and more blood is delivered to the foetus via the placenta. Data on thousands of pregnancies show that moderate increases in maternal blood pressure are associated with lower foetal mortality and that women with pre-existing high blood pressure have larger babies (Nesse and Williams, 1996).

Human chorionic gonadotrophin (HCG) is another hormone made by the foetus and secreted into the mother's bloodstream. It stimulates the continued release of progesterone from the mother's ovaries, blocking menstruation and allowing the foetus to stay implanted. According to Nesse and Williams (1996), HCG may have originated in the contest between foetus and mother over whether the pregnancy should continue. Up to 78% of fertilised eggs are never implanted, or are aborted very early in pregnancy. The majority of these aborted embryos have chromosomal abnormalities and this adaptation prevents continued investment in a baby that would die young or be unable to compete successfully in adult life. It is advantageous for the mother to cut her losses as early as possible (even if a few normal embryos are aborted), whereas the foetus will do everything it can to implant successfully. Producing HCG is an important early strategy for the foetus, and high levels of this hormone are probably interpreted by the mother's body as a sign of a viable foetus.

EARLY CHILDHOOD CONFLICT

As previously mentioned, the infant's strategy in parent–offspring conflict is predominantly psychological. Crying is a typical example of an honest signal to parents (of hunger, cold or other distress) which is also used deviously to gain extra food, warmth or attention. This may also be true of other childish behaviour, which is the basis of regression. Smiling and temper tantrums are further examples of such attention-seeking strategies aimed at eliciting additional parental care.

Parent–offspring conflict has also been used as an explanation for the existence of Freud's anal stage of psychosexual development. According to Badcock (1994), retention of urine and faeces may represent a psychological ploy by young children to suggest that insufficient food had been provided and therefore solicit additional care. Similar arguments have been advanced by Badcock for other stages of development, although these are not always totally convincing.

If faced with the choice of saving the life of one child or saving the life of another, the mother should prefer the older one because she has more invested in him. However, if the dilemma is less serious, such as the

Box 5.4 A comparison of first-born and later-born children

Characteristic	*First-born*	*Later-born*
Conformity	Higher	Lower
Openness	Lower	Higher
Seriousness	Higher	Lower
Antagonism	Higher	Lower
Popularity	Lower	Higher
Neuroticism	Higher	Lower
Anxiety	Higher	Lower
Assertiveness	Higher	Lower

provision of a particular morsel of food, she should prefer the younger one. This is because the older child is more capable of finding his own food unaided, and is the basis of weaning in mammals (Dawkins, 1989). Parents may not want to invest equal amounts of energy in each of their children, but may try to pick winners and losers and invest accordingly. In one study, two-thirds of British and American mothers confessed to loving one of their children more. According to Pinker (1997), children learn to cultivate favouritism. A first-born child would be expected to be a conservative and a bully; second-born children should become appeasers and cooperators. Later-born children should also avoid competing directly with their elder siblings (they are unlikely to be successful), and should find a different niche in which to excel. Expected personality characteristics of first-born and later-born children are summarised in Box 5.4.

ADOLESCENT CONFLICT

Several of the examples mentioned above may also be used as strategies to induce additional care during adolescence. Adolescent conflict can be extreme. Teenagers may want to do everything their own way and insist that no help of any sort is needed. Then, at the least difficulty, they are back in the regression act, apparently helpless and needy. However, we eventually reach a time when children become independent from their parents, and start to consider parenthood themselves.

Infanticide: cases of extreme conflict

Baby-killing is commonplace in nature. Fathers, mothers, siblings, close relatives and parents' new mates

Box 5.5 Infanticide by male house mice

Immediately after copulation, male house mice become highly aggressive towards mouse pups and attempt to kill them. The males remain prone to commit infanticide for about three weeks, but then gradually switch into paternal behaviour. They then protect and care for the young pups attentively until about fifty days have passed since intercourse. At this point, they regain their infanticidal tendencies.

This behaviour has obvious adaptive value. Female mice usually give birth three weeks after copulation. Attacks on pups during this period are almost definitely directed towards a rival male's offspring, reducing competition for the newborn young of the infanticidal male. After three weeks, a male that switches to paternal behaviour will almost invariably direct his care-giving to his own offspring. After fifty days, his weaned pups will have dispersed, so that once again infanticide can be practised advantageously (Alcock, 1993).

have all been known to destroy infants or eggs under certain circumstances. For example, infanticide by male house mice (*Mus musculus*) is described in Box 5.5. In black eagles, the first hatched (larger) chick harasses its sibling and monopolises the food, causing the second chick to starve to death (Mock and Parker, 1997). Similar patterns of infanticidal behaviour have also been observed in primates (Sugiyama, 1984).

A *runt* (weak or undersized offspring) bears just as many of its mother's genes as its siblings, but its life expectation is less. Depending on the circumstances, it may pay a mother to refuse to feed a runt, and allocate all of its share of her parental investment to its brothers and sisters. Indeed, Dawkins (1989) has argued that if a runt is so small and weak that its life expectancy is reduced to the point at which benefit to it from parental investment is less than half the benefit that the same investment could confer on its siblings, the runt should die 'gracefully and willingly'!

Similar calculations enter into human infanticide (which includes abortion). Maternal effort is a limited resource that has to be spent selectively and saved occasionally by infanticide (Hrdy, 1999). Women around the world let infants die in circumstances in which the odds of survival are low, as described in Box 5.6. For example, infanticide among Bolivian foragers almost

Box 5.6 Circumstances favouring a higher incidence of infanticide

- The infant is deformed or of 'low quality'
- The infant is one of twins
- The infant is fatherless
- The biological father is not the woman's husband
- The mother is young (and so can try again)
- There is a lack of social support
- The infant is born very soon after another child
- The family is overburdened with older offspring
- Inadequate parental resources

always takes place after the child's father has deserted the mother (Bugos and McCarthy, 1984). Such infanticide is viewed as an unavoidable tragedy, and may explain why certain societies try to distance their emotions from a newborn (by not touching or naming) until they are assured that it will survive. This issue of being able to cope with a new child may be linked to post-natal depression (See Chapter 15, page 135). The depression is most severe in the circumstances that lead mothers elsewhere in the world to commit infanticide, such as poverty, marital conflict, and single motherhood.

If infanticide represents a strategy for preserving future reproductive value, we might expect the frequency of infanticide to decrease as the mother's age increases. This is because the reproductive value of a mother

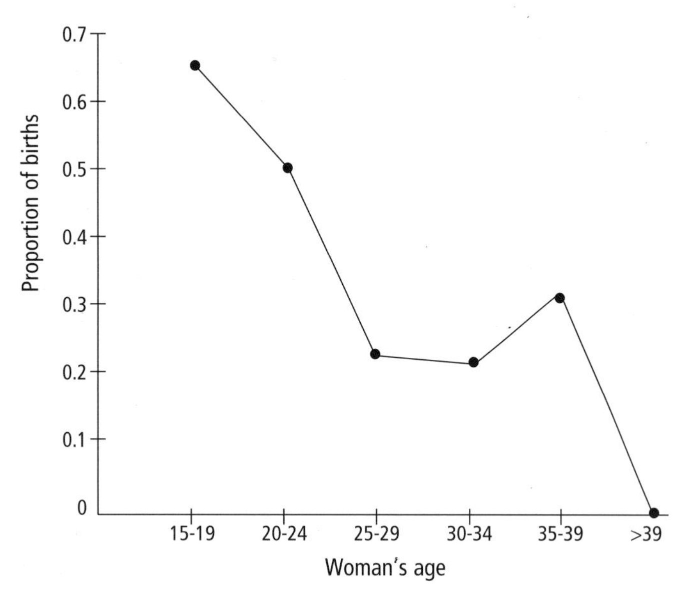

Figure 5.3 Rate of infanticide (proportion of births) versus age of biological mother

Figure 5.4 Are babies 'designed' to elicit tenderness?

declines as she ages. If less is at stake, less extreme behaviour may be expected. According to Daly and Wilson (1988), this effect has been seen both among Ayoreo Indians (Figure 5.4) and modern-day Canadians. Nevertheless, this data may be explained, at least in part, by the idea that women may become better mothers as they age or that younger mothers may suffer more social stress.

The child has only one weapon in the battle against infanticide: the instinctive bonding process with the mother. Babies appear to be genetically programmed to behave towards their mothers in ways that ensure survival (Hayes, 1994). Newborns smile, make eye contact, respond to speech and mimic facial expressions. They also have a unique geometry (large head and eyes, fat cheeks, and short limbs), which elicits tenderness and affection (Figure 5.4).

It seems likely that infanticide occurs in virtually all human populations, although the frequencies differ markedly, ranging from near zero to over 40% of live births (Hrdy, 1999). Biological parents are responsible for the largest proportion of infanticide, and marriage, inheritance systems, religious beliefs and social norms play central roles in parental decisions to terminate offspring. Where parental rank is correlated with the survival and breeding prospects of selected offspring, even the maintenance of parental status may take precedence over the survival of less favoured infants. Box 5.7 discusses the idea that the risk of infanticide is related to the reproductive value of the offspring.

Box 5.7 Risk of infanticide and reproductive value of offspring

Children have a reproductive value as the carrier of their parents' genes and as a potential source of grandchildren. This suggests that the value of a child will increase up to puberty and decrease as the child approached the end of its reproductive life. This idea lead Daly and Wilson (1988) to make the following predictions about the risk of infanticide and reproductive value of the offspring.

- Infanticide rates will fall as the age of the child increases from zero to adolescence
- The greatest increase in reproductive value will occur in the first year, hence infanticide rates should fall rapidly after the first year of life
- Infanticide by non-relatives will not vary with age in the same way since the children of other parents have a neutral reproductive value.

Data for infanticide has been shown to agree with these predictions (Daly and Wilson, 1988). However, the results may be due to the demands made by the child at certain ages, coupled with the length of time a parent is exposed to these demands, and younger children may also be easier to kill. It seems clear that further research is needed into this area.

Human infanticide is invariably sex selective and usually for socio-economic reasons. The Chinese, deprived of the chance to have more than one child, killed more than 250,000 girls after birth between 1979 and 1984 (Ridley, 1993). In one recent study of clinics in Bombay, of 8000 abortions, 7997 were of female foetuses (Hrdy, 1990). In the latter case, the main reason for infanticide was the need for large dowries when daughters were married off (one advertisement read: 'Spend six hundred rupees now, save fifty thousand later'). However, the preference for boys over girls is not universal. In very poor social classes, daughters are usually preferred. This is because a poor son is often forced to remain single, but a poor daughter can marry a rich man. In these societies, daughters are better vessels for producing grandchildren than sons.

By far the most common goals for parents committing infanticide involve the manipulation of family size, composition, or the adjustment of the timing of parental investment by the mother and/or father. Nevertheless, there exist a wide array of alternatives to infanticide, such as abandonment or the presence of other potential caregivers, which would be expected to be the preferred options where they are available. This is supported by Hrdy's (1999) observation that high rates of infanticide are inversely correlated with alternative opportunities to reduce parental effort.

Conclusions

In sexually reproducing species, parents and offspring are expected to be in conflict over the amount of parental investment the offspring receives. This is because the offspring are selected to attempt to gain more resources than the parents are selected to give. The conflict is expected to increase during the period of parental investment, which is characterised by a shift, from parents to offspring, in who initiates care. Parents are physically superior to offspring, more experienced and they control the resources at issue. Offspring are therefore selected to use psychological manipulation in order to induce greater investment. Overall there is no expected outright winner of the conflict.

Infanticide is an extreme form of parent–offspring conflict. It probably occurs in virtually all human populations, and marriage, inheritance systems, religious beliefs, economic status and social norms play central roles in parental decisions to terminate offspring. The risk of infanticide appears to be inversely related to the age of the mother and directly related to the reproductive value of the offspring. Infanticide is generally less common where there are alternative opportunities to reduce parental effort.

SUMMARY

- **Parent–offspring conflict** has been analysed from the point of view of the interests of adults and the young. The most common conflict arises when offspring, trying to maximise their own interests, attempt to manipulate feeding parents into providing extra resources. In extreme cases this conflict may lead to **infanticide**.

- The basis of parent–offspring conflict appears to be **genetic asymmetry**. A parent is equally related to each of its offspring, but an individual offspring is twice as related to itself as to its siblings. Parents will attempt to divide time and energy equally between their offspring, but individual youngsters are selected to want more than their fair share. Therefore, offspring tend to favour a longer period of parental investment than the parent is selected to give, resulting in conflict.
- When offspring are very young, the benefits of parental care are so large, relative to the costs, that the parent gains more by feeding the offspring than by ignoring it. However, the point will eventually arise when an individual youngster can do as well on its own as it can by receiving parental help. At this point the parent is selected to cease feeding, but the offspring is selected to continue to demand food. This is seen during **weaning conflict** in mammals. The conflict is expected to cease when the cost of investment by parents is exactly twice that of the benefit received by an individual offspring. Independence then becomes desirable for the offspring because its **inclusive fitness** is best served by the mother's production of new siblings.
- On theoretical grounds there is no expected winner of parent-offspring conflict, although arguments have been advanced in favour of both parents and young. In their attempts to manipulate each other, we would expect **adaptation** and **counter-adaptation** to occur, although the competition would not be expected to be too severe as they share genes.
- Parents are physically superior to offspring, more experienced and they control the resources at issue. Therefore, offspring usually employ **psychological** tactics and attempt to **induce** more investment than the parent is selected to give. These tactics include **regression** (reverting to infantile behaviour) and **temper tantrums**, as seen in pelicans, chimpanzees and human children.
- It has been suggested that the parents are heavily favoured to win the conflict. However, this argument does not stand up to examination by both theoretical arguments and mathematical models. **The most likely outcome is a level of investment intermediate between the best situation for parents and offspring**.
- Offspring may exhibit characteristic conflict behaviour throughout their development, ranging from the prenatal stage through to adolescence. During pregnancy the foetus may attempt to demand more resources than the mother will be adapted to supply. It is possible that **morning sickness, high blood pressure** and **pregnancy-related diabetes** are consequences of parent–offspring conflict during this stage. In early childhood, infants develop psychological tactics in the battle with their parents. **Crying, smiling** and **temper tantrums** are all examples of attention-seeking strategies aimed at eliciting additional parental care. These strategies often continue into adolescence. However, this is also the time when offspring become independent from their parents, marking the end of the conflict.
- **Infanticide** is commonplace in nature. Parents around the world let infants die in circumstances in which the odds of survival are low. Biological parents are responsible for the largest proportion of infanticide, and **marriage**, **inheritance systems**, **religious beliefs** and **social norms** play central roles in parental decisions to terminate offspring. The risk of infanticide appears to be inversely related to the age of the mother and directly related to the reproductive value of the offspring.
- Human infanticide is often **sex-selective**, being more common for female offspring. However, the preference for boys over girls is not universal. In very poor social classes, daughters are usually preferred. This is because a poor son is often forced to remain single, but a poor daughter can marry a rich man. In these societies, **daughters are better vessels for producing grandchildren than are sons**.
- The most common goals for parents committing infanticide involve the manipulation of family size or composition, or the adjustment of the timing of parental investment by the mother and/or father. Infanticide is generally less common where there are alternative opportunities to reduce parental effort.

6

HUMAN SEXUAL BEHAVIOUR

Introduction and overview

According to Miller (1998), the application of sexual selection theory to human behaviour has been the greatest success story in evolutionary psychology. Humans possess specific mental adaptations for choosing mates, selecting their sexual partners on the basis of viability and fertility (indicated by such factors as age, health, social status and disease-resistance). In sexually-reproducing species, it pays to be choosy as the genetic quality of your mate will determine half the genetic quality of your offspring. However, adaptations for mate choice are probably different for males and females, as what defines a 'good mate' from an evolutionary point of view will be different for the two sexes.

This chapter considers the nature of sexual selection in humans, examining mate choice, sexuality, and the wide variety of activities that form part of our sexual behaviour. I also review the influence that sexual selection may have had upon the evolution of the human mind and culture.

Sexual selection

Chapter 1 described the extent to which the behaviour of animals could be explained by evolutionary concepts. The general assumption in this approach is that evolution works almost exclusively through natural selection. However, Darwin himself was aware that natural selection could not explain all evolutionary processes. One major problem was to explain the evolution of certain behaviours or anatomical structures which appeared to *reduce* the probability of survival, such as the peacock's tail.

The tail of the peacock (*Pavo cristatus*) appears to have the dual disadvantage of attracting predators and impeding efficient flight, making escape difficult (Figure 6.1). If it was the case that such tails really

Figure 6.1 A peacock (*Pavo cristatus*) displaying his extravagant and cumbersome tail. The existence of such a structure is more readily explained by sexual selection than by natural selection.

increased fitness in some non-obvious way, one would expect them to be present in females also. As natural selection seemed to be unable to explain the existence of such a structure, Darwin proposed the theory of *sexual selection*. According to Darwin, sexual selection depends on the advantage which certain individuals have over others of the same sex and species solely in respect of reproduction (Darwin, 1871). In the case of the peacock, females appear to prefer males who possess the longest and most brightly-coloured tails. Therefore the effects of sexual selection outweigh the disadvantage of owning such a cumbersome appendage (Cronin, 1991).

Sexual dimorphism (the differences between the male and female sexes of the same species) is more marked among the apes and humans than among the monkeys (Crook, 1972). For example, during the EEA, male sexual strategy in humans involved rivalry in acquiring females and a certain amount of aggressiveness in protecting them from other men (McFarland, 1996). This may account for the man's greater size and strength, though it is more likely that this has to do with division of labour within the family (Passingham, 1982). Many of the differences between the sexes in humans can be attributed to natural selection, and to the differing roles of males and females in the Pleistocene era, rather than sexual selection. When considering sexually-selected traits, we must examine those different male and female features that appear to have no direct role in survival or reproduction. Examples of such features include the beard and other body hair of the man, the change in the male voice that occurs at puberty, and the protruding and rounded breasts of the woman (Wickler, 1967).

Humans are an extremely 'K-selected' species. This means that we have much slower development, larger bodies, fewer offspring, higher survival rates, and longer lifespans than more 'r-selected' groups, such as rabbits. The more K-selected the species, the more important sexual selection usually becomes compared to natural selection (Miller, 1998). We might expect that as humans evolved to be more and more K-selected, the relative importance of sexual selection increased. However, sexual selection also has a much greater effect in polygamous societies (see Chapter 4), and it seems likely that humans have become progressively more monogamous over time (probably in response to the increasing requirement for parental care). This implies that the influence of sexual selection has peaked in our recent past. It was probably during this 'peak period' that humans were selected to lose their body hair (Crook, 1972), and that our mental adaptations for mate choice were shaped. It should be noted that current opinion in evolutionary biology no longer identifies a distinction between natural and sexual selection. Rather, it focuses on the selection of traits that result in a higher number of reproductively viable offspring raised in a lifetime, compared with competing traits. The best approach is to simply use selection for fitness traits as a unified concept, although I will continue to consider sexual selection as a separate concept for the purposes of this chapter.

Evidence suggests that humans are a *mutually* sexually-selected species. In other words, both males and females have evolved preferences for certain behavioural and/or anatomical features in the opposite sex. According to Ridley (1993), 'People are attracted to people of high reproductive and genetic potential – the healthy, the fit and the powerful'. This brings us to the question of exactly how we choose our mates.

Mate choice: what is attractive?

One way to evaluate the role of sexual selection in human evolution is to compare our species with other primates (the *comparative* approach). We differ from other anthropoid apes in several respects, such as the nature of our facial features, and in having enlarged breasts and buttocks (females) and long penises (males). A great deal of research has been undertaken into the influence of selective mate choice on human facial features. This appears to suggest that average faces are attractive, but that females are preferred with more child-like features (large eyes, small noses and full lips), as are males with testosterone-enlarged features, such as strong jaws and large noses (Thornhill and Gangestad, 1993). We also seem to consider bilateral symmetry as an important feature of facial beauty, as described in Box 6.1. Furthermore, as Darwin (1872) suggested, human faces are extremely well developed for displaying a variety of emotions, many of which are used in courtship.

In addition to facial symmetry, we also appear to find bodily symmetry attractive. As suggested in Box 6.1, symmetry advertises biological quality, such as good

Box 6.1 The beauty of symmetry

Facial features may be a clue to genetic or nurtured quality. Studies have shown that men prefer photographs of women with symmetrical faces, and vice versa (Cartwright, 2000). It seems likely that symmetry (which shows a tendency to be inherited) equates with fitness. Development may be disturbed by parasites or other infectious agents, and only individuals with the best genes and food supplies will develop perfectly symmetrical faces. For example, the jawlines of males lengthen and broaden during puberty in response to increases in testosterone levels. However, testosterone also suppresses the immune system. Perhaps only the 'fittest' males can develop perfectly sculpted jaws in the face of immunity-damaging surges of testosterone. Facial symmetry is also the best predictor of body symmetry (see above). Therefore, the human face is probably the main guide to attractiveness and overall genetic fitness.

genes, reproductive vigour and an effective immune system. Recent research suggests that women with symmetrical male partners have the most orgasms, and women with symmetrical breasts are more fertile than those less evenly endowed (Cartwright, 2000). Males and females with near perfect body symmetry also report two or three times as many sexual partners as those with the most asymmetrical bodies. However, this does not necessarily mean that symmetry itself is directly attractive. For example, symmetrical males may be more dominant, or have higher self-esteem, and so be considered more attractive as a result. Furthermore, it has been suggested that we may prefer symmetrical bodies because symmetry is what our visual systems happen to respond to most strongly.

The penis of the human male is the longest, thickest and most flexible of any living primate. It appears that the main influence on the evolution of the human penis was female choice, probably owing to factors involved in sexual satisfaction and (indirectly) reproductive success (Eberhard, 1991). Likewise, female human breasts and buttocks have undergone sexual elaboration through mate choice by males. These organs store substantial amounts of fat, so could function as indicators of female nutritional status and hence fertility. Singh (1993) demonstrated that males prefer women who display a low waist-to-hip ratio (WHR), ideally about 0.7. This is concordant with enlarged buttocks, indicating sufficient fat reserves, and a narrow waist, indicating the absence of pregnancy. This idea is discussed further in Box 6.2.

Natural selection will favour males who prefer to mate with reproductively capable females. Unfortunately for males seeking to solve this problem, viability and fertility are not attributes that can be observed directly. Instead, males must be able to estimate the *age* of females (which is highly correlated with their reproductive capability), using physical attractiveness as a guide. The same arguments apply to female mate preferences, except that physical attractiveness will be less important, for reasons outlined in Box 6.3. Females should seek to mate with males who show the ability and willingness to invest resources connected with parenting, such as food and protection. For example, American men who marry in a given year earn about 50% more money than unmarried men of the same age, a fact probably due in part to female choice for male resources (Trivers, 1985). However, humans often mate at ages before a man's potential resources are fully known. Therefore, females have to rely on cues that predict the accumulation of resources, such as ambition, industriousness and intelligence (Willerman, 1979). It has also been speculated that expressions of love and kindness may provide reliable cues to a man's willingness to devote resources to a female and her offspring (Buss, 1987), and to the likelihood of females remaining faithful. It should be noted that the majority of these predictions have been supported by studies

Box 6.2 Vital statistics

Despite significant changes over time in the average weight of female centrefolds and beauty queens, one vital statistic has remained constant: the ratio of waist to hip size. Singh (1993) argues that, within reason, a man will find almost any weight of woman attractive so long as her waist is much thinner than her hips, with an ideal ratio of about 0.7. Furthermore, this ratio appears to be consistent across a wide range of cultures (Singh, 1995). Ridley (1993) suggests that this preference is due to sexual selection. Larger hips (or hips which look larger, compared to a slender waist) may indicate good childbearing capabilities. Alternatively, a thin waist would indicate the absence of pregnancy, something much less common in Pleistocene times than it is today. Thin waists are also associated with high levels of oestrogen and low levels of testosterone, a hormonal balance normally linked to high fertility.

Box 6.3 Physical attractiveness is more important in females than males

The physical attractiveness of females occupies a central place in male mate preferences. Males would be expected to use physical features (e.g. clear skin, white teeth), behavioural features (e.g. high energy levels) and reputation (e.g. information regarding the health and prior sexual conduct of a female) as reliable guides to age and reproductive capability. The preference for physical attractiveness should be stronger for males than for females for a number of reasons (Buss, 1995):

1 Female reproductive success is not as limited by the problem of obtaining fertile mates.
2 Male fertility is less dependent upon age.
3 Male fertility cannot be assessed as accurately from physical appearance (due to 2 above).

Box 6.4 Human mate choice

Dunbar (1995) studied the 'Lonely Hearts' columns of magazines and newspapers and found that men predominantly offer resources and seek attractiveness. The reverse is usually true in females (see the examples below). Buss (1989) found that the preference among women for power and earning capacity held across 37 different cultures, regardless of the status and financial position of the women concerned.

> *'Professional male (37) looking for attractive female (25-30) to share weekends in his country cottage and life in the city'*
>
> *'Attractive female (27) seeks professional male for friendship and possibly romance'*

Note that, in these examples, the male may be exaggerating his resources (indicated by 'professional', 'country cottage' and 'city'). Likewise, the female may lie about her attractiveness, reduce her real age, and try to imply coyness (by indicating that romance is only a possibility).

Figure 6.2 Males are expected to exaggerate their resources in order to attract females.
Copyright: Super Stock.

across a wide range of cultures (see Box 6.4). Finally, this account of evolutionary selection pressures yields specific predictions about the nature of male and female deception. Females would be predicted to lie about their age, alter their appearance, and conceal prior sexual encounters. Males would be expected to exaggerate their resources (Figure 6.2), inflate perceptions of their willingness to commit, and feign love to induce a female to mate with them (Buss, 1995).

Homosexuality

Homosexual behaviour represents a major puzzle for evolutionary psychology. Evidence suggests that genetic factors are involved in the development of male homosexuality (Stevens and Price, 1996). The genes in question probably reduce the sensitivity of the male foetus to testosterone. For example, dizygotic (fraternal) twins have a 25% chance of sharing a gay habit, but this becomes 50% for monozygotic (identical) twins. There is also good evidence that the genes are inherited from the mother, either on the X chromosome or in the mitochondria of the egg (Ridley, 1993). It is not clear whether female homosexuality is influenced by genetic factors to the same degree. However, it is difficult to account for the inclusive fitness of genes which predispose either sex to homosexual behaviour. Nevertheless, such genes must have some adaptive advantage, otherwise they would have been eliminated by natural selection.

One theory suggests that homosexuality is influenced by a number of genes, which are predominantly *recessive* (not expressed in the presence of other, *dominant* genes). These genes would be dormant in heterosexuals, but could provide reproductive advantages when combined with other genes in these individuals (and so transmitted to future generations). Alternatively, the recessive genes could be passed on through the relatives of an exclusive homosexual, because he or she helps his or her relatives to raise more children.

A second theory, the *dominance failure theory*, suggests that subordinate males are unable to find female partners and consequently develop a homosexual orientation. This could have an evolutionary basis if social dominance is determined, at least in part, by genetic factors. The dominance failure theory would also help to account for the fact that there are more male homosexuals than lesbians. Another solution to the problem of failure in inter-male competition is to assume a female role (*transvestism*) or identity (*transsexualism*).

Before the advent of AIDS, practising male homosexuals were far more promiscuous than heterosexual men. For example, a Kinsey Institute study of gay men in San Francisco found that 75% had more than 100 partners; 25% had more than 1000 partners (Symons, 1979). In addition, infidelity is acknowledged to be a greater problem in male homosexual partnerships than in heterosexual ones. In contrast, lesbians rarely engage in sex with strangers, and usually form long-term partnerships with little risk of infidelity. Most lesbians have fewer than 10 partners in their lifetimes (Symons, 1979). The reasons for these differences may be found in the evolved adaptations of the male and female psyche. Homosexual men have tended to be promiscuous because their partners are male, and males tend to seek sexual variety. (This is also characteristic of heterosexual men, as shown by the existence of relatively large numbers of female prostitutes). According to Symons (1979), homosexual men behave like men, only more so; homosexual women behave like women, only more so. It should be noted that one objection to evolutionary explanations of homosexuality is that they are *reductionist* arguments (see Chapter 3, page 23). There are many different explanations of gender role and gender identity and some psychologists argue that the evolutionary approach ignores the influence of social, developmental and cultural factors. As it happens, the main aim of evolutionary psychology is to integrate an understanding of these environmental influences with those of genes.

Further aspects of human sexual behaviour

ADULTERY AND JEALOUSY

Studies have shown that, in the UK, more than 20% of children are the offspring of males other than their ostensible father (Ridley, 1993). Adultery can be advantageous to both sexes within a monogamous marriage. In short, the male may increase the *quantity* of his mates (resulting in *more* offspring) and the female may increase the *quality* of her mates (resulting in *better* young). In evolutionary terms, the risk of adultery for women is that they will lose their male partner to another female, and therefore lose the protection and resources he supplies. Males, on the other hand, risk being cuckolded and investing a great deal of time and effort bringing up children that are not their own. Both sexes have therefore evolved tactics to counter infidelity by their partner.

Human females exhibit long periods of sexual receptivity, which encourages continued attentiveness from their male partner. They also conceal ovulation, meaning that males must copulate regularly with the same female to ensure fertilisation (see sperm competition, page 33) and that he must guard the woman against advances from other men if he is to be confident of paternity (Lovejoy, 1981). It has recently been suggested that human infants have been selected not to resemble their fathers (Pagel, 1997). Concealing paternal identity in this way is advantageous as a strategy to avoid paternal neglect, abuse or infanticide when there is a risk that the domestic father is not the biological father. Other research suggests that people are more likely to say of a baby, "he (or she) looks just like his father" than to say "he (or she) looks just like his mother", and that it is the mother's relatives who are most likely to say this (Wilson and Daly, 1992). Finally, an evolutionary perspective would also predict that males will place greater importance than females upon chastity. This appears to be supported by studies across a range of human cultures, as described in Box 6.5.

Evolutionary explanations of human sexual relationships may also explain jealousy. The main concern of

Box 6.5 The importance of chastity

Males who preferred chaste females in the environment of evolutionary adaptedness probably enjoyed greater reproductive success than males who were indifferent to this quality. This is because, prior to the use of modern contraception, female chastity would provide a cue to paternity certainty. As maternity is never in doubt, it is likely that females will place a lower value on chastity than males. However, chastity may also provide a cue to the *future* fidelity of a selected mate, in which case it could be favoured by both sexes.

There is great cultural variability in the absolute value placed on chastity (defined as "no prior experience in sexual intercourse"). For example, it is nearly three times as important in China as in the USA (Buss, 1989). In a sample of 37 different cultures, 23 (62%) showed sex differences in the expected direction, with males valuing chastity more than females. In the other 14 cultures, no significant differences were found. There were no samples in which females preferred chastity in potential mates more than males. It appears that this preference mechanism is more sensitive to cultural conditions than the relatively invariant sex differences found for youth and beauty.

males appears to be paternity. Although maternity is a certainty, paternity is always a matter of opinion. A man incapable of jealousy may have a greater risk of having an adulterous partner, with a resulting decrease in reproductive success. However, men who exhibit jealous behaviour will have an evolutionary advantage. Genes that predispose to male sexual jealousy will therefore be maintained in humans.

Although women are certain of maternity, they do face other risks. A philandering husband may lead to a loss of resources and the risk of sexually transmitted diseases. Cultural factors appear to play a greater role in female jealousy, perhaps reflecting reduced selection pressure for this behaviour (compared to males). A certain amount of jealousy by both partners appears to be effective in maintaining relationships, perhaps because it reflects the value placed upon the relationship (Mathes, 1986). However, the nature of this jealousy may vary between the sexes. In general, sexual jealousy is reported to be more intense for men than women. Buss *et al.* (1992) asked participants to imagine different sorts of infidelity by their partners, and to rate which one distressed them most. As predicted, men rated a sexual scenario, and women a love scenario, as the more distressing (Figure 6.3).

SPERM COMPETITION AND THE FEMALE ORGASM

An interesting feature of sexual activity in human males is *sperm competition*. This is based on the idea that the quantity of sperm transferred to a human female may affect the male's chance of egg fertilisation, given the possibility that his partner may also receive sperm from another male. If this is true, we would expect males to adjust the quantity of sperm donated to a partner in relation to the risk that she has received sperm from a rival male. This appears to be supported by experimental studies (Figure 6.4).

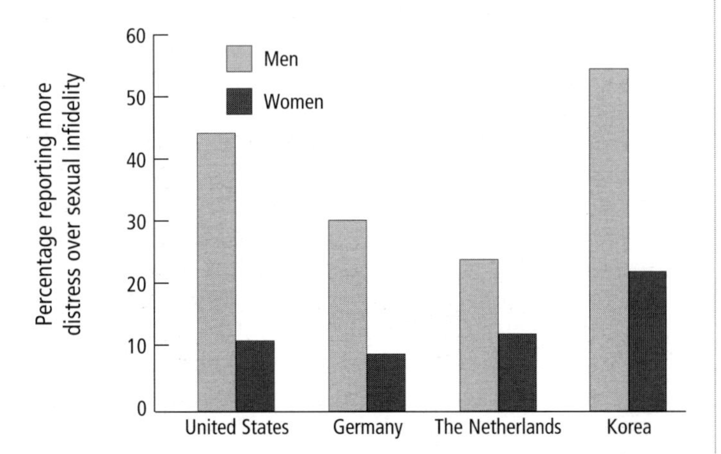

Figure 6.3 The percentage of respondents reporting more distress at cues indicating that their partner had shown sexual infidelity than at cues indicating emotional infidelity (Buss, 1999)

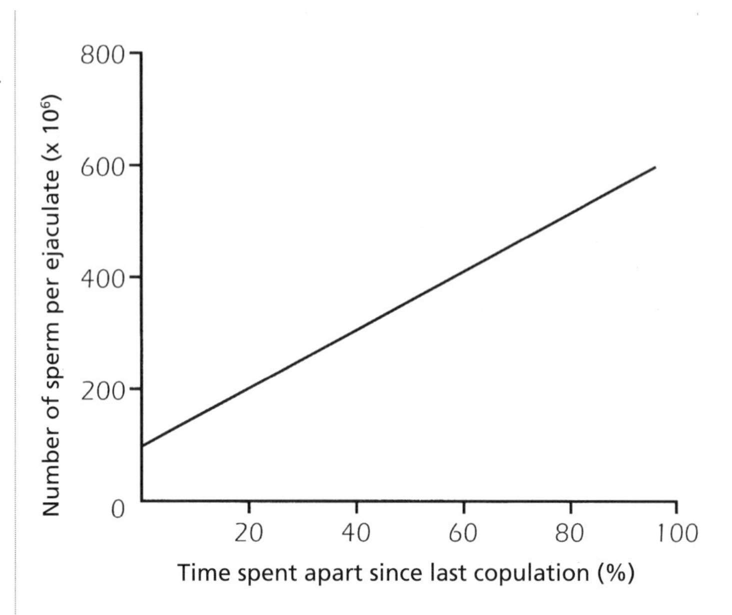

Figure 6.4 Sperm competition in humans. The number of sperm contained in an ejaculate increases as a function of the time a man and woman have spent away from each other since their last copulation (Baker and Bellis, 1989)

Eberhard (1985) has argued that male genitals often function as 'internal courtship devices' to stimulate females into accepting sperm from the copulating male. The length, variety, and vigour of human copulation suggests that this type of internal courtship has been highly elaborated in our species. Human female orgasm may function partially to suck sperm into the uterus, thereby promoting fertilisation by sexually exciting males (Baker and Bellis, 1995). Further aspects of the female orgasm are discussed in Box 6.6.

Box 6.6 The female orgasm

Copulation is likely to result in conception if the female has a 'high retention' orgasm during sex. This means that the female achieves orgasm less than a minute before the male, or up to 45 minutes after him, causing retention of most of the sperm in the vagina. Baker and Bellis (1995) found that in faithful women about 55% of the orgasms were high-retention. In unfaithful women, only 40% of the copulations with the partner were high retention, but 70% of the copulations with the lover were of this fertile type. Furthermore, the unfaithful women were having sex with their lovers at times of the month when they were most fertile. These two effects combined meant that an unfaithful woman could have sex twice as often with her partner as with her lover, but is still more likely to conceive a child by the lover (Ridley, 1993). These observations are consistent with the idea that an effective female strategy might be to marry a dependable and rich man (to provide resources), while also becoming pregnant by a handsome lover (to provide good genes).

RAPE: AN ADAPTIVE TRAIT?

Thornhill and Thornhill (1983) proposed that evolution has favoured males with the capacity to commit rape, under certain conditions, as a means to leaving descendants. According to this hypothesis, human males unable to attract willing sexual partners may use rape as a reproductive option of last resort. This idea is supported by the observation that victims of rape are often in their peak reproductive years. However, this observation could also be explained by the hypothesis that rape is a *maladaptive* by-product of the male reproductive psyche, associated with rapid sexual arousal, a desire for variety in sexual partners, and a readiness to engage in impersonal sex (Alcock, 1993). Furthermore, the 'rape-adaptation hypothesis' has been condemned for apparently placing an oppressive form of behaviour in a more positive light (it is 'adaptive'), and representing it as a natural characteristic of men ('they can't help it'). Evolutionary psychologists have to be very careful when attempting to explain anti-social behaviour, in case they appear to be justifying that behaviour (Edley and Wetherell, 1995).

Sexual selection and intelligence

It has been suggested that the human intellect is the result of runaway gene-culture coevolution (see Chapter 2, page 16). However, it seems more likely that the basis of the evolution of human intelligence is sexual selection, rather than natural selection (see Chapter 11, page 99). Ridley (1993) believes that big brains may have contributed to reproductive success, either by enabling men to outwit other men (and women to outwit other women), or because big brains were originally used to court and seduce members of the opposite sex. It may be, therefore, that human intelligence is a consequence of mutual sexual selection and that 'clever people are sexy people'.

The gradual evolution of language (see Chapter 12) was also important in the evolution of human intelligence. Language provides potential mates with an opportunity to access each other's minds, allowing more direct sexual selection. Also, language permits gossip, which can transform mate choice from an individual decision to a social decision that integrates information from family and friends. According to Miller (1998), the feedback loop between sexual selection, language complexity, and mental complexity was probably the mainspring of human mental evolution.

Sexual selection and human culture

Human culture may be a product of sexual competition between vast numbers of individuals pursuing different mating strategies in different display arenas. For example, sexual selection explains the origins of *cultural dimorphism* (male domination of political, economic and cultural life) by male efforts to acquire material resources for attracting and keeping females. On this basis, the production of art, music, and literature functions primarily as a courtship display. In other words, cultural displays by males increase their sexual success.

The genetic benefits of cultural displays are smaller for females because their reproductive success is constrained by greater parental investment. It seems that it may be more effective for a woman to exhibit her courtship displays to a few select males, who are capable of giving her the long-term care, attention and resources she desires. Thus cultural dimorphism is much more likely to reflect a difference in motivation and sexual strategy than a difference in basic mental capacity.

Conclusions

Evolutionary psychologists suggest that humans possess specific mental adaptations for choosing mates, selecting their sexual partners on the basis of viability and fertility. Both males and females have evolved preferences for certain behavioural and/or anatomical features in the opposite sex. Evolutionary psychology also provides plausible explanations of homosexuality, adultery, jealousy and rape. Furthermore, sexual selection theory may provide the basis for the evolution of human intelligence and culture.

SUMMARY

- The application of **sexual selection** theory to human behaviour has been the greatest success story in evolutionary psychology. Humans possess **specific mental adaptations for choosing mates**, selecting their sexual partners on the basis of **viability** and **fertility**. However, adaptations for mate choice are probably different for males and females, as what defines a 'good mate' from an evolutionary point of view will be different for the two sexes.
- Evidence suggests that humans are a **mutually** sexually-selected species. In other words, both males and females have evolved preferences for certain behavioural and/or anatomical features in the opposite sex. In general, **people are attracted to people of high reproductive and genetic potential – the healthy, the fit and the powerful**.
- When selecting a mate, we find **average** faces attractive. Females are preferred with more **child-like** features, as are males with **strong jaws** and **large noses**. We also seem to consider **bilateral symmetry** as an important feature of facial and bodily beauty. This may be because symmetry advertises **biological quality**, such as good genes, reproductive vigour and an effective immune system.
- **Sexual dimorphism** in humans may be partly explained by sexual selection. For example, it appears that the main influence on the evolution of the long human penis was female choice, probably due to factors involved in sexual satisfaction and reproductive success. Likewise, males prefer women who display a low **waist-to-hip ratio**. This is concordant with enlarged buttocks, indicating sufficient fat reserves, and a narrow waist, indicating the absence of pregnancy.
- Males must be able to estimate the **age** of females (which is highly correlated with their reproductive capability), using **physical attractiveness** as a guide. Females are less concerned with looks, and prefer males who show the ability and willingness to invest **resources** connected with parenting. On this basis, females might be expected to **lie about their age, alter their appearance,** and **conceal prior sexual encounters**. Males would be predicted to **exaggerate their resources, inflate perceptions of their willingness to commit,** and **feign love to induce a female to mate with them**.
- Evidence suggests that genetic factors are involved in the development of **homosexuality**. This may be in the form of recessive genes, which provide heterosexual 'carriers' with a reproductive advantage, or get passed on through the relatives of an exclusive homosexual because he or she helps his or her relatives to raise more children. Alternatively, the **dominance failure theory** suggests that subordinate males are unable to find female partners and consequently develop a homosexual orientation. This would also help to account for the fact that there are more male homosexuals than lesbians.
- **Adultery** can be advantageous to both sexes within a monogamous marriage. The male may increase the **quantity** of his mates and the female may increase the **quality** of her mates. The risk of adultery for women is that they will lose their male partner to another female, and therefore lose the protection and resources he supplies. Males, on the other hand, risk being **cuckolded** and investing a great deal of time and effort bringing up children that are not his own. Both sexes have evolved tactics to ensure fidelity by their partner and they are both capable of demonstrating **jealousy**.
- It has been suggested that evolution has favoured males with the capacity to commit **rape**, under certain conditions, as a means to leaving

descendants (the **rape-adaptation hypothesis**). However, an equally plausible hypothesis is that rape is a **maladaptive** by-product of the male reproductive psyche. Evolutionary psychologists must be very careful when attempting to **explain** such anti-social behaviour, in case they appear to be **justifying** that behaviour.

- It seems likely that the basis of the evolution of human **intelligence** is sexual selection, rather than natural selection. Sexual selection may also explain the origins of **cultural dimorphism**, a phenomenon which reflects a difference in motivation and sexual strategy rather than a difference in basic mental capacity.

PART 3
Prosocial and antisocial behaviour

7

ALTRUISM

Introduction and overview

Our ancestors have been members of social groups and engaging in social interactions for millions and probably tens of millions of years. Therefore, we would expect humans to have evolved a wide range of cognitive adaptations to social life. The third part of this book examines positive and negative aspects of human social behaviour from an evolutionary perspective. Chapter 7 considers helping behaviour, or *altruism*, and asks how such unselfish behaviour can evolve under the rules of natural selection. This chapter also looks at the cognitive adaptations that underlie altruistic behaviour, a theme we shall return to in Chapter 10. Chapters 8 and 9 are concerned with antisocial behaviour, and deal with *aggression* and *criminal behaviour* respectively.

People often donate money to charity, help someone who has collapsed in a public place, and do a multitude of large and small favours for relatives, friends and acquaintances. These acts are committed by nearly everyone, not just a few charitable individuals. Nevertheless, acts of selflessness are difficult to explain using Darwinian logic, which appears to emphasise the importance of individual survival and reproductive success. The aim of the present chapter is to examine the nature of altruism and how it can evolve under the selfish rules of natural selection. I discuss the idea that humans may have cognitive adaptations for altruism and look at *friendship* as a special case of prosocial behaviour.

What is altruism?

Evolutionary psychologists use the term altruism to refer to behaviour which helps another individual's fitness despite a cost (in terms of fitness) to the donor.

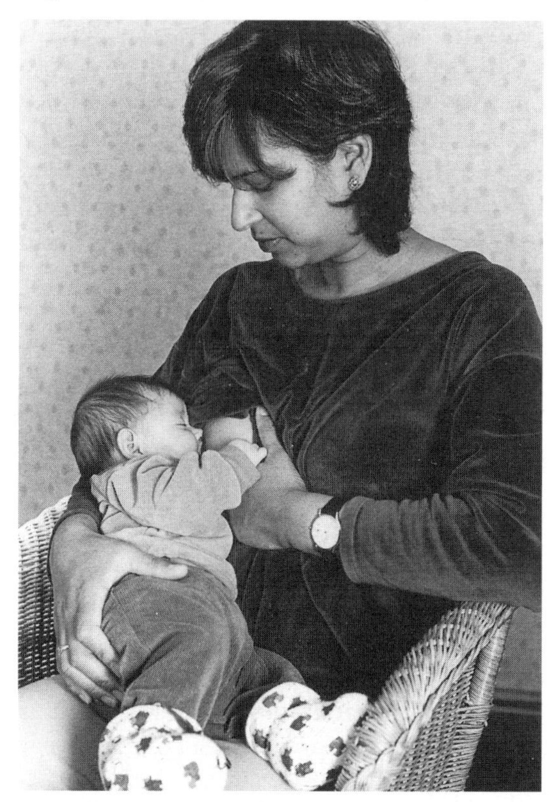

Figure 7.1 Parental investment appears to be altruistic, but it actually benefits the parents via an increase in fitness

Put another way, an altruistic act is one that lowers the direct individual reproduction of the organism committing the act (the *altruist*), while simultaneously raising the direct individual reproduction of another organism (the *recipient*). Care must be taken when labelling a behaviour as altruistic. For example, parental investment appears to be altruistic, because parents feed and protect their offspring at a cost to themselves (Figure 7.1). However, this is not true altruism as it actually benefits the parents via an increase in fitness.

Evolutionary theory argues that true altruistic behaviour should not occur since those who help others at a cost to themselves are less likely to survive to pass on their altruistic genes, compared to selfish individuals. Research suggests that instances of true altruism are only likely to occur on a non-voluntary or mistaken basis, due to deception or exploitation by a parasite such as the cuckoo. For true altruistic behaviour to continue, the costs must not be too great. In most cases, there is either a *genetic* reward (see 'kin selection theory' below), or a *long-term reward* (see 'reciprocal altruism', page 59). Therefore, most altruism is only *apparent* altruism.

According to Tooby and Cosmides (1996), aggression is more common than altruism for the same reasons that it is easier to break something than it is to construct it (or, to use a football analogy from Franey (1986), 'nobody with any skill plays in defence'). This means that altruistic adaptations will frequently require complex computations, and only be found in higher organisms, most commonly in humans. Therefore, if we are searching the animal kingdom for examples of true altruistic behaviour, we should start by looking at ourselves.

Kin selection theory

If people were really to perform behaviours that were selfless, surely they would rapidly lose the evolutionary race against those that were not? Selfish recipients would benefit without paying costs, altruists would encounter costs without benefits, and the selfish individuals would win hands down. At least that is what natural selection would predict in a competitive world.

Hamilton (1964) and Maynard-Smith (1964) proposed an explanation which could account for altruism between *kin* (related individuals). *Kin selection theory* suggests that traits which directed an individual's altruism towards its relatives, but not to non-relatives, would evolve. Only those sharing genes would benefit, thus promoting the survival of related individuals which are also likely to be genetically predisposed to be altruistic. The altruist thus *gains* through inclusive fitness (see Chapter 1, page 6). This can be summed up by a quotation from the biologist J.B.S. Haldane when he was asked if he would lay down his life for his brother. 'No,' he said, 'but for two brothers or eight cousins.' It should be noted that *selfish genes* (see Chapter 1, page 9) do not necessarily specify selfish organisms. Box 7.1 describes Hamilton's (1964) prediction of when kin-directed altruism will evolve.

According to kin selection theory, humans must be able to assess degrees of relatedness to themselves. They do this by using several kinds of information: who grows up together, who resembles whom, how people interact, what reliable sources indicate, and what can be logically deduced from other kin relationships. The decision to be altruistic to a relative depends upon the assumed degree of relatedness and the impact of the altruism on the relative's prospects of reproducing (Figure 7.2). Pinker (1997) proposed that mental programmes for familial love were calibrated in the course of evolution so that love correlated with the probability

Box 7.1 When will altruism evolve? (Hamilton 1964)

We would expect altruism to occur if the cost **(c)** of the behaviour to the altruist is low (c is small) and the benefit **(b)** to the recipient is great (b is large). The ratio of benefits to costs **(K)** can be expressed a **b/c** and we would except this figure to be large where altruism occurs – that is, for the benefits to exceed the costs. If **K = b/c**, then the higher the value of K, the greater the probability of altruism occuring. If the costs are too high, altruists are unlikely to survive to be altruistic, and if the gains are too small, the behaviour may not have significant effect on the recipient. Of course, the degree of kinship **(r)** matters too. Altruism should only occur when **K > 1/r**. This will only be fulfilled when either the cost/benefit ratio is very favourable, or when the degree of relatedness is very high (so 1/r is very small). This makes sense: individuals will risk more for close kin as they stand to gain more in terms of inclusive fitness.

Figure 7.2 Kin selection suggests that monozygotic twins are more likely to be altruistic to one another

during the environment of evolutionary adaptedness (EEA: see Chapter 1, page 1) that a loving (or altruistic) act would benefit copies of genes for loving (or altruistic) acts.

Burnstein *et al* (1994) used social-psychological rating scales to test whether people would follow predictions from inclusive fitness when making hypothetical decisions concerning whom to help, either when a small favour was involved or under life or death conditions. In each case, the respondents were asked to choose between a series of three hypothetical target individuals differing in kinship, and in other characteristics such as sex, age, health and wealth. The choice of whom to help followed kinship in the way predicted from inclusive fitness, particularly in response to the life or death scenarios. People also used other criteria which were likely to reflect inclusive fitness, such as preferring to help younger or healthier individuals under life or death conditions.

During the EEA, humans tended to live in small populations of related individuals. Under these conditions, it would probably pay to help any individual in the group, irrespective of calculations of kin. Hamilton (1975) showed that this is most likely to occur where the contrast between close kin and neighbours is unclear, but there is a sharp drop in relatedness at the edge of the group. Once humans had evolved under such conditions, people would probably act altruistically towards someone in trouble, even under modern urban conditions where the recipient was unlikely to be a close relative. This is because insufficient time has elapsed for the trait to be selected against, and/or because there may be other advantages to altruism (see 'reciprocal altruism' below).

Box 7.2 Xenophobia

Xenophobia (a dislike of strangers) is a feature of most human societies. For example, tribespeople in western New Guinea take it for granted that strangers will be killed if they stray into another group's territory (Diamond, 1991). Throughout our history, the criminal justice system has only applied to those regarded as part of that particular society. Outsiders have been persecuted, driven from their homes, tortured and killed. Furthermore, the nature of such killing is often on a large scale, well-planned and intentional.

The psychological mechanisms underlying xenophobia are probably strong identification with one's own group, and negative stereotyping of those from other groups. People are categorised on the basis of appearance, religion, customs, location, language or sexuality. An evolutionary perspective would suggest that xenophobia is ultimately based on kin selection. Outsiders are unlikely to be relatives, therefore we will be selected to compete, rather than cooperate, with those who are not members of 'our' group.

If altruism did evolve in small groups, there would have to have been a way of discriminating between those to whom it was offered and those from whom it was withheld. An evolutionary perspective would suggest that this should happen on the basis of group membership, as non-members were unlikely to be relatives. Hostility to strangers by group members, or *xenophobia*, has been demonstrated by most groups of people throughout human history. Box 7.2 provides a discussion of the nature of xenophobia.

Reciprocal altruism

Kin selection can only explain altruism when the helper and recipient are related, but in many cases they are not. Reciprocal altruism (Trivers, 1971) can be described as 'I'll scratch your back and you scratch mine'. One individual (the altruist) helps another, and is later 'repaid' by assistance from that unrelated recipient. The initial altruist suffers a short-term reduction in fitness, but both parties eventually achieve a gain in fitness. Box 7.3 describes cases of reciprocal altruism among olive baboons and vampire bats.

Box 7.3 Examples of reciprocal altruism

Packer (1977) provided evidence for reciprocal altruism from observations of olive baboons. Competition for fertile females is fierce and competitors will attempt to steal the female away from the *consort male* (the male defending a female who is ready to mate). Takeovers are more likely to be successful if intruding males form an alliance. A male seeking to depose a consort will enlist the help of an altruist. These two then threaten the consort male, causing him to desert his female. He is replaced by the soliciting male, while the altruist is potentially left to fight with the ex-consort male. However, the altruist ultimately benefits because he is more likely to receive reciprocal assistance if he subsequently

Figure 7.3 Reciprocal altruism in olive baboons. The males on the right have formed an alliance to compete with the consort male on the left.

solicits help (Figure 7.3). This system could be open to cheats, individuals who solicit help but do not reciprocate. To avoid this, males are able to recognise one another, and remember which individuals assisted them. As a consequence, a cheating strategy is usually ineffective.

Another example of reciprocal altruism is illustrated by vampire bats. Wilkinson (1984) studied kinship relationships between bats at a roost site. He found that bats were only altruistic to one another if they were either close relatives or unrelated individuals who were regular roost mates. A vampire bat without food will only survive for about two days. If it has been unsuccessful in finding a host from which to suck blood, it returns to the roost and solicits food from a neighbour who obliges by regurgitating blood. When the altruist and recipient are related, this can be explained by kin selection. Reciprocal altruism can explain regurgitation between unrelated individuals. The bats are aware of which individuals they help and receive help from, assistance being restricted to those who reciprocate.

Reciprocal altruism must entail the ability to recognise other individuals, in order to discriminate who is 'owed' a favour. It is likely that helping would evolve so as to occur selectively where the costs of helping were relatively low and the benefits relatively high, and where there was a way of identifying and excluding those individuals who received help but did not return it. This is an important point: reciprocal altruism is not evolutionarily stable unless most cheating does not pay.

Humans are an intelligent species, and unusual in how often they help unrelated individuals. It seems likely that our lifestyles and our minds are particularly well-adapted to the demands of reciprocal altruism (in fact this form of altruism may be quite rare in non-human species). People can trade food, tools, favours and information. As the only species with true language, the trading of information is unique to humans. It usually costs very little to give, but may be of enormous benefit to the recipient. Language also enables us to rapidly 'spread the word' about cheats in the reciprocal altruism contract, reinforcing the efficiency of this process. The demands of reciprocal altruism are probably also the source of many human emotions, as described in Box 7.4.

The principle of reciprocity leads to the prediction that people will generally be less helpful to strangers. Therefore, bystander intervention should be less common among larger anonymous communities than among smaller integrated ones, as indeed it is. Between strangers, helping is more likely when it exacts a low cost from the donor, and confers a high benefit on the recipient (Archer, 1995). For example, many of the reasons people offer for not helping someone after an accident involve costs to themselves. Furthermore, it is likely that help given to strangers also depends on considerations of shared group identity (see page 59).

Box 7.4 Human emotions: a product of reciprocal altruism? (Based on Pinker, 1997)

Emotion	Altruistic perspective
Liking	A willingness to offer altruism, usually directed at those who appear willing to reciprocate. We like people who are nice to us, and we are nice to people whom we like.
Anger	A response to exploitation (a refusal to reciprocate). The cheat is punished by severing the relationship or via aggression.
Gratitude	A strong desire to reciprocate because the altruistic act helped us a great deal and/or involved high costs to the altruist.
Sympathy	A feeling toward those in great need. Being altruistic to such individuals means that they will be very grateful. Therefore, the altruistic act will be very 'cost effective'.
Guilt	The emotion suffered by a cheat who is in danger of being found out.
Shame	The emotion suffered by a cheat who has been publicly exposed.

GAME THEORY REVISITED

To a selfish individual, reciprocal altruism is ripe for exploitation. Cooperation pays, but individuals may benefit more from cheating. This seems to present an obstacle to the evolution of cooperation; the best course of action for any individual is to pursue its own self-interest, and so everyone ends up worse off. However, game theory analysis suggests that this pessimistic approach is unwarranted.

A simple version of the 'Prisoner's Dilemma' was described in Chapter 1 (page 10), and a reminder of the pay-off grid is given in Box 7.5. I now want to take this idea further by examining the optimal strategy for *repeated* games of this type: *Tit for Tat* (TFT). TFT always cooperates on the first move, and then copies the opponent's previous move. Therefore it is never the first to defect. TFT will retaliate against defection by defecting on the next move, but subsequently forgives and forgets. It turns out that this highly cooperative strategy can evolve (provided that there are a number of other cooperators in the population), even when initially pitted against exploitative, readily-defecting strategies. TFT also represents an *evolutionarily stable strategy* (see Chapter 1, page 9), and is stable against any invasion by other strategies. It should be noted that game theory has been criticised for adopting a very simplistic approach to explain complex behaviour patterns (Cartwright, 2000), but it is still a useful tool for analysing the interactions between individuals.

Box 7.5 The prisoner's dilemma: a reminder of the payoff grid

		Player Y	
		Co-operate	*Defect*
Player X	*Co-operate*	Mutual co-operation (Investment pays off)	Sucker (exploited)
	Defect	Cheat (best net result)	Mutual defection (no pains, no gains)

Axelrod (1984) suggested that the success of Tit for Tat is due to three main factors; being *nice* (never the first to defect), *provokable* (retaliating against defection), and *forgiving* (letting bygones be bygones and resuming cooperation). In evolution, a strategy is represented in any generation in proportion to its success in the previous generation. So, the more Tit for Tat is successful, the more likely it will be to encounter itself and the more it will be able to reap the rewards of mutual cooperation. As Cronin (1991) says, 'Out of selfishness comes forth altruism.'

Social exchange

The concept of reciprocal altruism suggests that altruistic acts can be favoured by natural selection if they cause the target of the altruism to subsequently reciprocate the act. A population of reciprocators will be stable against invasion by non-reciprocators ('cheats') *if* they are able to detect and subsequently exclude non-reciprocators. Cosmides and Tooby (1992) have suggested that our ancestors should have evolved to detect violations of social conventions when those violations were interpretable as cheating on a social contract. In other words, human reasoning in social situations should involve a 'search for cheats' strategy.

Experimental psychologists have long known that our reasoning powers are affected by the content and not merely the logical structure of arguments (Cronin, 1991). This shows up in people's responses to the

Wason selection task, as described in Box 7.6. According to Cosmides (1989), humans are particularly adept at solving puzzles to do with social exchanges. These have the structure of a social contract: 'if you take the benefit, then you pay the cost'. The reason why we are so much better at applying a conditional rule when it involves a social contract is that we are operating a search-for-cheats procedure. We look for people who take the benefit (to ensure they have paid the cost) and for those who do not pay the cost (to check that they have not received the benefit). This is why we do so much better in the second example of the Wason selection task described in Box 7.6. Beer is a benefit that one earns through maturity, and cheats are underage drinkers. These basic findings have been replicated among the Shiwiar, a foraging people in Ecuador, suggsting that socially-biased problem solving is universal (Cosmides, 1989).

Box 7.6 The Wason selection task

The Wason selection task is a test of logical reasoning in which people are asked to determine whether a conditional rule has been violated (Wason, 1983). What is interesting about this task is that our ability to solve it depends a great deal on the way the problem is presented. For example, consider the following problem.

The four cards below have a letter on one side and a number on the other. *If a card has the letter D on one side then it must have the number 3 on the other side.* Indicate only those card(s) that you definitely need to turn over to see if this rule is violated.

D	F	3	7

The logically correct answer is to turn over only two cards: D (to check that it has a number 3 on the reverse) and 7 (to check that it does *not* have a D on the back). However, people generally perform poorly on a test like this, with only 4-10% of candidates being successful.

Now consider another problem involving a conditional rule.

The four cards below have information about four people sitting in a bar. One side of the card states what a person is drinking and the other side tells that person's age. *If a person is drinking beer, then they must be over 18 years old.* Indicate only those card(s) that you definitely need to turn over to see if any of these people are breaking this law.

drinking beer	drinking coke	25 years old	16 years old

The logic of enforcing the rule is, of course, exactly the same. The cards you need to turn over are 'drinking beer' (to check they are over 18 years old) and '16 years old' (to check they are not drinking beer). In this case, an example of detecting a 'cheat' in an example of social exchange, people are much more successful (typically around 75% selecting the correct reply). This suggests that humans may possess cognitive adaptations for social exchange (Cosmides and Tooby, 1992).

If Cosmides and Tooby are correct, we solve puzzles involving social contracts using the adaptive rules of mutual cooperation, not the rules of logic. Even though we *look* as if we are being more logical in these circumstances, this is purely coincidental. Therefore, if the rules for detecting cheats do *not* coincide with the rules of logic, we should stick with the 'look for cheats' response. According to Cosmides (1989) that is exactly what happens. This should not surprise us, as reciprocal altruists have no special need to ensure that others who pay costs receive their benefits, only that those who receive the benefit pay the cost. Natural selection, it seems, has endowed us with a propensity to pursue a search-for-cheats procedure because it is likely to be adaptively useful (Cronin, 1991).

In summary, reciprocal altruism is always vulnerable to cheats. For it to have evolved, it must be accompanied by cognitive mechanisms that remember who has taken a benefit and that ensure a cost is paid. Trivers (1985) predicted that humans, the most conspicuous altruists in the animal kingdom, should have evolved a hypertrophied cheat-detection algorithm. Cosmides may have found it.

Other theories of altruism

Many cases of altruism may not be directed at kin or to reciprocate favours, but may paradoxically be to the direct advantage of the altruist. For example, Arabian babblers (small brown birds found on the Arabian and Sinai peninsulas) actually *compete* for the position of sentinels to the flock, despite the apparent danger involved. According to Zahavi's (1987) handicap theory, they do this *because* of the danger – sentinel duty implies strength and stamina and only individuals of high quality could afford to handicap themselves so much. If serving as a sentinel acts as a testament of quality, we would expect sentinels to have increased reproductive success compared to those who are 'not up to the position' (at present, it is not clear whether this is the case). A similar argument may be advanced for humans. We may act in an altruistic manner to display our *ability* to help, which may be seen as a positive trait in the search for a mate.

Another theory of altruism arises from Dawkin's (1982) idea of the *extended phenotype*. Altruistic behaviour may genuinely be self-sacrificial, but the altruist is acting under the influence of another organism. In other words, the genes in individual A cause individual B to behave altruistically (the extended phenotypic expression of A's genes), and this altruism benefits the genes in A. An example may help. Consider a cuckoo's unwitting hosts, sacrificing themselves and their own offspring to satisfy their demanding foster-child. In this case, the behaviour of the hosts may be an adaptation that benefits the cuckoos; the adaptive phenotypic effect of a manipulative gene in the cuckoo's body (Dawkins, 1982).

It could be said that with manipulation we have at last found true, although involuntary, altruism. With kin selection, reciprocal altruism or handicapping theory, there is a benefit to the altruist or to copies of its altruistic genes. The altruist appears to experience only cost in cases of manipulation. However, what benefits from altruism in this case is still a gene for altruism – it just happens to sit in an organism distinct from the altruist. So, from a gene-centred point of view, manipulation turns out not to be a special case. We are left with no true altruism, just many examples of *apparent altruism*.

Friendship: a special case?

Information presented in this chapter suggests that people are good at detecting cheats and are fitted with moralistic emotions that motivate them to punish the cheats and reward the cooperators. This implies that Tit for Tat underlies much of the widespread cooperation observed in our species. Pinker (1997) argues that even moderately good friends privately remember the most recent Christmas gifts and dinner-party invitations, and calculate the appropriate way to reciprocate. However, are the altruistic adaptations that underlie *friendship* really based on the standard model of reciprocal altruism (Figure 7.4)?

Figure 7.4 Friendship: a special case of reciprocal altruism?

Tit for Tat does not cement a friendship; it strains it. 'Exchange couples', who keep close track of what each has done for the other, are the couples who are the least happy (Gross and McIlveen, 1998). It has been suggested that friendship has rules of its own. Friends feel as if they are in each other's debt, but these debts are seldom measured and the obligation to repay can be very satisfying. (This in itself might represent a benefit to the individual and might exceed the costs involved, therefore not necessarily representing true altruism.) We feel a spontaneous pleasure in helping a friend, without anticipating payment or regretting the favour if payment does not come. Only if the favour-trading becomes very imbalanced for a long period of time do we consider terminating the friendship. However, this still implies that we *are* measuring the benefits of friendships, but that some tolerance in terms of immediacy of reciprocation is exercised.

Friendship does not actually contradict the theory of reciprocal altruism, but it does demand a more flexible approach. Tooby and Cosmides (1996) have tried to explain how such a relationship may have evolved, using an idea called the 'Banker's Paradox'. This is explained in Box 7.7.

Box 7.7 The Banker's paradox

Bankers have a limited amount of money, and must choose who to invest it in. Each choice is a gamble: taken together, they must ultimately yield a net profit, or the banker will go out of business. Paradoxically, this means that bankers are most likely to loan money to people who do not need it. Individuals who need money desperately are likely to be the poorest credit risks and, therefore, the least likely to receive a loan.

The same logic applies to altruism among our ancestors. A person considering an altruistic act must worry not only about cheats (is the recipient willing to repay?), but also about bad credit risks (is the recipient *able* to pay?). Unfortunately, it is the bad credit risks, the sick, starving and injured, who most need favours. How can we ensure that people will extend credit to us, even if misfortune were to make us a risk?

One strategy is to make ourselves irreplaceable. Possessing unique or valuable talents (and making sure that everyone knows about them) can make us too costly to abandon in times of need. It may be that the quest for status is in part a motive for making oneself irreplaceable. Another tactic is to associate with people who benefit from the things that benefit you. In pursuing our own interests, we may help someone else as a side-effect. Marriage is a good example of this: the husband and wife share an interest in their children's welfare. In this case, one delivers a benefit to someone without incurring a cost. Therefore we do not need a repayment to make the act worthwhile. This is really a case of *symbiosis*, where both participants benefit from the relationship.

Once we have made ourselves valuable to someone, they become valuable to us. We value them because if we were ever in trouble, they would have an interest in helping us (and *vice-versa*). The theme song to the TV show *Friends* says, 'I'll be there for you'. The point of friendship, in evolutionary terms, is to save you in hard times when it is not worth anyone else's trouble.

Conclusions

An altruistic act is one that lowers the direct individual reproduction of the altruist, while simultaneously raising the direct individual reproduction of the recipient. Such behaviour initially appears to present a problem for evolutionary psychologists, since those who help others at a cost to themselves are less likely to survive to pass on their altruistic genes, compared to selfish individuals. The main theories which seek to explain altruism are *kin selection theory*, *reciprocal altruism theory* and, to a lesser extent, *handicapping theory* and *manipulation theory*. According to all of these theories, the altruist ultimately *gains* from the act. Therefore, there is no true altruism, only *apparent altruism*. Nevertheless, it is possible that friendship may represent a special case of prosocial behaviour.

SUMMARY

- **An altruistic act is one that lowers the direct individual reproduction of the altruist, while simultaneously raising the direct individual reproduction of the recipient.** Evolutionary theory argues that true altruistic behaviour should not occur since those who help others at a cost to themselves are less likely to survive to pass on their altruistic genes, compared to selfish individuals.
- **Kin selection theory** suggests that traits which directed an individual's altruism towards its relatives, but not to non-relatives, would evolve. Only those sharing genes would benefit, thus promoting the survival of related individuals which are also likely to be genetically predisposed to be altruistic. The altruist thus **gains** through inclusive fitness.
- According to kin selection theory, **humans must be able to assess degrees of relatedness**. The decision to be altruistic to a relative depends upon the assumed degree of relatedness and the impact of the altruism on the relative's prospects of reproducing. Recent studies suggest that humans do follow predictions from inclusive

fitness when making hypothetical decisions concerning whom to help.

- If, as expected, altruism evolved in small populations, there would have to have been a way of discriminating between those to whom it was offered and those from whom it was withheld. An evolutionary perspective would suggest that this should happen on the basis of group membership, as non-members were unlikely to be relatives. Hostility to strangers by group members, or **xenophobia**, has been demonstrated by most groups of people throughout human history.
- Kin selection can only explain altruism when the helper and recipient are related, but in many cases they are not. These latter cases are often examples of **reciprocal altruism**. One individual (the altruist) helps another, and is later 'repaid' by assistance from that unrelated recipient. **The initial altruist suffers a short-term reduction in fitness, but both parties eventually achieve a gain in fitness**.
- Reciprocal altruism must entail the ability to recognise other individuals, in order to discriminate who is 'owed' a favour. It is likely that helping would evolve so as to occur selectively where the costs of helping were relatively low and the benefits relatively high, and where there was a way of identifying and excluding those individuals who received help but did not return it. **This is an important point: reciprocal altruism is not evolutionarily stable unless most cheating does not pay**.
- To a selfish Darwinian, reciprocal altruism is ripe for exploitation. **Cooperation pays, but cheating could pay the cheat even better**. However, cooperation can evolve if certain strategies are employed, such as **Tit for Tat** (an evolutionarily stable strategy). Tit for Tat is successful because it is **nice**, **provokable** and **forgiving**.
- It has been suggested that **human reasoning in social situations should involve a 'search for cheats' strategy**. We look for people who take the benefit (to ensure they have paid the cost) and for those who do not pay the cost (to check that they have not received the benefit). Natural selection, it seems, has endowed us with a propensity to pursue a search-for-cheats procedure because it is likely to be adaptively useful.
- **Many cases of altruism may not be directed at kin or to reciprocate favours, but may paradoxically be to the direct advantage of the altruist**. The **handicap theory** suggests that we may act in an altruistic manner to display our **ability** to help, which may be seen as a positive trait in the search for a mate. The **extended phenotype (manipulation) theory** argues that altruistic behaviour may be genuinely self-sacrificial, but the altruist is acting under the influence of another organism. However, from a gene-centred view, manipulation is just another example of **apparent altruism**.

8

AGGRESSION

Introduction and overview

Aggression may be defined as physical or symbolic behaviour that is carried out with the intention of harming someone (Berkowitz, 1993). This may be considered as a fairly narrow definition as it excludes aggression used in self-defence, or the constructive aggression sometimes observed in goal-orientated behaviour. These latter two cases may be considered adaptive, whereas the definition suggested by Berkowitz appears to describe maladaptive behaviour. It seems clear that there are many types of aggression, as shown in Box 8.1. Nevertheless, evolutionary psychologists believe that aggression is (or at least was) adaptive.

This chapter considers the evolutionary psychology view of aggression and examines theories of aggressive behaviour, sex differences in aggression, ritualised aggression and conflict between groups. I start by looking at the idea that aggression is an innate trait in all of us – the *instinct theories*.

Box 8.1 Types of aggression

- *Altruistic aggression*: aggression to help others
- *Hostile aggression*: aggression whose main purpose is to inflict pain and suffering on the victim
- *Displaced aggression*: aggression against someone or something that is not to blame
- *Instrumental aggression*: aggression which is a means to achieving another goal
- *Resource aggression*: aggression used to secure resources, such as food, mates or a territory

The instinct theories of aggression

FREUD'S PSYCHOANALYTIC APPROACH

Freud (1920) proposed the existence of an instinct for aggression, which he called *Thanatos*. Aggression was seen as a reaction to frustration experienced in the pursuit of 'pleasure' or the satisfaction of *libido* (the sexual energy of the life instinct). This instinct drives us towards self-destruction, death and the return to an inanimate, lifeless state. The only way to realistically satisfy this instinct is to turn it outward, and to destroy some other thing or person if we are to avoid destroying ourselves (avoiding the release of aggression causes psychological disorders, such as depression, suicide or masochism). This results in periodic acts of aggression to discharge the aggressive energy that has been built up (similar to a discharge of sexual energy through sexual activity). According to Freud, just as we need to eat, drink and express our sexual needs periodically, so too

Figure 8.1 Is aggressive behaviour an inevitable part of our society?

Box 8.2 The biological basis of aggression

Biological factors implicated in aggression may have a genetic basis, an environmental basis (such as diet or drugs), or a combination of both. For example, Mednick *et al* (1984) found that adopted children with biological fathers who were aggressive criminals were more likely to become aggressive criminals themselves (see Chapter 9), thus supporting a genetic link. However, there is also a strong correlation between alcohol abuse (an environmental phenomenon) and violent behaviour.

It has been suggested that brain differences may account for individual differences in aggressive behaviour. Tumours in the limbic system are associated with aggressive behaviour, and lobotomies have been performed to reduce aggression. However, the cerebral cortex normally plays an important role in regulating aggressive behaviour, which is therefore influenced by experience. Brain chemistry may also be important, with aggression being negatively correlated with levels of serotonin. Other body chemicals, such as adrenalin, testosterone and progesterone are also associated with aggressive behaviour.

Overall, a biological approach may help to explain individual but not cultural differences in aggressive behaviour. Certain factors, such as hormones, may be a cause or an effect of aggression, and no physiological system has been found to have an invariant effect on aggressive behaviour (Siann, 1985).

must our hostile and destructive impulses be expressed (Gross and McIlveen, 1998). Aggression, it appears, is inevitable (Figure 8.1). Perhaps in partial support of Freud's ideas, several biological factors have been linked with aggressive behaviour, and these are summarised in Box 8.2.

Some support for Freud's theory comes from Megargee's (1966) study of people who had committed brutally aggressive crimes. These crimes were often committed by people who commonly repressed their anger (*overcontrolled individuals*), causing a build-up of aggression. Minor events can trigger aggressive outbursts in such individuals and, following the cathartic release of aggression, they tend to revert to a very passive state. However, Freud's theory is difficult to test empirically. It is based on a vague concept (Thanatos) that provides no testable hypotheses and gives us little insight into the true causes of aggressive behaviour. Furthermore, to assume aggressive behaviour is due to an *instinct* does not help to explain the occurrence of such behaviour. One concept, namely observed behaviour, is simply replaced by another, namely the assumed basic drive. Nevertheless, some of Freud's ideas were incorporated into later theories of aggression, such as the *frustration-aggression* hypothesis (see page 68).

LORENZ'S ETHOLOGICAL APPROACH

Lorenz (1966) also saw aggression as being instinctive, with aggressive energy needing to be released from time to time if it is not to build up to dangerously high levels. He believed that aggression is adaptive because it is closely related to survival prospects and reproductive success. For example, fights between rivals serve to select the strongest and healthiest leaders of the group. Through within-species aggression, a hierarchy is established within a social unit which places the 'best' individuals at the highest levels (Figure 8.2). According to Lorenz, most aggression is related to competition between members of the same species. However, animals usually refrain from killing each other in battles over territories or mates, because of 'built-in safety devices'. Two such devices are *ritualised fighting* and *appeasement displays*, which allow conflicts to be resolved without the competitors suffering serious injury (see page 68).

Figure 8.2 Dominant males, such as this red deer, are a feature of many species

Lorenz saw humans as different to most other species, because although aggression is still basically adaptive, it is no longer under the control of rituals. This is not to say that our appeasement gestures (such as cowering and begging for mercy) are ineffective, but that our *methods* of fighting negate the use of these gestures. Once we acquired the ability to kill each other from a distance, through advances in weapon technology, our appeasement rituals became ineffective (Lea, 1984).

Lorenz's theory has been subjected to much criticism. There are many cases of aggression in non-human animals that result in the death of the loser (Lea, 1984). The degree of ritualised aggression also seems to depend on the context. For example, antelopes are more likely to engage in ritualised aggression when fighting over territory, than when competing for a sexual partner. Furthermore, many psychologists have questioned Lorenz's view that most aggression is spontaneous rather than reactive (Hinde, 1974). Most evolutionary psychologists consider Lorenz's ideas as too inflexible, believing that human aggression is predominantly reactive and modifiable by a variety of internal and external conditions (Gross and McIlveen, 1998).

Figure 8.3 Boxing: a useful way to 'let off steam'?

Finally, both the Freudian and ethological approaches to aggression propose that the most effective way of reducing this instinct is through *catharsis* (the discharging of aggression, or 'letting off steam'). However, this view is not well-supported by experimental evidence. Watching televised violence, attacking inanimate objects, and participating in or attending sporting events, would all be expected to reduce aggression (Figure 8.3). Most studies appear to show that this does not happen. Indeed, there is evidence that aggression may actually be *increased* in such conditions (Baron and Byrne, 1994).

Other theories of aggression

The frustration-aggression hypothesis (Dollard *et al*, 1939) combines Freudian ideas on aggression with learning theory, and states that aggression is always a consequence of frustration. In other words, aggression is an innate response but it is only elicited in frustrating situations (and perhaps in the presence of certain *environmental cues*, see Box 8.3). Early studies appeared to provide some support for this idea (Barker *et al*, 1941), but the frustration-aggression hypothesis has otherwise

Box 8.3 The aggressive cue theory (Berkowitz, 1989)

According to Berkowitz, there are two conditions which act together to produce aggression when frustration occurs. The first is a readiness to act aggressively and the second is the presence of certain environmental cues. These cues may be associated with a frustrating person or object, or with aggressive behaviour in general.

In an experiment by Berkowitz and Le Page (1967), angry participants were given the opportunity to deliver electric shocks to people. For one group of participants, there was a shotgun and a revolver on a table next to the shock key; for a second group, two badminton rackets and some shuttlecocks; and for a third group, no objects. As expected, the participants delivered more shocks if the weapons were nearby (objects associated with violence) than when neutral objects (or no objects) were present. As Berkowitz (1968) put it, 'Guns not only permit violence, they can trigger it as well'. In other words, aggression can be 'pulled' by external stimuli as well as being 'pushed' from within.

been heavily criticised. Frustration may be necessary but not sufficient to induce aggression, and aggression is only one of several possible responses to a frustrating situation (Miller, 1941). Both situational and personal factors can influence the probability of aggressive behaviour, and the frustration-aggression hypothesis is unable to explain many instances of aggressive and non-aggressive behaviour. Furthermore, Kulik and Brown (1979) showed that frustration was more likely to cause aggression if it was not anticipated and if people believed that the individual responsible for frustrating them did so deliberately and without good reason, showing the importance of cognitive factors as cues for aggressive behaviour.

Social-psychological theories of aggression suggest that we *learn* both aggressiveness and how to express aggression through a variety of mechanisms. These include direct reinforcement (conditioning theory), indirect reinforcement (observational learning), identification (with role models or significant others) and imitation (modelling). Box 8.4 shows how our aggressive behaviour owes much to the environment and to distortions and deprivations of socialisation. There is a considerable body of evidence supporting the influence of environmental factors on aggressive behaviour, and this should be considered when evaluating genetic theories of aggression (Gross and McIlveen, 1998). Nevertheless, as mentioned in Chapter 1 (page 1), evolutionary psychology attempts to integrate the influences of genes and the environment.

Box 8.4 Social-psychological theories of aggression

Bandura (1977) suggested that aggressive behaviour is largely learned (although he acknowledged that there is certainly some biological component). Socialisation into aggressive behaviour may be through a straightforward conditioning process or else through observational learning.

Behaviour is established and maintained through rewards (such as social status or social approval) and punishments. Patterson *et al* (1989) observed two hundred families and concluded that coercive home environments may create aggressiveness in a number of ways. For example, aggression may be rewarded, or harsh discipline may result in a child becoming resistant to punishment, and progressively harder to restrain. In addition, parents may solve disputes aggressively, providing children with inappropriate role models.

Bandura *et al* (1963) showed that, if children watch someone behaving aggressively towards a doll, they were more likely to be aggressive and to imitate specific actions when they were placed on their own with the doll. This became even more likely if the child identified with the model and if the model was rewarded. However, the validity of these studies has been questioned, and much of the observed behaviour may have been due to demand characteristics.

Individual differences in aggression may reflect differences in the ability to process information about social situations (which may be an evolved mechanism). These differences may relate to the interpretation of social cues, or the selection of an appropriate response. Aggressive people tend to have a hostile attributional bias. In other words, they are more likely than non-aggressive people to attribute hostile intent to others' actions.

Finally, it should be noted that environmental factors can influence aggressive behaviour, such as noise, air quality, heat, or the effects of alcohol and other drugs.

Aggression in males

Sexual rivalry is a universal and sometimes deadly source of conflict in humans; a substantial proportion of homicides can be seen as the outcome of dangerous confrontational competition amongst men over women (see Chapter 9). Sociobiologists generally considered aggressive behaviour to be adaptive, and predominantly concerned with mating strategies and/or social organisation (see Chapter 4). Evidence to support this idea included the relationship-specificity of human violence; circumstances that elicit it are threats to fitness, and the targets of violence are generally those with whom the aggressor has substantive conflict and, hence, something to gain from subduing them.

Aggression represents an important part of the male mating strategy and may be aimed at winning access to females, or wooing the choosing females in cases where aggression is equated with dominance and status. Aggression would, therefore, be expected to be directly related to reproductive success. However, this sociobiological view could not explain *why* females choose aggressive males, aggressive behaviour unrelated to mating strategies (if it exists) and aggression in females (see below). The evolutionary psychology approach to male aggression extends the original sociobiological ideas to answer these questions.

Aggressive behaviour in males is related to *status* and *paternity certainty*. In other words, aggression is used to enhance status (compared to other males) and to ensure paternity (by warning off other males and forcibly controlling the behaviour of females). Thus it serves to attract mates and reduce the risk of cuckoldry, thereby enhancing fitness. Aggression is directly related to success as a warrior and hunter, and to dominance over other males. In turn, this elevated status is often converted into sexual, marital and reproductive success (Daly and Wilson, 1994). As we shall see in Chapter 9, young male adults are the principal perpetrators of potentially lethal violence, as well as its main victims. During the EEA, young men had to display powers in hunting, warfare and the ability to defend their status, if they were to acquire a mate. Compared to other male mammals, young adulthood is particularly competitive among humans because our social complexity can make the consequences of differential performance in that stage enduring and hence even more critical.

According to Daly and Wilson (1994), young men are biologically and psychologically specialised to embrace danger and confrontational competition. Two pieces of evidence which may support this assertion are the attitudes of male car drivers (younger drivers underestimate risks and overestimate their own skills, compared with older drivers), and the relatively high rates of suicide among young men in western societies (compared with the figures for young women), representing the cost of perceived failure in this intense competition.

Despite the fact that women are the main resource for which men compete, male aggression against female partners is far from rare. This behaviour may represent a mechanism to deter a wife from pursuing courses of action that are not in the man's interests. Likely sources of marital conflict are those which relate to fitness, including sexual infidelity, cuckoldry, desertion, and conflicts over allocation of parental effort. Although male violence towards wives is universal, the *contexts* in which it occurs are remarkably few: infidelity, threatened desertion and male sexual jealousy. Consistent with this argument is the finding that men kill their estranged wives much more often than estranged wives kill their husbands, and that jealousy is the leading motive in spousal homicide (Daly and Wilson, 1988). Nevertheless, it should be noted that marital dissatisfaction, alcohol and drug abuse, and low socio-economic status have been found to correlate highly with serious partner abuse. These factors need to be considered when espousing an evolutionary view of male violence.

Aggression in females

Human females are generally viewed as less aggressive than their male counterparts. However, it is unclear as to whether this is truly the case. It may be that *physical* aggression is less common (see 'The biological basis of aggression', Box 8.2), but that *symbolic* aggression is greater than that seen in males (with no overall difference in aggressiveness between the sexes).

According to evolutionary psychology, most female aggression is related to *ensuring offspring quality* (Cronin, 1991). This is manifested in two main ways; emotional/sexual jealousy, and infanticide. Jealous aggression results from a threat to offspring quality caused by potential male desertion, or by a reduction/withdrawal of resources by the male. The likelihood of aggressive behaviour in females would therefore be related to mating strategies and social organisation (see Chapter 4), as well as to the degree of parental care required by offspring (see Chapter 5). Jealous aggression would be expected to be maximal in a monogamous system where a great deal of parental care is required, such as that found in humans.

Infanticide in females may be considered to represent aggression (although the act itself is not usually particularly aggressive) and would be expected to occur more frequently when the infant in question is of low quality in some way, such as a runt (Dawkins, 1989). Depleted resources, perhaps as a result of paternal desertion, may also cause the female to opt for infanticide, even if the offspring are perfectly healthy. Similarly, very young single mothers or those lacking social support would also be at risk from this particular type of behaviour. These circumstances have been observed to be related to the incidence of female infanticide in natural environments, and both would help to achieve the overall aim of ensuring the quality (if not the quantity) of offspring (see Chapter 5, page 43).

Fighting, fleeing and ritualised aggression

According to Lorenz (1966), ritualised aggression helps to preserve species against internecine bloodshed and the threat of possible extinction. However, this idea is based on the fallacy that animals evolve to benefit the species. It cannot explain why an aggressive mutant that never surrendered, and that killed surrenderers, would not become dominant and soon characterise the species. In order to fully understand the basis of an animals decision to fight, flee, or engage in ritualised aggression, we need to employ *game theory* (see Box 8.5).

Fighting every time to the bitter end is a poor strategy for an individual, because the chances are that his or her opponent has evolved to do the same thing. The loser ends up injured or dead, and has lost the resource at issue. The victor gained the resource, but has often paid for it in terms of energy or injuries. It would be far better for the two parties to agree on the likely winner beforehand, and for the underdog to concede. This is the basis of 'sizing up' your opponent and has lead to ways of exaggerating size and/or aggressiveness. A fight is only likely if the contestants are very evenly matched and the stakes are sufficiently high.

Box 8.5 To fight or not to fight: a game theory approach

In Box 1.7 (page 10), I used the 'Prisoner's Dilemma' to outline the basic ideas behind game theory. This approach can also be used to analyse decisions made during an aggressive conflict.

Consider a relatively simple situation involving competition between two strategies. Individuals which act in an aggressive manner at the onset of conflict, but always back down if they are challenged, are known as *doves*. Those which always fight in competitive situations are known as *hawks*. Let us suppose that two people compete for a resource that is worth X points to the winner and zero to the loser.

Let us also suppose that the serious injuries inflicted by hawks when they fight cost Y points. If a hawk meets a dove, the hawk wins X points and the dove scores zero. If a dove meets a dove, they engage in a brief ritualised contest that each has an equal chance of winning. Therefore, on average, a dove will win X/2 from conflict with other doves. Finally, when a hawk meets another hawk, there will be an unrestrained fight. The winner will gain X points and the loser will suffer serious injury, costing it Y points. If a hawk has an equal chance of winning or losing, its average payoff will be (X – Y)/2. The four payoffs can be summarised as below (written from the viewpoint of contestant 1).

		Contestant 2	
		Hawk	*Dove*
Contestant 1	*Hawk*	(X – Y)2	X
	Dove	0	X/2

In a population mainly consisting of doves, the hawk strategy will be favoured because its average payoff will be twice as high (X > X/2). In a population consisting mainly of hawks, a dove would win zero and a hawk would win (X – Y)/2. Which strategy is favoured depends on the relative values of X and Y.

X > Y Hawk is the best strategy and restrained fighting does not evolve.

X < Y Hawk is best when dove is common, but dove is best when hawk is common.

Calculations have shown that if the gain from winning is half the cost of losing (X = Y/2), we should expect the population to contain 50% hawks and 50% doves. The strategy that natural selection produces is the ESS (Evolutionarily Stable Strategy). If only hawks are present, it is known as a 'pure' ESS. If both hawks and doves are present, it becomes a 'mixed' ESS.

Repeated ritualised contests within a group may result in a 'pecking order', which correlates with the probability that each individual would win an all-out dual. Often there will be two dominance hierarchies, one for each sex. The females compete for resources; the males compete for females. Dominant males mate more often because they can fight off rival males, and because females prefer to mate with them (increasing their fitness as high-ranking males will tend to sire high-ranking sons, who will provide the female with more grandchildren than low-ranking sons).

Humans do not have rigid pecking orders, but in all societies people recognise a kind of dominance

Figure 8.4 Dominant males, such as Bill Clinton, are a feature of all human societies

hierarchy, particularly among men (Figure 8.4). High-ranking men are deferred to, have a greater voice in group decisions, often have a greater share of the group's resources, and always have more wives, more lovers, and more affairs with other men's wives (Pinker, 1997). Men strive for high status and are more likely to be successful in this quest if they look the part. Big men have an obvious advantage in physical battles for supremacy, but this also appears to be true in other inter-male contests. In the USA, taller men are employed more, are promoted more, earn more ($600 per inch in annual salary), and are elected president more (the taller candidate won twenty of the twenty-five elections between 1904 and 2000). Throughout history, men have often tried to exaggerate their size in the battle for status.

The evolution of language has provided men with another weapon in the battle for dominance: *reputation*. Size and observed success in aggressive conflict have become less important, and a reputation for being a tough opponent (whether physically or in the boardroom) counts for a great deal. Winning one battle means that the word is spread and further battles will be won more easily. However, losing the battle means losing face, and everyone gets to know about it! The rise of mass media in recent decades has served only to exaggerate this phenomenon in high-profile contests.

Group conflict

Many studies have suggested that social groups enhance aggressive behaviour. For example, analysis of lynchings has found that the larger the mob, the more vicious the violence to the victim (Mullen, 1986). Jaffe and Yinon (1983) found that students in groups who had been angered by another subject gave increasingly large shocks, much more than those given by individuals. It seems that there is more hostility when groups are involved because norms are formed which support more extreme, risky attitudes towards opposing groups. This phenomenon can be observed in cases of football hooliganism.

Social identity theory offers an explanation of why stereotypes of other groups are usually negative, and why people think so highly of their own groups (Gross and McIlveen, 1998). Essentially, this idea is simply an extension of individual resource holding potential (RHP). 'In-group' favouritism enhances the perceived status of members of the group and helps to avoid negative mood states (see Chapter 15). Even if we find ourselves in a low-status group (such as being working-class), we look for new dimensions for comparison, on which our group does better. An interesting point on this matter is that in-group bias appears to be greater if perceived differences in power or status are large. Furthermore, the likelihood of in-group bias (and therefore conflict) is larger if the differences in power or status are seen as illegitimate and unstable, leaving open the possibility of change. An example of this may be seen in Palestinian groups living in Israel. The state of Israel has existed only since 1948 and this short history is chequered with conflicts. Furthermore, the Palestinian people believe that they have a right to land and power in the region. This (apparently) illegitimate repression of Palestinians in an unstable country has led to repeated conflicts.

Le Bon (1897) based his account of violence in crowds on the behaviour of mobs during the French Revolution. He thought that crowds regressed to primitive and irrational behaviour, and this was due to three factors – *anonymity*, *contagion* (the sharing of an emotional state) and *suggestibility*. However, some large crowds do not become emotional, and some become emotional but not violent. It is not clear what factors influence the onset of aggressive behaviour in a crowd, but one important factor may be the initial intentions of some or all of the group members. If these people are actively seeking conflict, then violence is much more likely to occur. Nevertheless, there has been much less industrial violence, much less political violence and less violence in the community since the Second World War. This may be partly due to less extreme inequality in wealth over the last fifty years.

War is rare in the animal kingdom. Only the social insects, chimpanzees, dolphins and humans appear to form coalitions to attack other members of their species. Aside from the social insects, whose unusual genetic system makes them a special case, these species are generally considered among the most intelligent. This may suggest that war requires sophisticated mental machinery (Pinker, 1997). But why would intelligent beings opt for a course of action which represents a very good chance of getting killed? The answer may be that the coalition acting together can gain a benefit that its members acting alone cannot, and that the benefits are distributed according to the risks taken (and translated into reproductive success).

It has been suggested that, one of the main reasons that men go to war is the pursuit of women, as described in Box 8.6. However, the risk in this strategy is that many children will grow up without a father, reducing their survival chances. If the group in question is relatively properous, the survival chances may not diminish too much and it could still pay men to raid. Therefore, men should be more willing to fight when their group is secure in food than when it is hungry, a supposition supported by observational evidence. Females are unlikely to form coalitions and raid neighboring villages for husbands, as their reproductive success is not ususally limited by the number of available mates (see Chapter 6). If war is a game that benefits men, then men should bear the risks.

Box 8.6 Fighting for females

It has been suggested that, in foraging societies, men often go to war to get or keep women (Pinker, 1997). Access to women is the limiting factor on males' reproductive success, and no other resource has as much impact on evolutionary fitness. Raiders will frequently kill all the men, abduct the young women (often raping them) and allocate them as wives. Studies of primitive societies have shown that successful warriors have significantly more wives and children than those who had never been to battle.

It appears that similar events occur in warfare among western people. Rape appears to have been systematically practised by the Germans invading Eastern Europe in World War II, the Japanese in China, American soldiers in Vietnam, and, more recently, the Serbs in Bosnia. Leaders may encourage rape as a terror tactic, which is often effective because the soldiers are keen to implement it. However, this approach frequently backfires as it gives the defenders the ultimate incentive to fight back. Finally, even when abduction and rape are not part of our warfare, the status associated with success in battle can significantly increase a man's sexual attractiveness and his reproductive success.

Attempts to explain war in terms of individual aggressiveness are generally judged to have failed (Wrangham, 1999). However, according to evolutionary psychology, conflict is related to status, resource holding power and reproductive success, whether between individuals, tribal groups or nations. Our shared psychological architecture, coupled with social factors favouring aggressive behaviour in large groups (anonymity, contagion and suggestibility) and the development of language to communicate information about the enemy, make war a common feature of our species. Nevertheless, this does *not* mean that war is inevitable. Our evolved information-processing abilities mean that virtually all group conflict can be avoided if we decide that the costs outweigh the benefits. In fact, under most environmental conditions, war is extremely unlikely owing to the costs involved. It is important to remember that evolutionary psychology argues for mental strategies that weigh up such costs and benefits and we would expect co-operation, not conflict, to evolve (see Chapter 7). Evolutionary psychology therefore accounts for peace just as much (if not more so) as it accounts for war.

Contrary to the arguments advanced at the end of the last paragraph, one reason why war may be more common than psychologists expect, is that we may *not* be able to accurately assess the costs involved. Indeed, Wrangham (1999) has argued that military incompetence (the inability to accurately assess costs) is itself adaptive, as explained in Box 8.7.

Box 8.7 Is military incompetence adaptive?

War may be more common than would be predicted by a simple evolutionary psychology model because we do *not* accurately assess the costs involved. According to Wrangham (1999), this inability to assess costs may even be adaptive, because it gives us an advantage when engaged in conflict.

A commonly reported reason for military battles is a failure of assessment: both opponents hold positive illusions and believe they will win. In other words, there is no such thing as a 50:50 battle as both sides think the odds are in their favour. Wrangham explains this in terms of two mechanisms by which positive illusions tend to promote victory:

- The Performance Enhancement Hypothesis: those engaged in the conflict will suppress negative thoughts or feelings.
- The Opponent-Deception Hypothesis: positive illusions increase the probability of a successful bluff.

As a result of these two mechanisms, military incompetence may be the result of adaptive strategies of self-deception, which unfortunately promote an increased intensity of violence.

Conclusions

Evolutionary psychology generally considers aggression to be an adaptive trait. This represents an extension of the relatively inflexible instinct theories of aggression, taking the view that human aggression is predominantly reactive and modifiable by a variety of internal and external conditions. Aggression represents an important part of the male mating strategy and is directly related to status and paternity certainty. Most female aggression is related to ensuring offspring quality. Conflict is generally greater between social groups than between individuals, probably due to the combined effects of anonymity, contagion and suggestibility. The inability to accurately assess the costs of conflict may itself be an adaptive trait.

SUMMARY

- **Aggression may be defined as physical or symbolic behaviour that is carried out with the intention of harming someone**. Evolutionary psychologists believe that aggression is (or at least was) **adaptive**.
- The **instinct theories** suggest that aggression is an innate trait in all of us. **Freud** proposed that we have an instinct (**Thanatos**) that drives us towards self-destruction, death and the return to an inanimate, lifeless state. This results in periodic acts of aggression to discharge the aggressive energy that has been built up. However, Freud's theory is difficult to test empirically. It is based on a vague concept that provides no testable hypotheses and gives us little insight into the true causes of aggressive behaviour.
- **Lorenz** also saw aggression as being instinctive. It is an adaptive trait because it is closely related to survival prospects and reproductive success. However, animals usually refrain from killing each other through **ritualised fighting** and **appeasement displays**. This may not be true for humans as our aggressive behaviour is no longer under the control of rituals. Most evolutionary psychologists consider Lorenz's ideas as too inflexible, believing that human aggression is predominantly reactive and modifiable by a variety of internal and external conditions.
- Other theories of aggression include the **frustration-aggression hypothesis** and **social-psychological** theories. The former idea suggests that aggression is always a consequence of frustration. However, frustration may be necessary but not sufficient to induce aggression, and aggression is only one of several possible responses to a frustrating situation. Social-psychological theories suggest that we **learn** both aggressiveness and how to express aggression through a variety of mechanisms. There is a considerable body of evidence supporting the influence of environmental factors on aggressive behaviour, and this should be considered when

evaluating instinct and evolutionary psychology theories of aggression.

- **Aggressive behaviour is predominantly concerned with mating strategies and/or social organisation**. Aggression in males is related to **status** and **paternity certainty**. It seems that young men are biologically and psychologically specialised to embrace danger and confrontational competition. Although male violence towards wives is universal, the **contexts** in which it occurs are remarkably few: **infidelity, threatened desertion** and **male sexual jealousy**. Nevertheless, it should be noted that marital dissatisfaction, alcohol and drug abuse, and low socio-economic status are also associated with serious domestic violence. Most female aggression is related to **ensuring offspring quality**. This is manifested in two ways; **emotional/sexual jealousy** and **infanticide**.
- Ritualised aggression results in **dominance hierarchies**, which may be different for each sex. Females compete for resources; males compete for females. Humans do not have rigid pecking orders, but in all societies people recognise a kind of dominance hierarchy, particularly among men.
- Many studies have suggested that **social groups enhance aggressive behaviour**. This may be due to norms being formed that support more extreme, risky attitudes towards opposing groups, and to the influence of **anonymity, contagion** and **suggestibility**.
- According to evolutionary psychology, conflict is related to status, resource holding power and reproductive success, whether between individuals, tribal groups or nations. However, this does **not** mean that war is inevitable. Our evolved information-processing abilities mean that virtually all group conflict can be avoided if we decide that the costs outweigh the benefits. However, we may not be adapted to accurately assess the costs of conflict and **military incompetence may be adaptive**.

9

CRIMINAL BEHAVIOUR

Introduction and overview

A gene has been identified that is associated with uncontrollable violent outbursts (Dershowitz, 1994). Neuroanatomical and biochemical abnormalities have been used in the defence of individuals charged with murder (Pinker, 1997). Is there any reliable evidence that the 'criminal mind' has a genetic basis, or that crime is in any way adaptive? In other words, can evolutionary psychology help us to understand criminal behaviour?

The aim of this chapter is to examine the evidence for a biological basis to criminal behaviour, and to consider evolutionary psychology explanations of two of the most severe crimes: *murder* and *rape*. The chapter concludes with a consideration of whether these undesirable aspects of human nature are in any way inevitable.

The biological basis of criminal behaviour

One recent study examined a Dutch family in which several of the men had carried out violent assaults (Hamer and Copeland, 1999). Most of them shared a variant form of a gene whose product is involved in the transmission of impulses between nerve cells. Faced with circumstances which would not perturb most men, these males fly into a rage. However, it is not yet known how common the variant is among law-abiding members of the community, and it is unlikely that there is a single gene responsible for all criminal behaviour. If crime has any genetic basis, it probably consists of multiple genes interacting with a stressful environment to produce adaptive behaviour. Furthermore, the ultimate aim of such behaviour is probably not the commission of crimes, but survival.

As most serious crime is committed by males, most research has focused on the male criminal mind. There are three main internal indicators which seem to contribute to male criminality: low serotonin levels; low resting heart rate; and high testosterone levels (Hamer and Copeland, 1999). Serotonin levels are 20-30% lower in men than in women, at their lowest in adolescent males, and associated with an increased sex drive. It has been suggested that low serotonin levels in males increases the aggressiveness necessary to capture or kill food, establish territories and acquire elevated status through the accumulation of resources. This serves to attract females and (via the increased sex drive) enhance reproductive success.

Criminals tend to have a significantly lower pulse rate than do their well-behaved counterparts. This lower heart rate may reflect fearlessness, or be a useful adaptation in a hunter (who would have to be able to remain perfectly still for long periods, but still act aggressively at a moment's notice). Hunting would also be aided by high testosterone levels, which help build muscle mass and stamina.

It seems that the better a hunter our male 'criminal' ancestor was, the more resources he acquired. Men were aggressive during the EEA, and in most cases are aggressive today, because aggression is the key to the acquisition of resources and hence reproductive success.

Box 9.1 Diathesis-stress model for criminal behaviour

Predisposing factors +	**trigger** →	**outcome**
Genetic predisposition	adverse family circumstances (e.g. poverty)	criminal behaviour
and/or biological factors (low levels of serotonin; low resting heart rate; high testosterone levels)	*and/or* major life events	
and/or increased sensitivity to psychosocial factors	*and/or* traumatic experiences	

If these arguments are valid, then the 'criminal tendency' of all men will be approximately the same (and significantly higher than that for women). Therefore, it must be the environment that determines who commits crime and who does not (see Box 9.1).

Murder

In 1990, there were 2,467 cases of actual or attempted murder or manslaughter in what was then West Germany. The figures of other European countries are comparable, and those for the USA even higher (Archer, 1995). Psychologists are particularly interested in finding out what causes someone to kill another person, because by identifying the causes we may find a means of controlling and reducing aggressive behaviour (see Chapter 8).

It is clear that *maleness* is by far the biggest risk factor for violence. On average, men kill men twenty-six times more often than women kill women. Trivers (1972) proposed that the greater the potential fitness benefits, the more males would risk their lives in competing with other males to obtain them. The figures for criminal convictions for serious crimes show a pronounced peak for young males, but not for females. Daly and Wilson (1988) showed that same-sex killings also occur predominantly among young males in all societies that have been studied, and are particularly prevalent among those with little to lose (see Box 9.2). The disputes are usually about status within a masculine subculture or directly over women.

Box 9.2 Murderers: nothing to lose?

Most murderers (and their victims) are male, uneducated, single, poor, and often unemployed. Human reproductive success varies enormously among males, and the fiercest competition can be at the bottom of the pecking order. Men attract women by their wealth and status, so if a man does not have them and has no way of getting them, he is a potential genetic dead-end. In other words, a young unmarried man without a future should be willing to take any risk to improve his resource holding potential (RHP). The combination of maleness, youth and hopelessness seems to make certain men reckless in defending their reputation. Young men commit crimes, drive too fast, ignore illnesses, and pick up dangerous hobbies like drugs and extreme sports.

Throughout the English-speaking world, the common law recognises three circumstances that reduce murder to manslaughter: self-defence, the defence of close relatives, and sexual contact with the man's wife (these also happen to be the three main threats to Darwinian fitness). Jealous rage at the sight of a wife's adultery is often cited as one of the ways a 'reasonable man' can be expected to behave (Cartwright, 2000).

In many foraging societies, a boy receives manly status only after he has killed. A man's respect increases with his success in aggressive conflict, giving rise to customs like dualling and scalping (which helps to verify the body count). This does not seem to apply, however, in most western societies. In this case, the state effectively prevents widescale violence through legal means. This is not the case in some foraging societies (where there is no true 'state'), or in various 'no go' areas in cities around the world. Furthermore, the assets of many people in the western world, such as houses and bank accounts, are hard to steal. This makes it difficult to acquire status by taking it from someone else. Nevertheless, the main reason why violence is rare among say, teachers and lawyers in the UK, is that they are not generally male, poor and young (see Box 9.2).

Who murders whom?

Murder rates differ over time and from place to place. However, when we take a broad look at who murders whom and why, we find an astonishingly steady pattern repeating itself down the centuries and across cultures (Daly and Wilson, 1998). Murders are overwhelmingly committed by men and there is no known human society in which the level of lethal violence among women ever begins to approach that among men. What is more, these male murderers are generally young. For example, despite enormous differences between murder rates in England and Wales and Detroit, USA, the median ages of males who killed unrelated males were 25 and 27 respectively (Figure 9.1).

Murder statistics are an important kind of evidence for theories of human relationships. In a typical American city, a quarter of all murders are committed by strangers, a half by acquaintances, and a quarter by 'relatives' (Pinker, 1997). However, these are rarely *genetic* relatives. They tend to be spouses, in-laws, and step-relatives (see page 78). Only about one in twenty-five murder victims are killed by their genetic relatives.

Figure 9.1 Who murders whom?

Figures represent the age-specific and sex-specific rates of killing nonrelatives of one's own sex in England and Wales and Chicago for the period shown. Although the absolute numbers differ enormously (the murder rate being over fifty times greater in Chicago), the shapes of the curves are very similar. (Adapted from Cronin, 1991).

When you consider that you spend much more time with genetic relatives than with other people, this figure is probably an overestimate. If we examine people who live together, so that the opportunities for interacting are held constant, the risk of being killed by a genetic relative is very small indeed.

The Cinderella effect

Child-rearing is a costly, long-term undertaking. As a result, we would expect parental care to vary as a function of the prospective fitness value of the child in question. One obvious determinant of this value is whether the child is biologically related to the parent. When people are asked to perform parental roles towards unrelated children, evolutionary theory would lead us to predict a reduction or absence of parental care.

Stepchildren are enormously more at risk from abuse and infanticide than natural children (Daly and Wilson, 1998). For example, in 1967 a North American child living with one or more substitute parents was 100 times as likely to be fatally abused as a child living with natural parents, even when confounding factors – poverty, the mother's age, the traits of people who tend to remarry – are taken into account. Furthermore, in North America as a whole, stepparents are more overrepresented among murders than among non-fatal abuse cases.

The excess risk of fatal abuse to stepchildren as compared to natural children is maximal for the youngest children (Figure 9.2). These findings are probably due to the greater costs involved in taking on a younger child and therefore a greater resentment of the obligation. The presence of stepchildren is also a source of *marital* conflict and therefore of relevance to the risk of violence against wives (see Chapter 8). Daly, Singh and Wilson (1993) reported that women with children sired by previous partners were much more likely to be assaulted than those whose children were all sired by the present partner.

It is possible that abuse in stepparent households is not really more prevalent than in natural-parent households, but is just more often detected or reported. However, if this was the case then detection and reporting biases should be least influential with the most severe forms of abuse. It is precisely these cases where stepparent overrepresentation is maximal. Alternatively, there is some evidence that abusive parents were themselves abused as children (Egeland, 1987), and such experience may be associated with high rates of marital break-up and abuse of children.

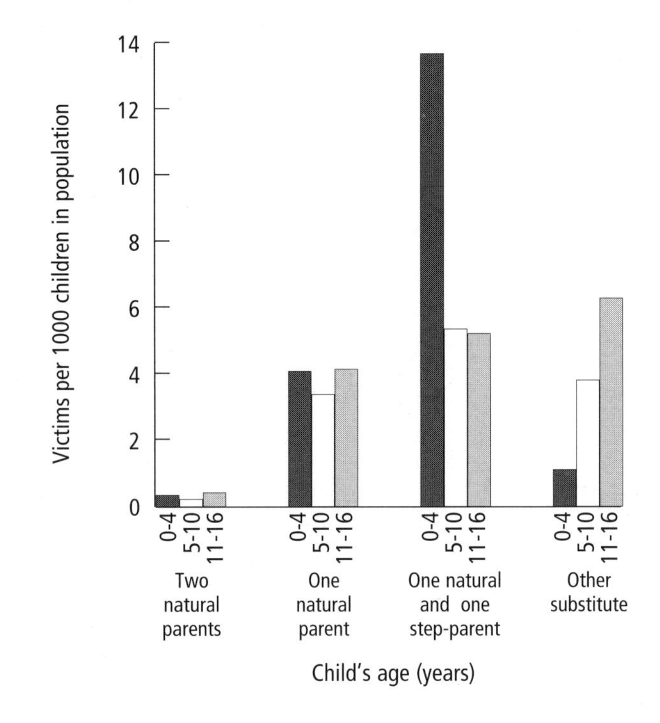

Figure 9.2 Child abuse victimisation rates by age and household type (adapted from Daly and Wilson, 1997)

However, this cannot account for the fact that abusive stepparents are discriminative, typically sparing their natural children within the same household (Lightcap *et al*,1982).

What about adopted children? There are several reasons why adoptive parents would be expected to be lower-risk substitutes than stepparents. Adoptive parents are often strongly motivated to provide a 'healthy' family environment, having chosen their course of action (rather than having it thrust upon them). They are also carefully screened by agencies and usually financially secure. Finally, if the adoption (or the marriage) fails, the couple can return the child, which happens more often than is generally realised (Kadushin and Seidl, 1971).

In one study of emotionally healthy middle-class families in North America, only half the stepfathers and a quarter of the stepmothers claimed to have 'parental feeling' toward their stepchildren, and fewer still claimed to 'love' them (Pinker, 1997). However, this is not to imply that stepparents are more cruel than other people who are not genetically related to the children. For obvious evolutionary reasons, parents are adapted to want to make sacrifices for their own children, but not for anyone else. Nevertheless, if you are a stepparent, this is exactly what you have to do. But why do they take on the 'burden' of stepchildren? Females (stepmothers) may benefit from access to the father's resources and males (stepfathers) may benefit from access to future reproduction. It is possible that these benefits exceed the costs incurred in bringing up stepchildren (especially if parental investment is less than it would be for their own children). In other words, the adults may simply be tolerating stepchildren in order to receive the benefits that the new spouse has to offer.

Finally, it is important to make clear the fact that abusing or killing a stepchild may not be (nor ever was) adaptive. Killing is often an overreaction and is likely to elicit costly reprisals, therefore having a negative effect on fitness. However, discriminative parental care probably *is* an evolved adaptation, being directly related to the child's expected contribution to parental fitness. This can apply just as well to biological offspring, whose treatment can vary with sex, age, birth order and gender of previous children. These factors relate to the *reproductive value* of the children, as described in Chapter 5 (page 45).

Rape

The competition among males for sexual partners is evident in the readiness of some males to engage in coercive sex, including criminal rape (Alcock, 1993). This behaviour has been reported from every culture that has been studied to date, despite the fact that rape is often severely punished. There are two main evolutionary explanations for rape: first, that it is an adaptive tactic used by some males to increase reproductive success; second, that it is a *by-product* of adaptive mechanisms controlling male sexual behaviour. Box 9.3 summarises some of the predictions derived from these alternative hypotheses.

Thornhill and Thornhill (1983) proposed that sexual selection has favoured males with the capacity to commit rape *under certain conditions* as a means of increasing reproductive success. According to this view (sometimes known as the mate deprivation hypothesis), men who are unable to attract willing sexual partners (poor and/or unattractive men) might rape as a reproductive option of last resort (Alcock, 1993). In line with this hypothesis, raped women do sometimes become pregnant, even in

Box 9.3 Two alternative hypotheses on why some human males commit rape, and some predictions derived from these hypotheses (adapted from Alcock (1993))

Hypothesis	Predictions
Rape is an adaptive tactic used as a reproductive option of last resort by men who are unable to attract willing sexual partners	Victims of rape are likely to be in their peak reproductive years
	Victims of rape will sometimes become pregnant by the rapist
	Rapists are likely to be unmarried, poor men
Rape is a maladaptive by-product of male sexuality	Victims of rape are likely to be in their peak reproductive years
	Rapists will come from all socio-economic classes
	Rapists will be individuals with an unusually high sex drive

modern societies which employ widespread chemical contraception. In our evolutionary past, when chemical contraception and abortion procedures were unavailable, it seems likely that rapists would have had a higher probability of reproductive success through forced sex.

An alternative hypothesis to account for rape is that this behaviour is a maladaptive by-product of male sexuality. Ease of sexual arousal, a desire for variety in sexual partners, and a readiness to engage in impersonal sex are all features of the male psyche that probably have a net positive effect on fitness (see Chapter 6). However, an incidental effect of these motivating systems may be a willingness to occasionally engage in coercive sex (even if this usually has a negative effect on *female* fitness, as described in Box 9.4).

Discriminating between these two evolutionary hypotheses of rape is difficult, given that they generate many of the same predictions (see Box 9.3). For example, both the rape as by-product and rape as adaptive tactic hypotheses predict that rape victims will be young, fertile women with a good chance of becoming pregnant. Figure 9.3 suggests that this prediction is correct, but it does not enable us to discriminate between the two hypotheses.

Official crime statistics suggest that young, poor men commit rape at a disproportionately high frequency, apparently supporting the rape as adaptive tactic hypothesis. However, this evidence is questionable as

Box 9.4 The costs of rape

In human evolutionary history, rape may have resulted in a reduction in female fitness in the following ways:

1 Rape may cause injury.
2 Rape may prevent women from choosing the timing and circumstances for pregnancy and childrearing.
3 Rape prevents women choosing the father of their offspring, often meaning that a lower quality male will be the father.
4 Rape of a pair-bonded woman may adversely influence the levels of protection, parental investment and resources provided by her mate.

In summary, female fitness is reduced following rape due to physical trauma, reduced mate choice, and reduced parental care from males (owing to doubts about paternity).

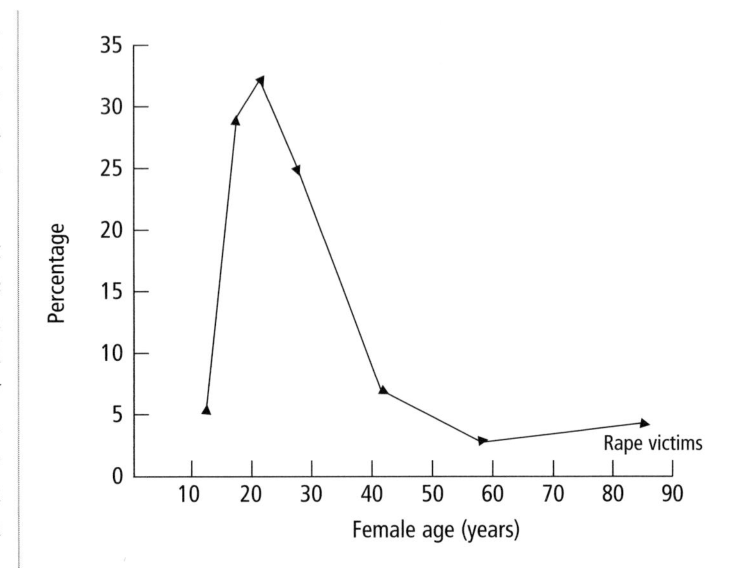

Figure 9.3 An analysis of the age of rape victims (Data comes from 1974-75 police records for 26 cities in the USA; adapted from Alcock (1993))

men of low social status are more likely to be prosecuted for criminal acts than are their high-ranking counterparts. Rape by married men of high social status does occur, but may be underreported in official statistics. Care must be taken when using such statistics to test the adaptive tactic hypothesis.

The rape as by-product hypothesis suggests that rapists will have unusually high levels of sexual activity with consenting as well as non-consenting partners. Although there is some evidence in support of this prediction, it is insufficient to resolve this matter (Alcock, 1993). At this point in time, it remains unclear as to which of the evolutionary explanations of rape is the more valid.

The aftermath of rape

According to Thornhill and Thornhill (1989), human mental pain is an adaptation designed by natural selection to guide cognition, feelings, and behaviour toward solutions to social problems that reduced inclusive fitness in human evolutionary history (such as rape, loss of social status, death of a relative, or desertion by a mate). The pain also informs decision-making processes, so that similar problems are avoided later in life. Furthermore, the magnitude of mental pain is expected to correlate with the reduction in inclusive fitness. For example, the death of a high-reproductive-value relative will be more painful than the death of a low-reproductive-value relative.

Thornhill and Thornhill (1989) have examined the aftermath of rape from an evolutionary psychological perspective. They suggest that reactions to rape are particularly revealing about the psychology of male sexual attitudes. Men often reject raped women as 'damaged goods', sometimes accusing the victims of having provoked or enjoyed the rape. Thornhill and Thornhill argue that the act of coerced copulation, although it represents a threat to the husband's fitness, is not his main cause for concern. Rather, the husband worries that the sexual act might have involved the woman's complicity, and therefore be predictive of further infidelities (with consequent threats to fitness and the risk of cuckoldry).

If the argument above is valid, it seems likely that men's jealous concerns in the aftermath of rape will actually be reduced by evidence of coercion, such as injury to the woman. This hypothesis also predicts that much post-rape emotional trauma and difficulties in relations with male partners will arise out of men's reactions to rape victims. These reactions may be more favourable in the more brutal and hence less equivocal incidents. It appears that this is the case. Studies have shown that physical injury to a woman during rape is associated with less post-rape difficulties with male partners (Alcock, 1993).

Further predictions from the Thornhills' evolutionary hypothesis are: the aftermath of rape will be more traumatic for women in a relationship than for single women (who do not have to face a male partner whose paternity may be questioned as a result of the rape); and rape will be more problematic for women of reproductive age, compared to those of pre-pubertal or post-menopausal age (as only reproductive-aged females can become pregnant as a result of rape). Initial studies appear to provide evidence in support of the second of these predictions (Figure 9.4). However, more research is needed to demonstrate the specificity of certain information-processing in the event of rape versus other crimes perpetrated against women. For example, if reproductive-aged women are more traumatised by *theft* than other women, this phenomenon would not be restricted to rape (in fact the trauma is more likely to correlate with the value of the stolen property).

Figure 9.4 Rape victims seeking psychiatric assistance

The figures represent the ratio of the number of victims seeking help to the number that would be *expected* to seek help, all other factors being equal. In other words, reproductive-aged women seek help much more often (and nonreproductive-aged women seek help much less often) than would be expected (data from 781 women; adapted from Thornhill and Thornhill (1990))

Finally, Thornhill and Thornhill (1990) suggest that women are adapted to cope with fitness-reducing problems in the event of rape, rather than to prevent rape from occurring. It seems reasonable to suggest that women may have psychological adaptations that are specifically designed to detect the *risk* of rape, and motivate avoidance of dangerous situations. These adaptations would be expected to process information about female vulnerability to rape, such as age and the social status of the male in question, and adjust anxiety and fear accordingly. These hypothetical adaptations require further investigation.

CRITICISMS OF EVOLUTIONARY EXPLANATIONS OF RAPE

Thornhill and Thornhill's rape-as-an-adaptation hypothesis is very controversial and subject to much debate in the scientific press. The supporting evidence is limited at present and many psychologists believe that other (non-biological) hypotheses are just as valid. Furthermore, it appears that the mate deprivation hypothesis outlined on page 80 is not supported by certain psychological studies.

In a study by Lalumiere *et al* (1996), a group of young heterosexual males were questioned about their sexual

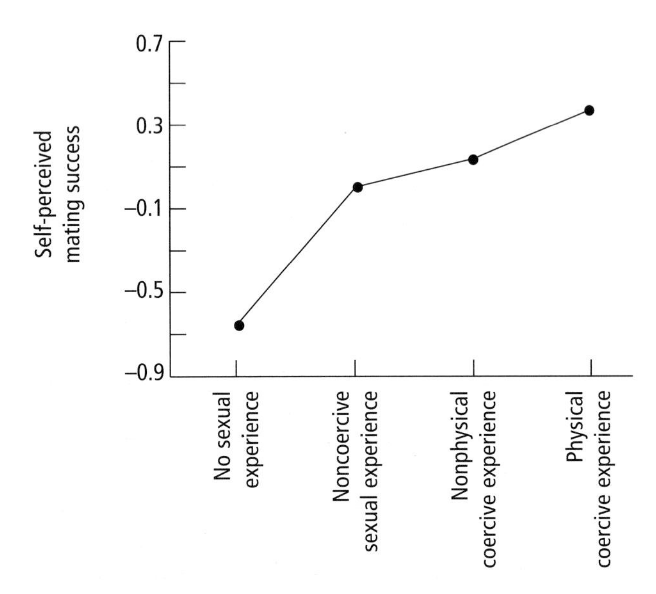

Figure 9.5 Self-perceived mating success and sexual aggression

experience, including whether they had ever used non-physical coercion (persuasion) or physical coercion (aggression) in order to have sex with a woman. The men were also assessed in terms of their self-perceived mating success. Background socioeconomic status and perceived future income potential were also measured. The results, shown in Figure 9.5, appear to contradict the mate-deprivation hypothesis of sexual aggression. Men who scored high on high-perceived mating success (and future earning potential) tended to use non-physical and physical coercion more often. However, it is possible that these men use coercion during periods of difficulty in securing sexual access and further investigations are required.

It seems clear that, because of the sensitive nature of this controversial topic, the debate surrounding evolutionary explanations of rape will continue. Nevertheless, until we are convinced that there is no validity in the work of Thornhill and Thornhill, their hypothesis on this subject will require careful consideration.

The ethics of evolutionary psychology

As mentioned in Chapter 3, evolutionary psychology has been criticised for apparently supporting anti-social behaviours such as murder and rape. The idea that discriminative parental care or rape (under certain circumstances) are *adaptive* seems to condemn humans to these behaviours. However, evolutionary psychologists do not agree with this deterministic argument and strongly argue that no behaviour is inevitable. Once again, it is worth emphasising the idea that evolutionary psychology is a discipline that attempts to *explain* human behaviour; it does not attempt to *justify* the behaviour.

Conclusions

Murder is generally committed by young, poor men. These men live in a competitive world, where status and resources are vital to reproductive success, and they are prepared to use violence to achieve this success. As predicted by an evolutionary perspective, murder of genetic relatives is rare. Stepchildren are particularly at risk from abuse and infanticide, and it seems likely that discriminative parental care is an evolved adaptation.

There are two main evolutionary explanations for rape: the rape-as-by-product and rape-as-adaptive-tactic hypotheses. At present, it remains unclear as to which hypothesis is the more valid. An evolutionary approach to the aftermath of rape, predicting that married women of reproductive age will be the most traumatised, appears to be supported by recent studies. However, further research is needed into this area.

SUMMARY

- It is unlikely that there is a single gene responsible for all criminal behaviour. **If crime has any genetic basis, it probably consists of multiple genes interacting with a stressful environment to produce adaptive behaviour**.
- There are three main internal indicators which seem to contribute to male criminality: **low serotonin levels**; **low resting heart rate**; and **high testosterone levels**. These factors may have improved hunting abilities, the accumulation of resources, and consequent reproductive success in the past EEA.
- **Maleness** is by far the biggest risk factor for violence. The greater the potential fitness benefits, the more males will risk their lives competing with other males to obtain them. Murder is often the result of a dispute about status within a masculine subculture or directly over women, and **most murderers are young, poor men**.
- **Murder statistics are an important kind of evidence for theories of human relationships**. Although approximately 25% of murders are committed by relatives, these are rarely **genetic** relatives. They tend to be spouses, in-laws and step-relatives. **The risk of being killed by a genetic relative is very small indeed**.
- **Stepchildren are enormously more at risk from abuse and infanticide than natural children.** This is true even when we take into account the confounding factors of poverty, the mother's age, and the traits of people who tend to remarry. In addition, stepparents are more over-represented among murders than among non-fatal abuse cases.
- **The excess risk of fatal abuse to stepchildren as compared to natural children is maximal for the youngest children.** This is probably due to the greater costs involved in taking on a younger child and therefore a greater resentment of the obligation. The presence of stepchildren is also a source of **marital** conflict and therefore of relevance to the risk of violence against wives.
- It is important to make clear the fact that **abusing or killing a stepchild may not be (nor ever was) adaptive.** Killing is often an overreaction and is likely to elicit costly reprisals, therefore having a negative effect on fitness. However, **discriminative parental care probably *is* an evolved adaptation**, being directly related to the child's expected contribution to parental fitness.
- The competition among males for sexual partners is evident in the readiness of some males to engage in coercive sex, including **criminal rape**. There are two main evolutionary explanations for rape: **the adaptive tactic hypothesis** and **the by-product hypothesis**.
- The adaptive tactic hypothesis suggests that sexual selection has favoured males with the capacity to commit rape **under certain conditions** as a means of increasing reproductive success. According to this view, men who are unable to attract willing sexual partners might rape as a reproductive option of last resort. The by-product hypothesis proposes that rape is a **maladaptive** by-product of male sexuality. The sexual motivating systems that generally have a net positive effect on fitness may also result in a willingness to occasionally engage in coercive sex. At this point in time, it remains unclear as to which of the evolutionary explanations of rape is the more valid.
- An evolutionary perspective on the aftermath of rape enables us to make three predictions about the trauma suffered by victims. First, **the trauma will be greater for women in a relationship than for single women**. Second, **rape will be more problematic for women of reproductive age**. Third, **physical injury to a woman during rape will be associated with less post-rape difficulties with male partners**. Initial studies appear to provide some evidence in support of these predictions. However, **evolutionary explanations of rape are the subject of much debate and the supporting evidence is limited**. Further research is needed into this sensitive and controversial issue.
- Evolutionary psychology has been criticised for apparently supporting anti-social behaviours such as murder and rape. However, it is important to remember that **it is a discipline that attempts to *explain* human behaviour; it does not attempt to *justify* the behaviour.**

PART 4
Cognition

LEARNING

Introduction and overview

Cognition is a general term used to refer to the 'higher' mental processes, including learning, thinking, memory, perception, intelligence and language. Cognitive abilities, like the reproductive and social behaviours discussed in Parts 2 and 3 respectively, are the product of evolutionary change. The fourth part of this book (Chapters 10-12) considers the evolutionary basis of three important cognitive attributes of humans; *learning*, *intelligence* and *language*.

The aim of the present chapter is to examine the nature of learning. I will begin by looking at what psychologists mean by learning, and then review some of the traditional theories about how we learn (including the limitations of these theories). I will then conclude by considering how evolutionary psychology can improve our understanding of the processes involved in learning.

What is learning?

The standard view of learning is that it is a relatively permanent change in behaviour as a result of past experience. From an evolutionary viewpoint, most instances of learning take the form of adaptive changes that increase our effectiveness in dealing with the environment, increasing our chances of survival. Anderson (1995) defines learning as '... the mechanism by which organisms can adapt to a changing and non-predictable environment'.

Traditional theories of learning

IMPRINTING

Imprinting is a highly constrained type of learning in which offspring form a rapid and permanent attachment to the first moving object they see (known as *filial imprinting*). Under normal circumstances, when this is their mother, it would be an adaptive behaviour. Such a response would ensure they were fed and protected, and would only approach their mother, rather than other adults who may attack them. Imprinting also provides a model from which to learn the appearance of an adult of their species of the opposite sex. This is known as *sexual imprinting* and serves as a guide to later courtship. It is clear that effective sexual imprinting will have adaptive value in terms of reproductive success.

The first detailed studies on imprinting were conducted by Konrad Lorenz (1935). The features which he believed to be characteristic of imprinting are listed in Box 10.1, together with modifications arising from subsequent research in this area. Current opinion suggests that imprinting is sufficiently flexible to be adaptive if the environment changes, but is

Box 10.1 The nature of imprinting

Characteristic feature (Lorenz, 1935)	*Modification*
Only precocial (born at a relatively advanced state of development and require less parental care) species imprint	Imprinting is *more common* in precocial species, but is also observed in some altricial (born relatively undeveloped and require more parental care) species
Imprinting must occur during a critical period	*Critical period* replaced by *sensitive phase*
The effects of imprinting are irreversible	Imprinting is *resistant* to reversal
Imprinting governs filial and sexual behaviour	*Governs* replaced by *influences*
Imprinting is different from other forms of learning	Imprinting shares several features with other forms of learning, such as conditioning

pre-programmed in order to occur rapidly to provide immediate security.

From an evolutionary viewpoint, it is often important that mating should only occur between members of the same species and that parents should care only for their own offspring. Imprinting tends to occur in species in which attachment to parents, to the family group, or to a member of the opposite sex is an important aspect of social organisation (McFarland, 1996). Sexual imprinting may be more important for kin recognition than for species recognition. Bateson (1979) suggests that sexual imprinting enables an animal to choose a mate that appears slightly different, but not too different, from its parents and siblings. This may enable the animal to strike a balance between the advantages of inbreeding and outbreeding. Some researchers have suggested that humans tend to choose mates that are socially, psychologically and physically similar to themselves (Lewis, 1975). However, there is also evidence that satisfactory marriages are not formed between people who spend their early childhood together (Wolf, 1970). Although human relationships are complicated by cultural factors, the evidence for some biologically-based negative imprinting is considerable.

Imprinting is an important component of the *attachment* process in humans. Attachment is a close emotional bond between a caregiver and an infant that is characterised by mutual involvement and a desire to maintain proximity. This behaviour appears to be primarily instinctive, with babies being genetically programmed to behave towards their mothers in ways that ensure their survival (Hayes, 1994). Bowlby (1951) believed that the mother also inherits a genetic blueprint which programmes her to respond to the infant, leading to attachment (Figure 10.1). Nevertheless, there appears to be no evidence that mothering skills are innate or instinctive, and the caregiver could just as easily be the father or, more commonly, both parents.

Figure 10.1 Mothers may be genetically predisposed to respond to their babies, leading to attachment.
Copyright: Life File © Terence Waeland.

CONDITIONING

The mechanisms of *classical conditioning* and *operant conditioning* are well documented in the psychological literature (see Clamp and Russell, 1998), and do not warrant further description here. Instead, I shall concentrate on human examples of conditioning and the limitations of this explanation of learning.

Box 10.2 The case of Little Albert

Little Albert was the son of a nurse who worked at the same children's hospital as J.B. Watson. At the age of 11 months, Albert became the subject of a classical conditioning experiment by Watson and Rayner (1920).

While Albert was playing with a white rat (neutred stimulus), Watson made a loud noise (unconditioned stimulus) behind the boy by banging a hammer on a steel bar. This elicited a fear response (unconditioned response) and crying. After seven trials, over a period of seven weeks,

Albert demonstrated a fear response (conditioned response) to the rat (conditioned stimulus), even though its appearance was no longer accompanied by the loud noise. Albert's fear became generalised to objects similar to the rat, such as a fur coat, cotton wool and even a Santa Claus mask. The fear response was still evident a year later. It is not clear whether Watson and Rayner intended to remove the fear response (conditioned response) because Albert's mother withdrew him from the experiment.

Fear conditioning, as illustrated by the case of Little Albert, may take place after only one pairing of a neutral stimulus with an unconditioned stimulus. It is also highly resistant to extinction.

Classical conditioning has been used to explain many aspects of human behaviour, such as the acquisition of phobias (see Chapter 14). In a classic study, Watson and Raynor (1920) conditioned a fear response in an 11-month-old boy, known as 'Little Albert'. This study is described in Box 10.2. However, the case of Little Albert represents a deliberate inducement of a fear response. Can classical conditioning also help to explain how fears are acquired in everyday life? One example, suggested by Richard Gross (1996), relates to the development of a fear of dentists (Figure 10.2).

In addition to fear, other human reflexes have also been subjected to classical conditioning experiments. Menzies (1937) asked participants to place their hands in ice-cold water whenever a buzzer sounded. This caused vasoconstriction (constriction of the blood vessels) in the hands. Eventually, vasoconstriction occurred just in response to the sound of the buzzer.

Before conditioning
Drill hitting a nerve (**UCS**) → Pain/fear (**UCR**)
Sound of the drill (**NS**) → No response

During conditioning
Sound of the drill (**CS**) + drill hitting nerve (**UCS**)
→ Pain/fear (**UCR**)

After conditioning
Sound of the drill (**CS**) → Fear (**CR**)

(NS = neutral stimulus; UCS = unconditioned stimulus; UCR = unconditioned response; CR = conditioned response; CS = conditioned stimulus).

Figure 10.2 A classical conditioning explanation for the development of a fear of dentists.

Advertisements often make use of classical conditioning. Advertisers attempt to couple their products with an unconditioned stimulus that will produce pleasant emotions, such as happiness or sexual arousal. Classical conditioning may result in the product becoming associated with these positive feelings, encouraging people to part with their money. Coffee has been paired with romance, cornflakes with happy family life and ice-cream with sex.

Operant conditioning has been used to explain many aspects of human behaviour, such as the acquisition of language by shaping (see Chapter 12) and superstitious learning. Shaping initially involves reinforcing any response which is even vaguely related to the behaviour in question. Subsequent reinforcement of closer and closer approximations to the required behaviour may result in its successful acquisition. Once an animal has been conditioned to perform a particular behaviour, it tends to generalise and use this as the basis of further behaviour. Skinner (1957) suggested that most skills in humans are learned in this manner.

Superstitious behaviour, such as avoiding walking under ladders, may arise through operant conditioning. The behaviour is strengthened, by chance, because it happens to precede a reinforcement. For example, a footballer may put his left boot on first when getting ready for a match and his team may subsequently win the game. He may then continue with this ritual because he believes that it brings him (or the team) good luck. (It should be remembered that the relationship between the behaviour and the reinforcer is accidental; the reinforcer would have occurred anyway). It is possible, however, that if the footballer truly believes that his actions bring him luck, the consequent increase in confidence may actually help him play better!

One major way in which operant conditioning has been put to practical use is *behaviour modification*. This involves the setting of a specific behavioural goal and then systematically reinforcing the individual's successive approximations to this goal (see Box 10.3). This technique has been used in places such as classrooms, mental hospitals, factories and prisons.

Box 10.3 Behaviour modification

Most behaviour programmes follow a broadly similar pattern, involving a series of steps. First, the behaviour to be changed is specified as precisely as possible and this behaviour is monitored for several days before treatment commences. This monitoring process provides a baseline behaviour which may be used to assess the effectiveness of the therapy. Second, a reinforcement or punishment (or both) strategy is decided upon, and the treatment is planned. Finally, the treatment begins and progress is closely monitored (the programme may be changed if necessary).

One example of behaviour modification, using positive reinforcement, was described by Gross and McIlveen (1996). The case in question was a 40-year-old male schizophrenic who had not spoken to anyone for nineteen years. One of the therapists discovered that the patient was very keen on chewing gum, and decided to use it as a positive reinforcer to encourage the man to speak. The behaviour modification process used in this case is outlined below.

Therapist held up a piece of gum.
Patient received the gum for looking at it.

↓

Patient only given the gum if he moved his lips.

↓

Patient had to make a sound to receive the gum.

↓

Patient given the gum for saying the word 'gum' (prompted by therapist).

↓

After 6 weeks of therapy, the patient spontaneously said, 'Gum, please', and soon afterwards began talking to the therapist.

If conditioning works in the same way for all species, it should be possible to produce general laws of learning. Two such laws have been suggested.

1 The law of contiguity: events which occur close together in time and space are likely to become associated with each other.

2 The law of preparedness: animals are biologically prepared to learn actions that are related to their survival (see Box 10.4). These actions are learned very quickly (often in just one trial) and are highly resistant to extinction. However, other behaviours are learned with great difficulty, if at all.

Many conditioning studies appear to obey the law of contiguity. In addition, the idea of biological preparedness is supported by research evidence suggesting that most human phobias relate to fears of dangerous animals or places (see Chapter 14). However, *taste aversion* experiments are an important exception to the law of contiguity (see Box 10.4) and the majority of psychologists believe that we cannot apply basic principles of learning to all species in all situations (Bolles, 1980). Overall, it seems unlikely that there are any general laws of learning.

Box 10.4 Taste aversion experiments (Garcia and Koelling, 1966)

Laboratory rats were given saccharin-flavoured water (NS), which they had not previously encountered. This was followed by the administration of a drug (UCS) which, after a time delay, induced severe intestinal illness (UCR). The precise time-lapse between tasting the solution and the onset of illness ranged from five to 180 minutes. In each case, a conditioned aversive response (CR) to the saccharin-flavoured water (CS) was acquired, regardless of the time elapsed. Such taste aversion experiments represent an important exception to the law of contiguity.

It seems that rats are specially prone to associate feeling ill with the last novel food they ate or liquid they drank: a wonderful mechanism for an explorative animal, used to foraging opportunistically on a wide range of dietary possibilities, to learn which items are poisonous. Humans also seem prone to this kind of food-aversion learning, which probably has survival value (Byrne, 1995).

There are significant limitations to conditioning explanations of learning. They are generally considered to be too simple and tend to ignore the influence of *social*, *genetic* and *cognitive* factors in learning.

The influence of social factors on learning

A major alternative to the conditioning theory of learning is *social learning theory* (Bandura, 1977). Social learning theorists do not deny the importance of classical and operant conditioning, but also emphasise the importance of *observational learning* (learning through watching the behaviour of another person). Observational learning takes place without any reinforcement, but *imitation* (copying the learned

Box 10.5 The role of cognitive factors in social learning

Bandura (1974) argued that there are five major functions involved in social learning:
1 Attention: the learner must attend only to the relevant clues in the stimulus situation.
2 Coding: a visual image or semantic information must be encoded into the memory stores.
3 Memory permanence: this is needed to retain the stored information over long periods.
4 Motor coordination: this requires a number of trials to enable the learner to reproduce the observed motor behaviour accurately.
5 Motivation: the learner must be motivated in order to learn and perform the behaviour.

behaviour) depends on the consequences of the behaviour, both for the model and the learner. Effective social learning requires certain cognitive processes, which are described in Box 10.5.

Social animals have additional advantages in how they can learn about the world. They can learn from the trials and errors of other individuals, in some cases even individuals from previous generations. I outlined in Chapter 2 how skills may be learned via cultural transmission, predominantly through imitation. However, Byrne (1995) has suggested that this type of social learning is considerably less common than first thought (most of the cases observed were already part of the animal's behavioural repertoire and performance was reliant on reinforcement), and that true imitation may even be exclusive to humans.

Teachers always tell us that knowledge is nothing without understanding. It seems obvious that copying new behaviour by imitation is a 'cheap' way of appearing clever, a sham of intelligence. It would take us a long time to learn anything if we could only produce exact copies of observed behaviours. Real learning takes place by generalising from examples. Children generalise from role models, or from their own behaviours that are rewarded or punished. For example, a child who observes that Alsatian dogs sometimes bite should generalise to other similar dogs. An interesting point about this example is that the *stimulus generalisation* must be innate, otherwise the child would generalise to everything or to nothing. The same idea is probably true for other features of conditioning, and presents a problem for the inherently empirical view of behaviourists.

The influence of genetic factors on learning

It is now known that animals do *not* find all events equally easy to associate. Garcia and Koelling (1966) gave rats water that was novel to them, either in its taste (sweet or salt) or in that a flashing light and clicking noise always accompanied drinking. They paired these stimuli with aversive reinforcement, either by illness (brought on by X-rays), or by electric shocks. If rats feel ill after they have drunk novel-tasting water, they then avoid water with this taste in the future; but if they feel only a shock, they do not seem to associate this with their novel drink. The opposite happens after drinking 'bright-noisy' water. The pain of an electric shock causes the rats to avoid bright-noisy drinks in future, but nausea has no effect (see Box 10.3).

It is clear that animals are equipped to learn some things better than others. Genetic preparedness arguments have been used to explain song learning in birds (see Box 10.6) and human fears of spiders and snakes, as described in Chapter 14. What have evolved are tendencies to learn efficiently just those specific kinds of information that have favoured survival and reproductive success (Seligman, 1970).

Box 10.6 Song learning in birds

The chick of a bird like the chaffinch has a *genetic predisposition* to listen to sounds that approximately resemble the song of its own species. This predisposition, or *template*, is moulded (by listening to the song of a mature male) into the 'proper' song for a chaffinch. The chick then remembers this song until it is sexually mature, when it begins singing itself. At first, its own song is only an approximation to a proper chaffinch song. However, by listening to itself sing, and matching the output with the memorised version, it gradually changes its singing until it is a perfect match to the song it heard as a juvenile. The specificity of this innate template is known from experiments: if the chicks are reared by hand and played only blackbird song, they are not influenced by it. If they are played both blackbird song and reversed chaffinch song, they later give an accurate copy of the reversed chaffinch song.

Preparedness arguments can also be applied to imprinting (see page 85). Bateson (1973) found that chicks will not imprint on just anything – they too have innate preferences. By focusing their attention on whatever best fits their innate idea of what should be followed, they learn its characteristics in greater detail. In this way, they successively narrow down their preferences to one particular conspicuous object, selecting their own mother rather than any other hen. The same argument presumably applies to imprinting in humans.

An evolutionary interpretation of classical conditioning is that it is a correlation-learning device (Dickinson, 1980). This enables an animal to automatically learn the pattern of event probabilities in its environment, increasing chances of survival. Similarly, operant conditioning has been likened to evolution by natural selection (Skinner, 1981). Like natural selection, it is an automatic process by which behaviour patterns with beneficial consequences are selectively increased in frequency. However, the mechanism is quite different in the two cases. In operant conditioning, *responses* increase in frequency or become 'extinct'. Natural selection is more drastic and slower to produce change, since whole individuals survive or die, and the selection effect on genes is therefore much less efficient. Rapid changes of behaviour in response to changing environmental circumstances *only* come about by learning. Operant conditioning has adaptive value in that it ensures that an individual profits from experience and does not repeat errors.

The influence of cognitive factors on learning

Mackintosh (1978) suggested that conditioning is more complex than it seems. He believed that animals learn about the *relationship between events*. They discover what it is that signals an important event, such as food or danger, and respond appropriately to this signal. For example, in Pavlov's classic study, one could say that the dogs were *expecting* food to follow the bell. In other words, presentation of the bell enables the dog to retrieve a mental representation of the food from memory (a cognitive event), with salivation being caused by that representation.

Bandura (1977) claimed that expectation also plays a significant role in operant conditioning. The way an animal behaves is largely determined by the expectations of future events. The processes of reinforcement and punishment provide the learner with information about the likelihood of future pleasant or unpleasant outcomes by giving animals feedback about their behaviours. Similarly, the phenomenon of *learned helplessness* also suggests that cognitive factors play a role in operant conditioning.

Insight learning may be defined as a perceptual restructuring of the elements that constitute a problem situation, whereby a previously missing 'ingredient' is supplied and all the parts are seen in relation to each other, forming a meaningful whole (Gross, 1996). In contrast to the trial-and-error of operant conditioning, insight learning usually involves a sudden solution to a problem. What is learned is not a specific set of conditioned associations, but a cognitive relationship between a means and an end and this makes generalising to other, similar problems easier. Koestler (1970) may have been an unwitting evolutionary psychologist when he suggested that the ability to use insight to solve certain problems was, to a certain extent, innate (an idea similar to the 'preparedness' theory of Seligman (1970)). Insight may be a vital component of *intelligence*, which is discussed in Chapter 11.

Gagné (1985) suggested that there is a continuity between simple and complex forms of learning. He suggested that there were eight major varieties of learning, hierarchically arranged, with the more complex forms being built on simpler abilities. Gagné's hierarchy of learning is summarised in Box 10.7.

Box 10.7 Gagné's hierarchy of learning

1 Signal learning	The establishment of a simple connection in which a stimulus takes on the properties of a signal (*classical conditioning*)
2 Stimulus-response learning	The establishment of a connection between a stimulus and a response where the response in a voluntary movement and the connection is instrumental in satisfying a need or motive (*operant conditioning*)
1 and 2 are prerequisites for:	
3 Chaining	The connecting of a sequence of two or more previously learned stimulus-response connections

4 Verbal association	The learning of chains that are specifically verbal, important for the acquisition and use of language. Enables a number of learned connections involving words to be emitted in a single sequence
3 and 4 are prerequisites for:	
5 Discrimination learning	Making different responses to similar stimuli. Involves more than simply making isolated stimulus-response connections because it is necessary to deal with the problem of interference between similar items
5 is a prerequisite for:	
6 Concept learning	Learning to make a common response to stimuli that form a class or category but which differ in their physical characteristics. Requires representing information in memory, classifying events and discriminating between them on basis of abstracted properties
6 is a prerequisite for:	
7 Rule learning	A rule is a chain of two or more concepts (e.g. 'if A then B')
7 is a prerequisite for:	
8 Problem-solving	Involves recombining old rules into new ones, making it possible to answer questions and solve problems, especially important for real-life human problem-solving situations

Learning and evolutionary psychology

The traditional behaviourist view of the mind of a newborn is that it is *tabula rasa*, or a 'blank slate', which is gradually filled in by learning about the environment. However, evolutionary psychologists believe that humans have an *instinct for learning* (see Figure 10.3). In other words, learning is made possible by innate machinery designed to do the learning (Pinker, 1997). This is not a new idea. Harlow (1949) suggested the concept of a *learning set*, or 'learning how to learn'. A learning set involves learning a general skill applicable to a whole new class of problems, or learning a simple rule based on a conceptual relationship. Harlow argued that the greater the number of sets, the better equipped the learner is to adapt to a changing environment and a very large number of different sets 'may supply the raw material for human thinking'. If we replace the word 'set' with 'instinct' and assume that 'learning how to learn' is, to a certain extent, hard-wired into the human brain, this makes Harlow one of the earliest evolutionary psychologists!

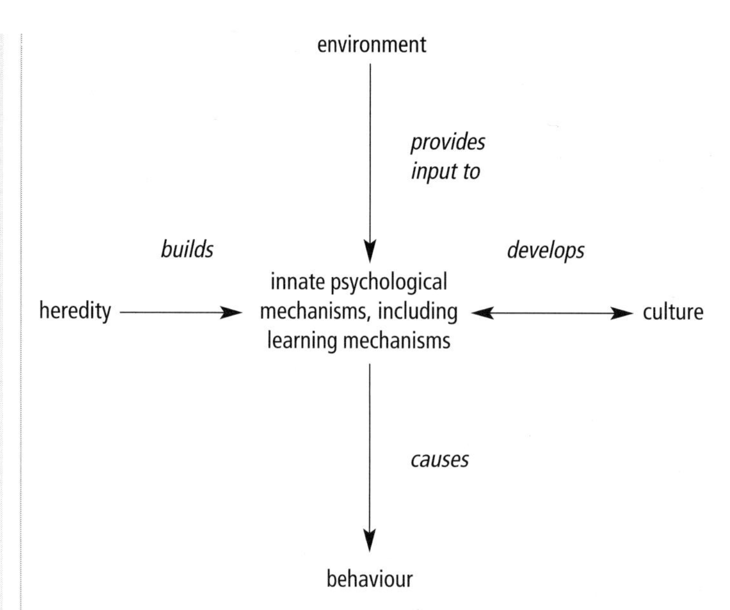

Figure 10.3 An instinct for learning (adapted from Pinker (1994))

Even when a trait starts off as a product of learning, it does not have to remain so. Evolutionary theory, supported by computer simulations, has shown that when an environment is stable, there is a selective pressure for learned abilities to become increasingly innate (Box 10.8). Nevertheless, some 'pure' learning will always be needed to cope with environmental unpredictability (see Chapter 11).

Box 10.8 Learning and innateness (adapted from Pinker (1997))

Imagine an animal controlled by a neural network with twenty connections, each either innately on or off. The network will only work if all twenty connections are correctly set. In a population of animals whose connections are determined at random, an individual with all the right connections will only appear about once every million genetically distinct organisms. Furthermore, sexual reproduction will ensure that this advantage is lost in the next generation, when genomes are mixed. In computer simulations of this situation, no adapted network has ever evolved.

Now consider a population of animals whose connections can come in three forms; innately on, innately off, or settable to on or off by learning. These animals will go through life trying out the learnable connections at random until it hits upon the 'winning' combination. It then retains these settings, ceasing trial and error. From then on it enjoys a higher rate of reproduction. The earlier in life the animal acquires the right settings, the longer it will have to reproduce at the higher rate. Among the descendants of these animals (in a relatively stable environment), there are advantages to having more and more of the connections innately correct. This means that it will take less time to learn the rest, and the chances of going through life without having learned them get smaller. In computer simulations, the neural networks evolved more and more innate connections, although they never became completely innate. As more and more of the connections are fixed, the selection pressure to fix the remaining ones tapers off, because every organism will learn them quickly. Learning leads to the evolution of innateness, but not complete innateness.

Learning mechanisms for different spheres of human experience, such as language, morals, foraging, and social interaction, are often found to work at cross-purposes. A mechanism designed to learn the right thing in one of these domains learns exactly the wrong thing in the others. This suggests that learning is accomplished not by some single general-purpose device (the behaviourist view), but by different modules or 'mental organs'. These mental organs have functions useful for survival and reproduction in the environments in which humans evolved. This does not mean, however, that all aspects of the mind are adaptations, or that the mind's adaptations are necessarily beneficial in evolutionary novel environments like twentieth-century cities (Pinker, 1994).

In summary, the term 'learning' as used by behaviourists is not really an explanation for anything, but is rather a phenomenon that itself requires explanation. Evolutionary psychologists view learning as a diverse set of processes caused by a series of intricate, functionally organised cognitive adaptations, implemented in neurobiological machinery.

Conclusions

This chapter began with a review of the traditional theories of learning and the limitations of these theories. It seems clear that the processes involved in learning are more complex than originally thought, involving significant contributions from social, cognitive and genetic factors. An evolutionary perspective suggests that learning is an evolved adaptation and is best considered as a range of specific abilities which improve our chances of survival and reproductive success.

SUMMARY

- **Learning** may be defined **as a relatively permanent change in behaviour as a result of past experience**. From an evolutionary viewpoint, most instances of learning take the form of adaptive changes that increase our chances of survival. From this perspective, learning is best defined as **the mechanism by which organisms can adapt to a changing and non-predictable environment**.
- **Imprinting** is regarded as a highly constrained form of learning in which offspring form a rapid and permanent attachment to the first moving object they see (**filial imprinting**) and also learn the appearance of an adult of their species of the opposite sex (**sexual imprinting**). These behaviours are generally adaptive in that they are associated with survival and reproductive success.
- Imprinting is an important component of the **attachment** process in humans. Attachment behaviour appears to be primarily instinctive, with babies and mothers being genetically programmed to behave towards each other in ways that ensure the survival of the offspring.

However, there appears to be no evidence that mothering skills are innate or instinctive, and the caregiver could just as easily be the father or both parents.

- **Classical** and **operant conditioning** have been used to explain many aspects of human behaviour including the development of phobias and the acquisition of language. However, it does not seem possible to produce any general laws of learning for all species in all situations. Conditioning explanations of learning are generally considered to be too simple and to ignore the influence of **social**, **genetic** and **cognitive** factors.
- In addition to classical and operant conditioning, **social learning theory** emphasises the importance of **observational learning**. Social animals can learn from the trials and errors of other individuals, and can **imitate** successful behaviours. However, pure imitation is a very limited way of learning. Effective learning involves **generalising** from examples.
- It is now known that animals do **not** find all events equally easy to associate and that they are equipped to learn some things better than others. **Genetic preparedness** arguments have been used to explain song learning in birds and human fears of spiders and snakes. What have evolved are tendencies to learn efficiently just those specific kinds of information that have favoured survival and reproductive success.
- Mackintosh suggested that conditioning is more complex than it seems. It appears that animals learn about the **relationship between events**. They discover what it is that signals an important event, such as food or danger, and respond appropriately to this signal. The way an animal behaves is also largely determined by the **expectation** of future events. This implies that **cognitive factors are important in learning**.
- In contrast to the trial-and-error of operant conditioning, **insight learning** usually involves a sudden solution to a problem. What is learned is not a specific set of conditioned associations, but a cognitive relationship between a means and an end and this makes generalising to other, similar problems easier. The ability to use insight to solve certain problems may be, to a certain extent, innate.
- Evolutionary psychologists believe that humans have an **instinct for learning**. In other words, learning is made possible by innate machinery designed to do the learning. It seems unlikely that learning is accomplished by a single general-purpose device, but rather by different modules or **mental organs**. These mental organs have functions useful for survival and reproduction in the environments in which humans evolved.
- The term 'learning' as used by behaviourists is not really an explanation for anything, but is rather a phenomenon that itself requires explanation. Evolutionary psychologists view learning as **a diverse set of processes caused by a series of intricate, functionally organised cognitive adaptations, implemented in neurobiological machinery**.

11

THE EVOLUTION OF INTELLIGENCE

Introduction and overview

Intelligence has long been considered to be a feature unique to human beings, giving us the capacity to devise elaborate strategies for solving problems. However, like all our other features, intelligence is the product of evolutionary change and can be observed in varying degrees in a range of species. The aim of this chapter is to consider the nature of intelligence, the possible selective advantages of intelligent behaviour and theories of the evolution of intelligence. I begin by trying to define what is meant by *intelligence*.

What is intelligence?

Many attempts have been made to define intelligence, with varying degrees of success. Binet and Simon (1915) described intelligence as 'the faculty of adapting oneself to circumstances'. Wechsler (1944) thought that intelligence was 'the aggregate or global capacity of the individual to act purposefully, think rationally, and to deal effectively with the environment'. A key point in both of these definitions is that intelligence contributes to the *adaptability* of an individual, a concept introduced in Chapter 1. With this idea in mind, a useful definition of intelligence is 'the ability to devise flexible solutions to problems'.

It seems unlikely that intelligence is a single entity. It is best considered as a collection of aptitudes, including learning a wide range of information; applying this knowledge in new situations; thinking, reasoning and original planning. Together, these abilities produce behaviour we see as 'intelligent'. Byrne (1995) suggested that human intelligence encompasses both special-purpose, hard-wired abilities serving particular needs (such as *social exchange*, see Chapter 7), and flexible, general-purpose cognitive functions which can be applied widely. To date, psychologists have tended to emphasise the latter abilities. However, the evolutionary psychology view is that we possess many more special-purpose abilities than previously thought.

Intelligence: nature or nurture?

Both genetic and environmental factors occurring before or after birth can influence the development of intelligence (Carlson, 1988). A large number of prenatal environmental factors are known to have harmful effects on development, such as maternal diet, diseases, drugs (such as cigarettes and alcohol), maternal stress and maternal age (McIlveen and Gross, 1997). Postnatal fluctuations in measured intelligence (IQ) are also related to disturbing factors in an individual's life. Despite the relative stability of IQ over time, these short-term fluctuations pose problems for a simple genetic theory of intelligence.

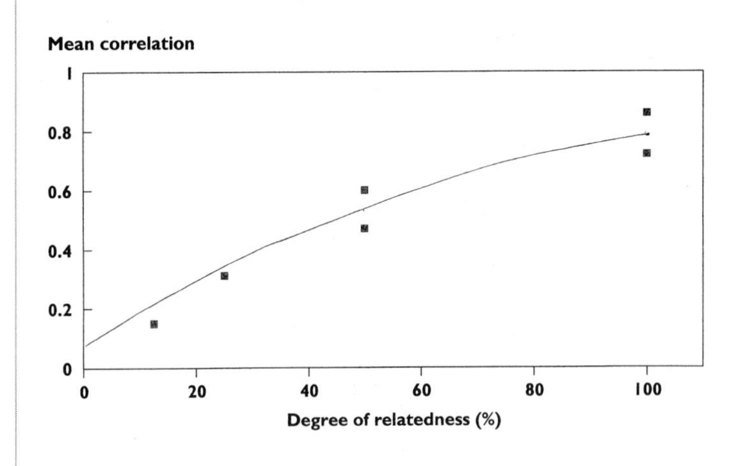

Figure 11.1 The relationship between degree of relatedness and familial correlation for IQ

GENETIC INFLUENCES

Family resemblance studies suggest that the correlation in IQ between cousins is weaker than that for parents and their offspring, while that for unrelated people reared separately is almost zero. The strongest correlation of all is for identical, or monozygotic (MZ), twins (Figure 11.1). These findings are consistent with a genetic basis for intelligence (Bouchard and McGue, 1981). However, as the genetic similarity between people increases, so their environments tend to become more similar (parents and offspring usually live in the same household, whereas unrelated people usually do not). One way of overcoming this problem is to compare the IQs of MZ twins reared together with those raised separately. Although MZ twins reared together are more alike than those reared separately (supporting the influence of environmental factors), MZ twins reared separately are still more similar than dizygotic (DZ) twins of the same sex reared together (suggesting a major role for genetic factors). These family resemblance studies have received further support from studies of adopted children, as described in Box 11.1 (McIlveen and Gross, 1997).

Box 11.1 Adoption studies into the genetic basis of intelligence

Adopted children share half their genes but little or none of their environment with their biological parents, and they share at least some of their environment but no genes with their adoptive parents. Studies have shown that there is generally a much stronger correlation between the IQ scores of adopted children and their biological parents than between adopted children and their adoptive parents. Also, by the end of adolescence, the IQ scores of adopted children are correlated only weakly with their adoptive siblings who share the same environment but are biologically unrelated (Plomin, 1988). These studies appear to support the influence of genetic factors on the development of intelligence.

One of the problems with adoption studies is the difficulty in assessing the amount of similarity between the environments of biological and adoptive parents. Evidence suggests that when these environments are very different, substantial changes in IQ scores can be observed. However, when the environments of biological and adoptive parents is roughly equal, the IQs of adopted children tend to be much more similar to those of the biological parents than the adoptive parents (McIlveen and Gross, 1997).

ENVIRONMENTAL INFLUENCES

While not denying the role of genetic factors, supporters of the environmentalist position argue that the development of measured intelligence can be strongly influenced by environmental factors. Some of these factors are described in Box 11.2.

Box 11.2 Environmental influences on the development of intelligence

- Diet
- Disease
- Drugs and environmental toxins
- Family size and birth order
- Stressful family circumstances
- Child-rearing styles
- Educational intervention programmes

THE INTERACTION BETWEEN GENETIC AND ENVIRONMENTAL INFLUENCES

For most psychologists, intelligence can be attributed to an *interaction* between genes and the environment. Genes do not fix behaviour but establish a range of possible reactions to environmental experiences. In turn, environments can affect whether the full range of genetic variability is expressed. Recent assessments of the extent to which the variation in IQ scores can be attributed to genetic factors suggested a heritability estimate of 50-60% (Bouchard and Segal, 1988). Nevertheless, as I pointed out in Chapter 1 (page 3), genetic and environmental factors can never be isolated from one another. What is important for evolutionary psychologists is that genes *do* play a role in the development of intelligence, and so this ability can evolve.

Why intelligence?

The human brain is uniquely large among primates. This evolutionary increase in brain size must have been driven by strong selective advantages, because there are significant costs involved. Our large brain is energetically expensive; makes birth a prolonged, painful and sometimes dangerous process; and continuing growth and maturation of the brain post-birth results in the requirement for extended parental care. Intelligence must be worth all these costs!

According to Plotkin (1995), *unpredictability* is the core concept for an understanding of why intelligence evolved. Instincts (adaptive behaviours that are constructed by complex developmental processes from genetic instructions) can deal with some environmental variation, such as physiological and behavioural adaptations for maintaining body temperature in mammals. However, instincts are somewhat inflexible and intelligence will be selected for in a world of unpredictable change. The faster or more significant the changes, the greater the selection pressure will be for the adaptability provided by intelligence. In effect, intelligence is best viewed as an adaptation based on instincts, but which provides much greater flexibility in an unpredictable world. In other words, advanced intellectual abilities are spin-offs of the more fundamental forms of knowledge essential to survival, or 'instinct is the mother of intelligence' (Byrne, 1995).

The evolution of human intelligence

There are two main theories that attempt to account for the evolution of human intelligence; the *ecological* theory and the *social* theory. Both theories rely to a certain extent on the *comparative approach*. This was outlined in Chapter 1 (page 8), but warrants further examination.

THE COMPARATIVE APPROACH

Comparative psychology may be defined as the study of the behaviour of animals with a view to drawing comparisons (similarities and differences) between them. It also involves studying non-human animal behaviour in order to gain a better understanding of human behaviour (Clamp and Russell, 1998). With the aid of the comparative approach, the evolutionary history of intelligence can be inferred from its pattern of occurrence in surviving species. The basis of the approach is summarised in Box 11.3.

The comparative approach is most useful when restricted to relatively closely related species. In the case of humans, this means monkeys and apes (Figure 11.2). For example, monkeys and apes have brains that are twice as large as average mammals of their size, and humans have brains three times as large as a monkey or ape of human size (Cartwright, 2000). This brain inflation is accomplished by prolonging foetal brain growth for a year after birth. In fact, if our bodies grew proportionally during that period, we would be ten feet tall and weigh half a ton! A summary of human evolution is shown in Box 11.4 and Figure 11.3.

Learning (see Chapter 10) and memory (the storage of an internal representation of learned knowledge) are forms of intelligence common to humans and quite a range of other animals. The ability to manipulate stored knowledge (reasoning and thought) is a form of intelligence that is probably restricted to a small

Box 11.3 The comparative method (Byrne, 1995)

1 Find reliable differences in the intelligence of living animal species, and ascertain how these differences affect the species' ability to survive under different circumstances.
2 Deduce from 1 the likely intelligence of the species' extinct ancestors.
3 Look for plausible selection pressures that could have favoured the evolutionary changes uncovered, that is, problems to which they seem to be the solutions.

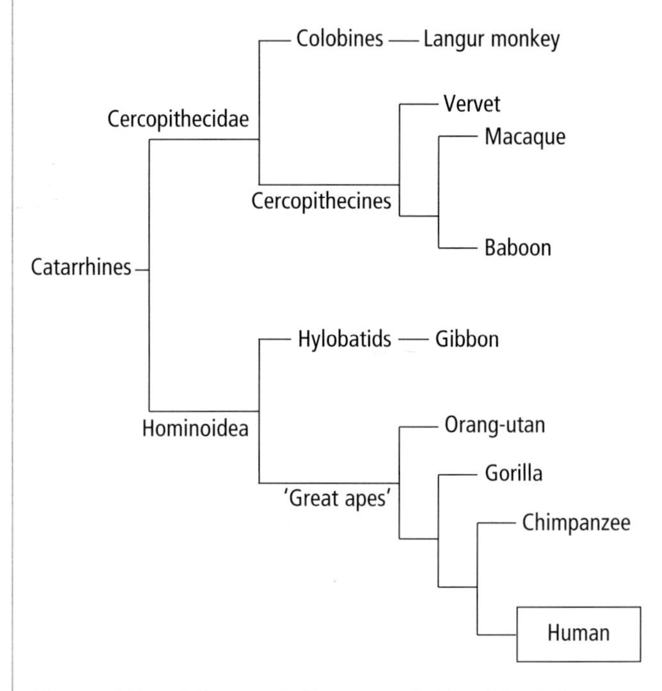

Figure 11.2 The evolutionary relationship between monkeys, apes and humans

Box 11.4 A summary of human evolution

Species	*Date*	*Brain size*
Chimp-hominid ancestor	6-8 million years ago	450 mm³
Australopithecus afarensis	2.5-4 million years ago	400-500 mm³
Homo habilis	1.6-2.3 million years ago	500-800 mm³
Homo erectus	300,000-1.9 million years ago	750-1250 mm³
Homo sapiens	Present-45,000 years ago	1350 mm³

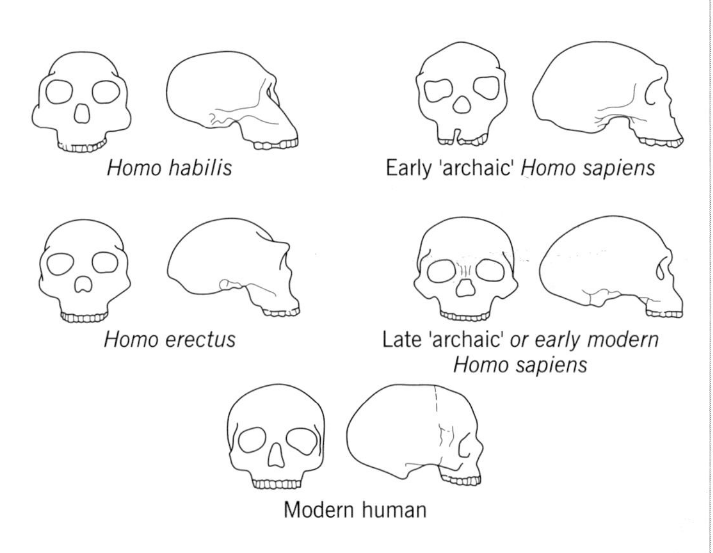

Figure 11.3 A summary of the changes in skull shape during human evolution

number of species. *Homo sapiens* is particularly good at this skill, and at sharing learned knowledge (culture), for which language is essential (see Chapter 12).

THE ECOLOGICAL THEORY

One of the main selection pressures that promoted the development of intelligence may have been efficiency in foraging. Many simian (monkey-like) primates have to balance their diets via wide-ranging and selective eating. To do this efficiently requires adaptations for finding and obtaining food. *Finding* particular foods over a wide area may require a *cognitive map* (memorised spatial knowledge). Although many species probably have some spatial knowledge, the idea that the advantages of a better cognitive map selected for greater intelligence was first introduced to explain primate intelligence (Byrne, 1995). This idea is supported by the remarkable navigational skills possessed by many monkeys and apes. *Obtaining* food involves several skills, such as hunting, tool use and complex food processing. These skills presumably also require intelligence, although objections have been raised to these arguments.

The first stone tools of *Homo habilis* appeared about two and a half million years ago in Ethiopia. These were very simple indeed (roughly chipped rocks) and barely improved over the next million years. They were then replaced by the hand axes and tear-drop shaped stone devices of *Homo erectus*. Again, nothing much happened for over a million years until about two hundred thousand years ago, when there was a sudden and dramatic expansion in the variety and sophistication of tools at about the time that *Homo sapiens* appeared. After that, tools became ever more varied and accomplished until the discovery of metal. However, all of this came too late to explain intelligence, which had been increasing ever since three million years ago.

Hunting explanations of intelligence suggest that this ability requires the skills of forethought, cunning and coordination . However, this logic applies equally well to lions, who seem to cope with much smaller brains than ourselves. Similar arguments have been advanced for *gathering* food, but this also applies to many other species. Baboons must know where to forage at what time, and whether to eat certain insects. Chimpanzees seek out a special plant whose leaves can cure them of worm infections, and they exchange cultural information about how to crack nuts. Most ecological explanations fail the test of applying only to humans (although they could conceivably apply *more strongly* to humans).

There is one final problem with the ecological theory of the development of intelligence. If intelligence evolved to cope with large range areas and highly selective diets, we would expect *neocortex ratio* (ratio of neocortex size to that of the rest of the brain) to correlate positively with the complexity of the environment. However, neocortex ratio appears to be unrelated to environmental complexity (Byrne, 1995). Therefore alternatives to the ecological theory must be considered.

THE SOCIAL THEORY

According to the social theory, interactions with other members of a social group present an intellectual challenge and primate intelligence has evolved in response to this challenge. Humphrey (1976) argued that the need to compromise between maximising individual gains (by manipulating others) and retaining the benefits of group living selects for those individuals with the greatest intelligence. In other words, *intelligence is an evolutionary adaptation for solving social problems.*

The most intelligent species are social: bees, parrots, dolphins, elephants, wolves, and, of course, monkeys, gorillas, and chimpanzees. (The urang-utan, clever but almost solitary, is a puzzling exception to this rule). Group living could have set the stage for the evolution of intelligence in two ways. First, sociality increases the value of having better information, because information is the one commodity that can be given away and kept at the same time. A more intelligent animal living in a group possesses both the benefit of the knowledge *and* the benefit of whatever it can get in exchange for the knowledge. Second, group living itself poses new cognitive challenges. Social animals send and receive signals to coordinate predation, defence, foraging, and sexual behaviour. They exchange favours, repay and enforce debts, punish cheats, and join coalitions (Pinker, 1997).

Apes and humans are particularly adept at *tactical deception* (deliberately deceiving others in order to secure a goal). Byrne and Whiten (1988) reports an incident in which Paul, a young baboon, saw an adult female, Mel, find a large edible root. He looked around and then gave a sharp cry. The call summoned Paul's mother, who 'assumed' that Mel had just stolen the food from her offspring or threatened him in some way, and chased Mel away. Paul ate the root. This piece of social manipulation by the young baboon required some intelligence: a knowledge that its call would bring its mother, a guess at what the mother would 'assume' had happened, and a prediction that it would lead to Paul getting the edible root. This type of reasoning is known as *Machiavellian intelligence*, and suggests that deceiving and detecting deception are the primary reason for the evolution of intelligence. In support of this idea, there is a strong positive correlation between neocortex ratio and the prevalence of tactical deception in various primates (Figure 11.4).

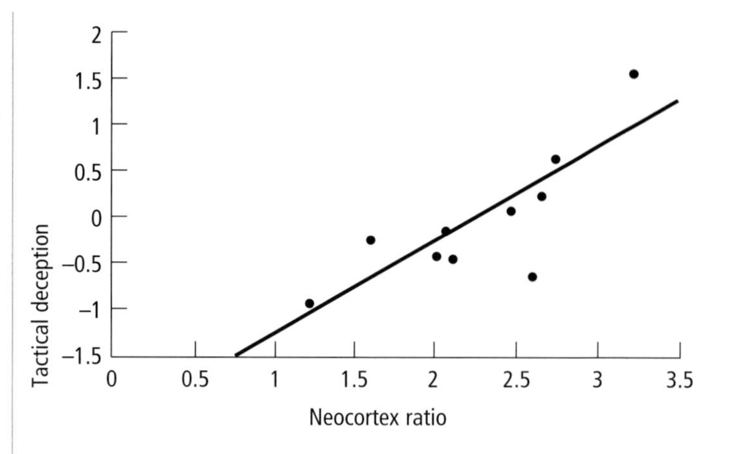

Figure 11.4 The relationship between the neocortical ratio and the prevalence of tactical deception for various primates (adapted from Byrne (1995))

In order to use tactical deception effectively, a species must have some understanding of the 'theory of mind' outlined in Chapter 2 (see page 15). Research suggests that some primates have a limited theory of mind; it is mainly confined to apes and humans. This idea fits in with observation studies suggesting that the habit of calculated deception is common in humans, occasional in chimpanzees, rare in baboons and virtually unknown in other animals (Ridley, 1993).

Several psychologists have proposed that the human brain is the outcome of a cognitive arms race set in motion by the Machiavellian intelligence of our primate forebears. As Pinker (1997) puts it, 'you had better think about what your opponent is thinking about what you are thinking he is thinking'. In other words, only humans themselves could provide the necessary challenge to explain their own evolution (Alexander, 1975). However, the Machiavellian theory applies to *every* social species. So how did humans break away from the pack? The answer to this question is not clear, but may relate to the changes in lifestyle required to cope with the *costs* of intelligence, such as large brain size, extended childhood, and so on. Only humans seem to have evolved these required changes in lifestyle, meaning that runaway selection for intelligence is unchecked in our species. Alternatively, advances in human intelligence could be the result of the development of language (see Chapter 12). Most animals use communication to manipulate each other, so perhaps our advanced communication system selected for greater deceptive abilities (and better deception-detecting skills), leading to increased intelligence.

On page 97, I stated that measures of environmental complexity are unrelated to neocortex ratio. However,

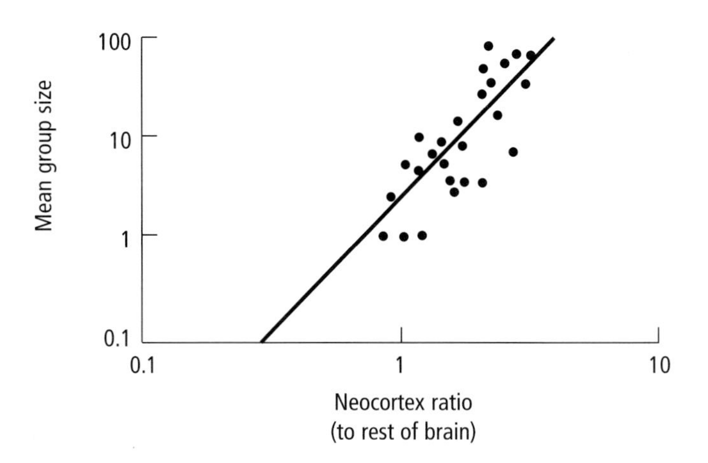

Figure 11.5 The relationship between group size (social complexity) and neocortex ratio for various primates (adapted from Byrne (1995))

group size (a measure of social complexity) *does* correlate positively with neocortical enlargement (Figure 11.5). This provides strong support for a social origin of human intelligence. However, all apes and monkeys show complex behaviour replete with communication, manipulation, deception and long-term relationships. Selection for Machiavellian intelligence based on such social complexities should predict much larger brains in other apes and monkeys than we observe. This means we still have a problem explaining *human* intelligence. It may be that we have to evoke the development of sophisticated language to explain human intelligence (see Chapter 12) and consider the possibility that one of the functions of language is to deceive. Alternatively, there may be other factors involved in the evolution of human intelligence, as described below.

OTHER THEORIES

According to Ridley (1993), the evolution of human intelligence was the result of sexual competition between individuals of the same sex. Males compete with males (and females with females) to attract and seduce attractive members of the opposite sex. In many ways, this may be seen as simply a version of the Machiavellian intelligence theory outlined above. But what could have made clever people more likely to win the inter-sex competition, and to have more children than their less intelligent counterparts? Answers to this question tend to focus on the idea of the brain as a courtship device to attract and retain sexual mates. Its specific evolutionary function is to stimulate and entertain potential partners, and to assess the stimulation attempts of others. Intelligent people are more attractive and are able to outwit their sexual competitors. The only way that sufficient evolutionary pressure could be sustained in one species to produce our extra-large brains is sexual selection. In other words, our brain is the human equivalent of a peacock's tail (see Chapter 1, page 5) and 'clever people are sexy people' (Ridley, 1993).

Surveys consistently place intelligence high in lists of desirable characteristics in both sexes, even above such things as beauty and wealth (Miller, 1998). Yet intelligence provides no indication of youth, status, fertility or parental ability, so evolutionists tend to ignore it. If, however, we view intelligence as being as measure of courtship ability, then mutual sexual selection could account for some of our impressive intellectual abilities.

One important type of courtship activity is the provision of food, predominantly by males (this may suggest a link between the ecological and sexual selection theories for the evolution of intelligence). It has been suggested that, during the EEA, hunting was overwhelmingly a male activity. Women tended to be busy with child-rearing duties, and men were psychologically and physically prepared for hunting because of their evolutionary history of killing each other (see Chapter 9). This enabled successful hunters to trade meat with females for sex, a behaviour observed in baboons, chimpanzees and most foraging societies (Pinker, 1997). Indeed, the exchange of resources for sexual access is still an important part of the interactions between men and women all over the world.

Selecting for big brains (intelligence) may also have influenced our mating systems (see Chapter 4). The large heads of human infants require that they are born helpless and premature at nine months (if they were as advanced at birth as apes, they would be twenty-one months in the womb), requiring the formation of long-term pair bonds to ensure that parental investment is adequate for survival. Montagu (1961) argued that humans are born more immature, and remain more immature for a longer period, than any other species. This feature, the retention of juvenile features into adult life, is known as *neotony*. However, although we look like baby apes, we breed at a relatively advanced age. The combination of a slow change in the shape of our head and a long period of youthfulness means that as adults we have astonishingly large brains for an ape. Ridley (1993) proposes that the mechanism by which apemen turned into humans was simply a genetic switch that slowed the developmental clock. Further discussions about the importance of neotony are provided in Box 11.5.

An alternative theory for the evolution of human intelligence has been proposed by Susan Blackmore (1999). Blackmore suggests that *memes* (see Chapter 2) could account for the explosion in brain size that occurred about 2.5 million years ago. The transmission of useful memes requires an ability to imitate, which probably requires a minimum of brain capacity. Reciprocal altruism and Machiavellian intelligence may have predisposed early humans to develop this minimum capacity and the influence of memes may then have set up further selection pressures for an increase in intelligence. Those individuals who are good imitators and who imitate other successful imitators will do better in the competition to survive and reproduce. According to Blackmore, this selection pressure will cause an increase in brain size by a process of positive feedback. As Blackmore observes:

> I suggest that the human brain is an example of memes forcing genes to build ever better and better meme-speading devices.
> (Blackmore, 1999, p119)

Furthermore, as brains become selected for imitating, language emerges more or less inevitably since language is one way in which memes can be propagated and obtained (see Chapter 12). Although this is an interesting idea, it suffers from a lack of supporting evidence.

Box 11.5 The importance of neotony in the development of human intelligence

The neotony theory may be closely linked with human mating strategies (see Chapter 4). If men began selecting mates that appeared youthful (for arbitrary reasons, or because youthfulness implied health and/or fertility), then any gene that slowed the rate of development of adult characteristics in a woman would make her more attractive at a given age than a rival. As a result, she would have more offspring, who would inherit the same neotony gene. Neotony, in other words, could be a consequence of sexual selection. Since neotony may be a major factor in the development of human intelligence (by enlarging the brain size at adulthood), it is to sexual selection that we should attribute our great intelligence.

A neotony gene would probably make males appear more youthful as well as females (there is no reason why it should be specific to the female sex in its effects). Therefore, it is possible that neotonous traits were favoured by *female* choice, rather than male choice. Younger males may have made more co-operative hunters and females that wanted meat picked younger-looking men. The conclusion is the same: increased intelligence is favoured by neotony, and neotony is a consequence of sexual selection.

A COMPARISON OF THEORIES

There are advantages and disadvantages in each of the theories presented in this chapter. (A summary of the key ideas underlying each theory is presented in Figure 11.6). It is possible that ecological factors, sexual selection and memes have all played a role in the evolution

Ecological theory

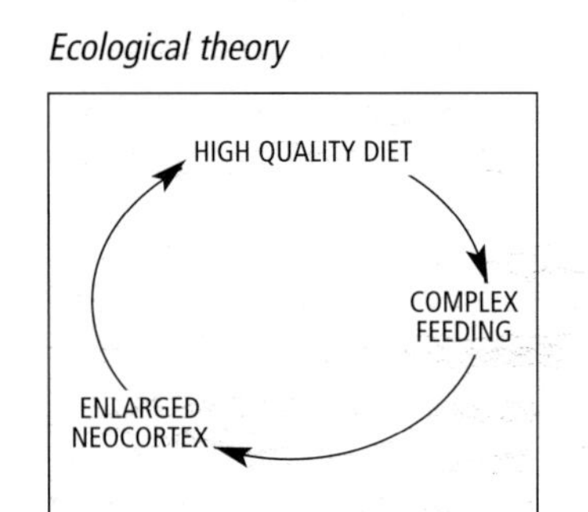

Social theory

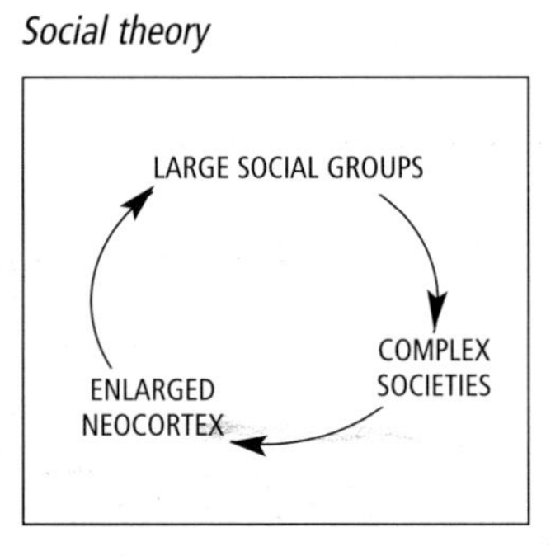

Meme theory

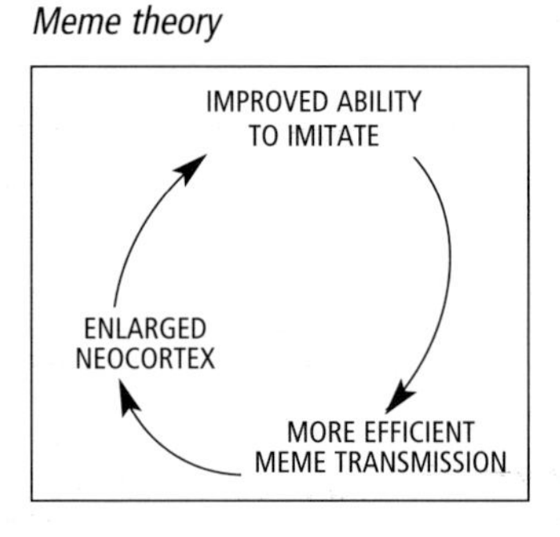

Sexual selection theory

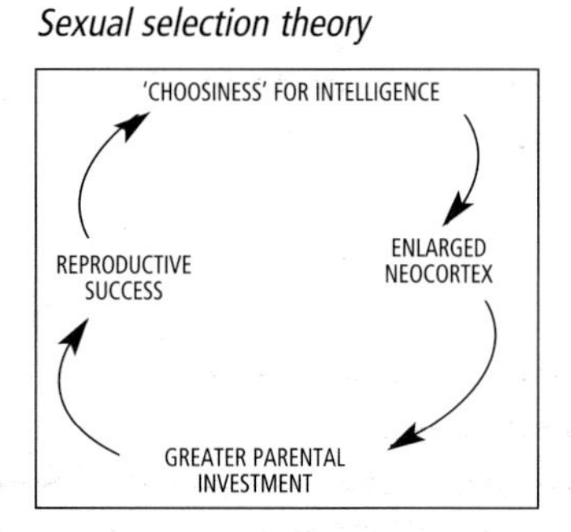

Figure 11.6 A comparison of the alternative models for the increase in intelligence during human evolution

of human intelligence. However, it is only the *social* function of the intellect that is supported by a significant body of evidence and sociality is probably the most important single factor contributing to the evolution of intelligence.

Conclusions

Intelligence is a key component of the *adaptability* of a species in that it provides the ability to devise flexible solutions to problems. Genetic factors play a significant role in the development of intelligence, and so this ability is subject to the forces of evolution. Two main theories have been proposed to account for the evolution of human intelligence; the *ecological* theory and the *social* theory. The current consensus in evolutionary psychology is that the social theory provides by far the most plausible explanation for the evolution of intelligence.

SUMMARY

- **Intelligence** has long been considered to be a feature unique to humans, giving us the capacity to devise elaborate strategies for solving problems. However, **intelligence is a product of evolutionary change** and can be observed in varying degrees in a range of species.
- Definitions of intelligence tend to emphasise its contribution to the **adaptability** of an individual. A useful way to view intelligence is as **the ability to devise flexible solutions to problems**. Byrne suggested that human intelligence encompasses both special-purpose, hard-wired abilities serving particular needs, and flexible, general-purpose cognitive functions which can be applied widely.
- Both **genetic** and **environmental** factors occurring before or after birth can influence the development of intelligence. **Family resemblance studies** suggest a genetic basis for intelligence, but the similarity of environments in these studies means we have to be careful when drawing conclusions. Nevertheless, research on **twins reared apart**, together with **adoption** studies, support the idea that **genetic factors are important in the development of intelligence.**
- A large number of pre-natal environmental factors are known to have harmful effects on intellectual development, such as maternal diet, diseases, drugs, stress and maternal age. Similarly, disease, family size, child-rearing styles, coaching and stressful family circumstances can influence the development of intelligence after birth.
- **Unpredictability** is the core concept for an understanding of why intelligence evolved. The more unpredictable the environment, the greater the selection pressure will be for the adaptability provided by intelligence. Intelligence is best viewed as an adaptation which is based on instincts, but which provides much greater flexibility in an unpredictable world. In other words, **instinct is the mother of intelligence**.
- There are two main theories that attempt to account for the evolution of human intelligence; the **ecological** theory, and the **social** theory.
- The ecological theory proposes that one of the main selection pressures that promoted the development of intelligence was **efficiency in foraging**. Intelligence is an adaptation that increases the efficiency of **finding** food (requiring a **cognitive map**) and **obtaining** food (which involves several skills, such as hunting, tool use and complex food processing).
- There are several problems with the ecological theory. Advances in tool technology were probably the **result** of increasing intelligence, not the **cause**. Foraging explanations fail the test of applying only to humans. Finally, **neocortex ratio** appears to be unrelated to environmental complexity.
- According to the **social** theory, the need to compromise between maximising individual gains (by manipulating others) and retaining the benefits of group living selects for those individuals with the greatest intelligence. In other words, **intelligence is an evolutionary adaptation for solving social problems**. This idea is supported by the positive correlation between group size (a

measure of social complexity) and neocortical enlargement.

- Apes and humans are particularly adept at **tactical deception**. This suggests that deceiving and detecting deception are the primary reason for the evolution of intelligence. In support of this idea, there is a strong positive correlation between neocortex ratio and the prevalence of tactical deception in various primates.
- The **sexual selection** theory proposes that the evolution of human intelligence was the result of sexual competition between individuals of the same sex. The brain functions as a **courtship device** to attract and retain sexual mates. Intelligent people are more attractive and are able to outwit their sexual competitors. The **meme** theory suggests that the human brain is an example of memes forcing genes to buid ever better and better meme-speading devices.
- There are advantages and disadvantages in each of the theories. It is possible that ecological factors, sexual selection and memes have all played a role in the evolution of human intelligence. However, it is only the **social** function of the intellect that is supported by a significant body of evidence and **sociality is probably the most important single factor contributing to the evolution of intelligence.**

12

LANGUAGE

Introduction and overview

Language has often been the subject of controversy in psychology. The issues debated include:

- what is language?
- is it unique to humans?
- how did language evolve?
- how do we acquire language during childhood?

The aim of this chapter is to address these questions and to present the case for an evolutionary psychology view of language – that humans are born with a 'language instinct' (Pinker, 1994).

What is language?

Brown (1965) defined language as: 'an arbitrary set of symbols which, taken together, make it possible for an individual … to transmit and understand an infinite variety of messages'. This ability is based on the accumulation of a vocabulary (the 'arbitrary set of symbols') and, just as importantly, a set of rules for the production of language, known as *grammar* (to permit the generation of 'an infinite variety of messages'). The major components of grammar are *phonology*, *semantics* and *syntax*, as shown in Figure 12.1.

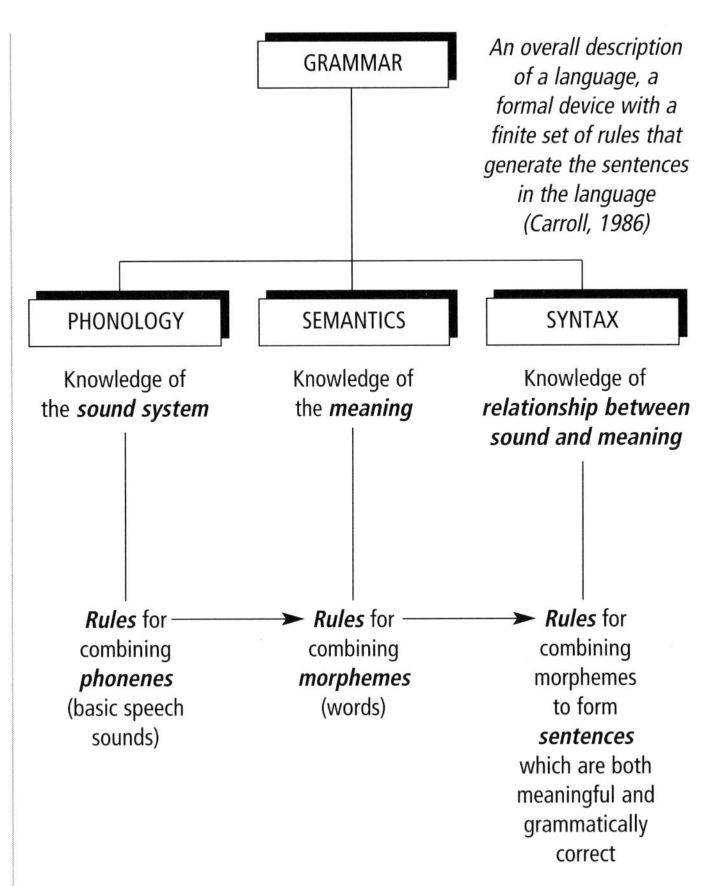

Figure 12.1 The major components of grammar (adapted from Gross, 1996)

Language *development* appears to follow a universal timetable. In other words, *all* children are thought to pass through the same sequence of stages at approximately the same ages (although there may be differences between children with respect to the rate of their development). The relative importance of innate programming, maturation, and environmental factors in this process is discussed on page 104. Note that language development may originally have been a much longer process, but gradually became more innate (although not totally innate) through a process similar to that described in Box 10.5 on page 89. The typical pattern of language development, together with underlying brain development, is shown in Figure 12.2. (A more detailed description of language development is beyond the scope of this book, but can be found in Gross and McIlveen's (1997) *Cognitive Psychology*).

The evolution of language

A COMPARATIVE APPROACH

Language, we might suppose, is a human characteristic that sets us apart from other animals. Darwin's theory of the evolutionary origin of species asserts that there

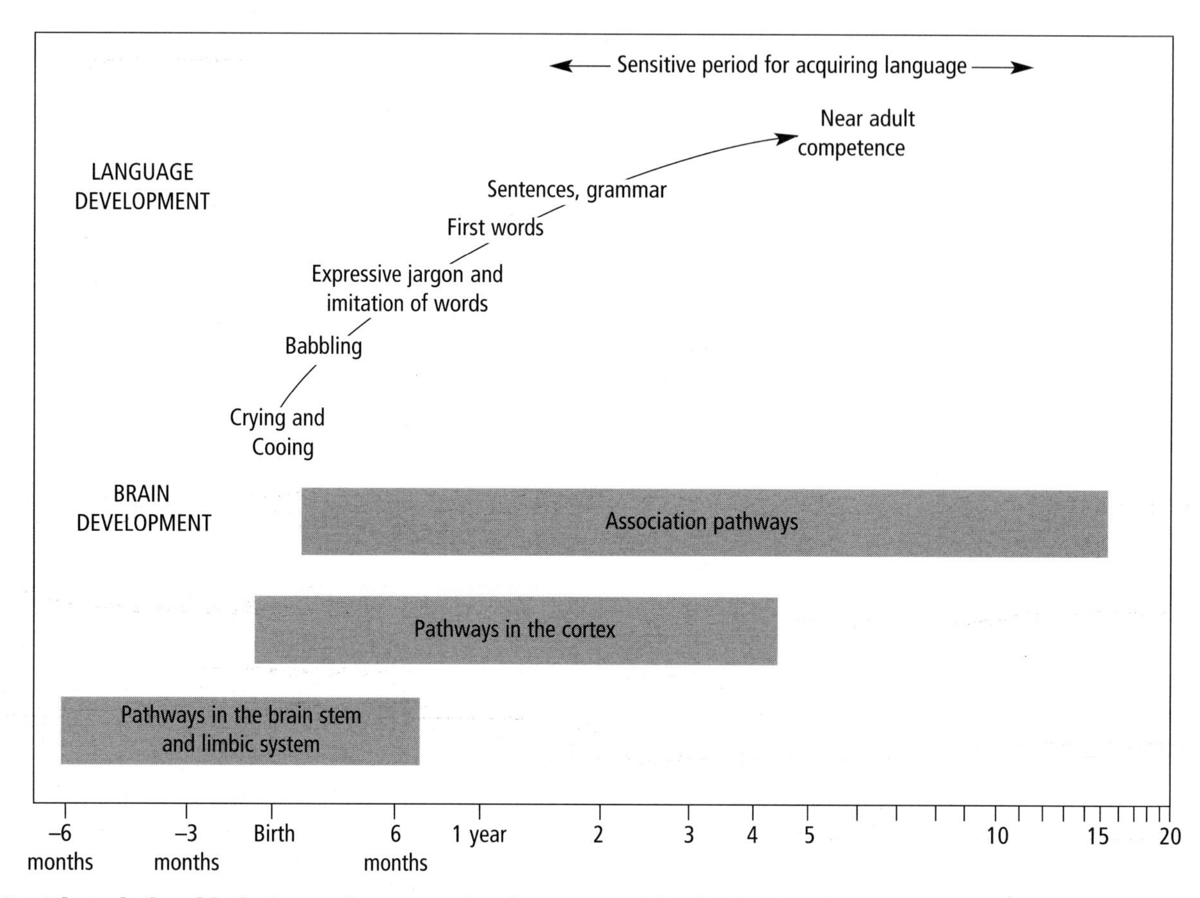

Figure 12.2 The relationship between language development and brain development. Early speech is associated with development of pathways in the cortex, but more complex speech depends on the development of association pathways in the cortex.

exists a genetic continuity between humans and non-human animals. If language is not a special characteristic of humans, research should indicate that non-human animals do have some sort of rudimentary language, or at least the capacity to learn it. But is true language unique to humans?

Box 12.1 describes the ten generalised features of language that can be used to assess its existence in non-human animals. Many animals, such as vervet monkeys, honey bees, and birds exhibit *some* of these features. However, it is debatable whether any non-human species satisfy them all (Clamp and Russell, 1998).

Chimpanzees use varied facial expressions, sounds and gestures to communicate (Goodall, 1965), but none seems complex or varied enough to constitute language. However, the ability of wild primates to learn complex skills, and to imagine a situation from the point of view of another individual, has been observed by Boesch

Box 12.1 Ten language criteria

The ten generalised features of language described below are used throughout this chapter to evaluate the existence of language in non-human animals.

Symbolic/ semantic	The system uses arbitrary symbols which have shared meaning for the communicators.
Specialised	The symbols used are employed only for communication, they are not the by-product of another behavioural system.
Displacement	Language can be used to describe things which are absent in time or space (e.g. past events or hidden objects).
Generativity	Language allows for the production of an infinite variety of novel utterances.

Phonological and lexical syntax	Language is dependent on a rule-based structure. This has rules for the combination of basic units (e.g. sounds or 'phonemes'), known as phonological syntax, and for the combination of higher level units (e.g. words), known as lexical syntax.
Spontaneous acquisition	Users acquire basic language spontaneously without formal instruction or reinforcement. Only then can subsequent languages, or language elements, be learned.
Critical period	The acquisition of fluency in a first language is limited to a phase early in life.
Cultural transmission	Language, with changes accumulated by one generation, is passed to the next by its use.
Interchangeable roles	Individuals can be both transmitters and recipients of language.
Conversation	By alternating roles, individuals can exchange information about a shared understanding.

(1991). These attributes could imply a capacity to learn language.

Boesch studied young chimpanzees learning to open nuts in their natural habitat. Many nuts are difficult to open, so chimpanzees use a tool (a large stone or stick) as a hammer. Adults foraging alone carry a suitable hammer, selecting nuts and cracking them deftly against an 'anvil'. When foraging with a youngster, however, a mother will supply not only nuts but also hammers to her offspring. Boesch observed mothers guiding the behaviour of their offspring when they encountered problems. One mother was seen to reposition nuts on an anvil to enable her son to use the hammer effectively. Another mother, having been handed the hammer by her daughter who had unsuccessfully attempted to open a nut, held the hammer where it was visible and rotated it in her own hand, to illustrate a more effective grasp. She then opened ten nuts and allowed her daughter to eat some of them before giving her the hammer. The daughter assumed the same grip and maintained this whilst varying other aspects of her behaviour, such as posture. She succeeded in opening four nuts in fifteen minutes. Boesch concluded that adult chimpanzees seem to have the ability to compare their offspring's performance to an internal concept of the way a behaviour should appear. From this, they can anticipate the effects of these actions and the consequences of modifications in performance which are essential to language. Being able to understand that there can be a different viewpoint from one's own, and predicting the likely outcome from a change in behaviour, is indicative of complex cognitive processes. These perspective and turn-taking skills are fundamental to aspects of language such as *cultural transmission, displacement* and *conversation.*

Further evidence for the ability of chimpanzees to consider the perspective of others has been provided by Povinelli *et al* (1992). Their work supports the idea that chimpanzees can appreciate the *symbolic* nature of language, its *displacement* quality, and that it can convey information from one individual to another. So even though chimpanzees demonstrate little by way of language in the wild, other aspects of their comprehension and behaviour suggest that they may have some skills which underlie the acquisition of language.

Attempts have been made to *teach* language to a variety of non-human species, including birds, cetaceans and primates. Several species appear to be capable of grasping some of the rudiments of language, but it is only really in chimpanzees that more sophisticated aspects of language are exhibited (see Box 12.2). Nevertheless, language remains a special feature of humans because no single species possesses all of the characteristics together, or to the same phenomenal extent, as human beings.

IS LANGUAGE AN ADAPTATION?

The idea of language as an adaptation is fully compatible with the Darwinian paradigm, in which complex biological systems arise by the gradual accumulation over generations of random genetic mutations that enhance reproductive success (as seen by the possession of the rudiments of language in several other species). Human language therefore probably evolved from the foundations of language seen in other species and in our immediate ancestors.

Even if we believe that the language instinct is unique to modern humans, this poses no more of a paradox than the trunk unique to modern elephants. For example, consider that a form of language first emerged after

Box 12.2 Panzee and Panbanisha, a language-reared chimp and bonobo

Rumbaugh and Savage-Rumbaugh (1994) were interested to know whether the success of teaching by immersion in language could also benefit other species which had shown lesser language skills using formal teaching methods. They reared two chimps, one *Pan troglodytes*, Panzee, and one *Pan paniscus* (bonobo), Panbanisha, of very similar ages, in the same 'language-rich' environment (Figure 12.3). Within two years, two findings were clear: that both species could learn without formal instruction, but that the bonobo was much more competent. Panbanisha and Panzee, like Kanzi, received no explicit training in language, they simply picked it up. As such, their learning fulfils the criterion of *spontaneous acquisition*, in a manner analogous to the language learning of a child. Early exposure to a language-structured environment lays the foundations for comprehension.

Figure 12.3 Panbanisha and Panzee using the lexigram keyboard.
Copyright: Dr Duane Rumbaugh, Georgia State University.

the branch of the evolutionary tree leading to humans split off from the one leading to chimpanzees. This could result in chimpanzees without language (or at least not a language as sophisticated as our own) and approximately 5 to 7 million years in which language could have gradually evolved in humans (the 'missing links', all those individuals with intermediate language abilities, are of course now all dead). The language of children, immigrants, tourists and aphasics demonstrates that there is a vast continuum of viable language systems, varying in efficiency and expressive power (Pinker, 1994). This is exactly what the Darwinian paradigm would predict.

Box 12.3 outlines the criteria which would have to be satisfied for a 'language instinct' to have evolved by natural selection. Even though there are no conclusive data on any of these issues, studies of the biology of language and evolution suggest that each of the criteria are quite plausible.

Box 12.3 The criteria which would need to be satisfied for a 'language instinct' to have evolved by natural selection

- There must have been genetic variation among individuals in their grammatical competence
- There must have been a series of steps leading from no language at all to language as we now know it
- Each 'improvement' in language must have been small enough to have been produced by a random mutation or recombination
- Each intermediate grammar must have been useful to its possessor
- Grammatical competence must have conferred a reproductive advantage
- The reproductive advantage of better grammar must have been large enough to become fixed in ancestral populations

Box 12.4 In support of language as an adaptation (based on Pinker [1994])

- Some people are born with an inherited condition in which they make grammatical errors of speech.
- Language is associated with certain physical areas of the brain, such as Wernicke's and Broca's areas.
- Language bears signs of apparent design for specialised functions.
- Children acquire language incredibly quickly, inferring grammatical rules from language spoken by others and applying them automatically.
- The human vocal tract appears to have been shaped to meet the demands of speech and the mechanisms of the human ear suggest that it is specialised for decoding speech.
- There is no correlation between the level of sophistication of a culture and the grammatical complexity of its language, indicating that language is not solely the product of culture.

Variation does exist in grammatical ability, and at least some of this variation is probably genetic. For example, Bever *et al* (1989) showed that right-handed people with a family history of left-handedness show less reliance on syntactic analysis and more reliance on lexical association than do people without such a genetic background. Similarly, Gopnik *et al* (1996) reported data suggesting that a genetic disorder can affect normal language learning mechanisms. Nevertheless, it is unlikely that we would find many examples of single gene deficits in grammatical ability as most grammar systems will be polygenic. Furthermore, different grammatical subsystems may generate superficially similar constructions, making genetically-based disorders difficult to detect.

Some psychologists have doubted that an evolutionary sequence of increasingly complex universal grammars is possible. The intermediate links, it has been suggested, would not have been viable communication systems. However, many of these arguments fail to stand up to rigorous examination. For example, Geschwind (1980) asked how a hypothetical beneficial mutation in grammar could have benefited its possessor, given that no one else could have understood him or her. This argument fails to grasp the point that *comprehension* abilities do not have to be in perfect synchrony with *production* abilities. Ungrammatical strings like *skid crash hospital* are quite understandable (Pinker, 1994), and I can do a reasonably good job understanding French newspaper stories based on a few words remembered from school lessons 19 years ago, and an appreciation of context. Nevertheless, grammatical sophistication is still advantageous, and will continue to be selected. Finally, it should be remembered that if a single mental database is used in production and comprehension, evolutionary changes in response to pressure on one performance would automatically transfer to the other (Bresnan and Kaplan, 1982). Box 12.4 summarises Pinker's (1994) arguments in favour of language as an adaptation.

WHY LANGUAGE?

Language is a complex cognitive process and considerable costs must have been involved in the development of this ability in humans. However, the benefits of language must have exceeded the costs, or it could not have evolved by natural selection. Dunbar (1998) has reviewed the circumstances in which language might evolve and has come to two important conclusions. First, language is closely related to sociality. Only animals which associate in relatively permanent groups will benefit from language, which serves a vital function in managing social relationships. However, several forms of 'communication' could fulfil this criterion, such as social grooming in baboons. This leads Dunbar to his second conclusion, that 'true' language is significantly more efficient as a means of cementing social relationships than traditional methods of communication. This is probably true for large social groups or complex societies, suggesting that language may have evolved in a similar way to intelligence, as described in Chapter 11. In fact, language may simply be a by-product of increased intelligence. Chomsky (1959) takes the view that language could have appeared as an emergent property from an increase in brain size without being the product of selective forces. It is interesting to compare this view with the more plausible description of language as an adaptation, given in Box 12.4. Finally, it seems likely that language may have a role in supporting social intelligence and that there may be a co-evolutionary circuit linking the advances in language with those of intelligence.

Can better grammars *really* provide reproductive advantages? Although the benefits of linguistic competence may seem minimal when compared to, say, access to a rich supply of food, there are several reasons why improved grammar may facilitate greater reproductive success. First, we should remember that tiny selective advantages are sufficient for evolutionary change. According to Haldane's (1927) class calculations, a variant that produces on average 1% more offspring than its alternative allele would increase in frequency from 0.1% to 99.9% of the population in just over 4000 generations. Even in long-lived humans, this fits comfortably into the evolutionary time-table. Secondly, there will be large selective advantages arising from: being able to learn in a way that is essentially stimulus-free; using language to promote cooperation in a hunter-gatherer community; using language to enhance resource holding potential (RHP). This last point receives support from Symons's (1979) observation that tribal chiefs are often both gifted orators and highly polygynous (see Chapter 4). Finally, Dunbar (1998) has suggested that what we talk about is socially useful information, otherwise known as gossip (see Box 2.5 on page 18). The relationship between human social complexity, the evolution of language, and intelligence is discussed in Box 12.5.

Box 12.5 Evolution and the social use of language

The social use of language probably played a key role in human evolution. This role is best appreciated by examining the dynamics of cooperation among individuals, which presents extraordinary opportunities for evolutionary gains and losses (see Chapter 7). The minimum cognitive apparatus needed to function effectively in a cooperative environment is memory for individuals and the ability to enforce social contracts of the form 'if you take a benefit then you must pay a cost' (Cosmides, 1989). This alone will select for linguistic skills that are powerful enough to distinguish subtle semantic differences. Furthermore, cooperation also opens the door to advances in the ability of cheaters to fool people into believing that they have paid a cost or not taken a benefit. This in turn selects for the ability to detect signs of such cheating, which selects for the ability to cheat in less detectable ways, and so on. This sets the stage for a cognitive 'arms race', which may be the basis for increased intelligence (see Chapter 11).

The ability to 'sell' an offer so that it appears to present maximal benefit and minimum cost to the buyer, and the ability to see through such attempts and to formulate persuasive counterproposals, would have been very useful skills in primitive negotiations, as they are today. So is the ability to learn of other people's desires and obligations through gossip, an apparently universal human vice (see Chapter 1). It seems that our ancestors lived in a world in which language was woven into the intrigues of politics, economics, family, sex, and friendship that played important roles in individual reproductive success.

Theories of language development

THE BIOLOGICAL APPROACH (CHOMSKY, 1957)

At one year of age nearly all human infants, regardless of which of the 5000-plus languages of the world they are being raised to speak, have a vocabulary of about ten words. The average vocabulary of five-year-olds is somewhere between 5000 and 10000 words. This extraordinary increase appears to occur in an unguided and unintended manner. Children develop highly specific and intricate language structures simply by being exposed to a language-rich environment.

Darwin thought that the ability to learn language was a special kind of instinct. However, this idea was lost for a while in a cloud of cultural relativism, which held that all languages were radically different from one another. The relativist viewpoint led linguists to concentrate on cataloguing the differences between languages rather than the commonalties which they all shared.

The biological approach argues that whilst the environment may supply the *content* of language (such as vocabulary), the *structure* of language (its *grammar*) is an innate, biologically determined capacity of human beings. According to this view, the process of language development is essentially one of *acquisition*, rather than learning (Gross and McIlveen, 1997).

Chomsky (1957) proposed the existence of an innate *language acquisition device* (LAD). This enables children to formulate and understand all types of sentences, even if they have never previously heard them (sometimes children are born with a genetic language impairment, leading to difficulties in language development, as described in Box 12.6). An important part of Chomsky's theory is the idea of *transformational grammar*, which is essentially a set of rules (*phrase-structure rules*) that specify what are and are not acceptable utterances in a speaker's native language When applied systematically, these rules generate sentences in *any* language. Some of Chomsky's phrase-structure rules are shown in Figure 12.4, which also shows how a sentence is produced using these rules (Gross and McIlveen, 1997).

Some sentences have different phrase structure but share the same meaning, whilst others have a similar structure but completely different meanings. Furthermore, certain sentences (such as 'The lamb was ready to eat') can have ambiguous meanings. This led Chomsky to distinguish between the *surface structure* (the actual words or phrases used) and the *deep structure* (the meaning) of a sentence. According to Chomsky, the language acquisition device enables us to transform the meaning of a sentence into the words that make it up (and vice versa).

The biological approach argues that children are equipped with the ability to learn the rules to transform deep structure into various surface structures, and they do this by looking for *linguistic universals* (features common to all languages, such as consonants, vowels

Rule (1) An S (sentence) consists of (or can be broken down into) NP (noun phrase) and VP (verb phrase)

Rule (2) NP ⟶ Article + (Adjective) + Noun

(The brackets denote 'optional')

Rule (3) VP ⟶ Verb + NP

Rule (4) Article ⟶ a(n), the

Rule (5) Adjective ⟶ big, small, red, etc.

Rule (6) Noun ⟶ boy, girl, stone, etc.

Rule (7) Verb ⟶ hit threw, helped, etc.

These are *Lexical Rewrite Rules*

The commas imply that only *one* word should be selected from the list

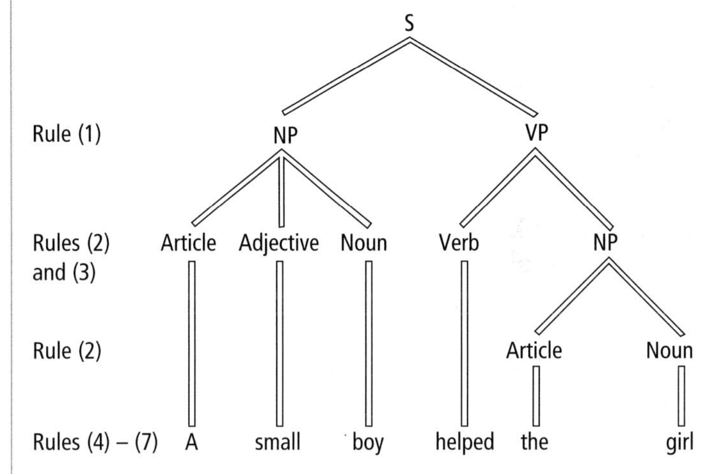

Figure 12.4 Some of Chomsky's phrase-structure rules and an example of a sentence produced by using them

Box 12.6 Genetic language impairment

It is well established that some children have great difficulty in acquiring their own native language, even though they seem otherwise normal. *Specific Language Impairment* (SLI) is defined as a developmental deficit of language in the absence of perceptual, motor, general cognitive, emotional or social problems. There is converging data from epidemiological studies and family studies that show that SLI aggregates in families. The increased concordance in monozygotic, as compared to dizygotic, twins suggests that this disorder is likely to be heritable. Gopnik et al (1996) suggest that the genetic factor (or factors) responsible for SLI must interfere with the establishment of neurological structures that underpin the acquisition of language. This, in turn, affects the ability to build the kinds of grammars that ordinary children build automatically and unconsciously, and provides support for the biological approach to language development.

Box 12.7 Evidence supporting the biological approach (Based on Gross and McIlveen, 1997)

- Human vocal organs, ventilation apparatus, auditory system and brain are all specialised for spoken communication
- Research suggests that babies are born with the ability to discriminate between different speech sounds (Eimas, 1975)
- All adult languages appear to have certain linguistic universals and transformational grammar is acquired in some form by virtually all people, irrespective of their culture or other cognitive abilities
- 'Invented' languages consistently possess a set of structures comparable to all known languages, supporting the view that humans are born with an already-formed knowledge of syntax.
- Studies of congenitally deaf children have shown the emergence of 'gestural language', even though the children received no encouragement or training from their parents.

and syllables). Collectively, linguistic universals provide the deep structure. In other words, all brains have the same 'language organ' (Ridley, 1993). Several studies have failed to find strong evidence for the application of Chomsky's rules when people speak and listen (Hampson and Morris, 1996). However, empirical studies of languages all over the world, from remote villages to busy cities, suggest that there *is* a constrained set of principles that underlies all languages and further evidence favouring the biological approach is summarised in Box 12.7.

In summary, nothing is more 'instinctive' than the predisposition to learn a language. It is genetically-determined and hard-wired into the brain, not learned. Nevertheless, this predisposition is almost infinitely plastic when it is applied to the development of vocabulary and syntax. The ability to learn a language, like almost all other human brain functions, is an instinct for learning (see Chapter 10).

THE LEARNING THEORY (SKINNER, 1957)

Skinner argued that language development can be explained by *operant conditioning* (see Chapter 10, page 87). Although the learning theory accepts that pre-linguistic vocalisations such as cooing and babbling are probably innate, it proposes that adults *shape* the baby's sounds into words by *reinforcing* those sounds which approximate the form of real words. Positive reinforcement may be in the form of physical rewards (such as receiving a biscuit for producing a word that sounds like 'biscuit'), or through parental encouragement and approval. Selective reinforcement also results in words being shaped into sentences, with correct grammar being reinforced and incorrect grammar being ignored. Finally, Skinner also saw *imitation* as playing an important role in language development.

Although there is some evidence to support Skinner's views, the importance of reinforcement in the development of language has been challenged by a number of researchers. For example, Brown *et al* (1969) reported that mothers respond to the presumed meaning of their children's language rather than to its grammatical correctness, and attempts to teach grammar appear have little effect (Tizard *et al*, 1972). Furthermore, Slobin (1975) found that parents often reinforce incorrect grammar. These studies suggest that parents pay little regard to grammatical correctness. Even if they do, this has little effect on language development.

The role of imitation in language development has also attracted much criticism. Imitation is probably far more important in the learning of accent and vocabulary than in the development of grammar. When children do imitate adult sentences, they tend to convert them to their own currently operating grammar and, since at least some adult language is ungrammatical, imitation alone cannot explain how children develop language.

If language is established through reinforcement, then we would expect that all children living in widely varying social conditions would acquire language in different ways. However, despite highly variable conditions, there appears to be a culturally universal and invariant sequence in the stages of language development. Even children raised by deaf parents seem to acquire language in the same sequence as other children (Slobin, 1986). Learning theory also fails to explain the *creativity* of language (the production and comprehension of an infinitely large number of novel sentences), or the spontaneous use of grammatical rules by children. Finally learning theory cannot account for children's ability to understand the meaning of *sentences* (as opposed to the meaning of *words*). The meaning of a sentence is not simply the sum of the meanings of the individual words. Learning theory may be able to account for how children learn the meaning of individual words, since these usually have an obvious reference. However, it cannot explain how the meaning of grammatical terms is acquired.

In summary, it seems that learning theory can only help to explain language development in a very limited way. Arguments for a biological approach are much more compelling, as would be predicted by evolutionary psychology. Indeed, if we view learning as an evolved instinct (see Chapter 10), we can consider the whole process of language development as being an evolutionary psychological phenomenon.

Conclusions

This chapter has addressed several key questions relating to human language. I have examined the nature of language, its exclusivity to humans, and language development. It seems clear that language, like other specialised biological systems, evolved by natural selection. Language shows signs of complex design for communication, and the only explanation for the origin of organs with complex design is the process of natural selection. The view from evolutionary psychology suggests that humans do indeed possess a 'language instinct'.

SUMMARY

- **Language** may be defined as **an arbitrary set of symbols which make it possible for an individual to transmit and understand an infinite variety of messages**. This ability is based on the accumulation of a vocabulary and a set of rules for the production of language, known as **grammar**.
- **Language development** appears to follow a universal timetable. In other words, **all** children are thought to pass through the same sequence of stages at approximately the same ages. The process of language development appears to depend on a combination of **innate programming, maturation** and **environmental factors**.
- There are **ten generalised features** of language that can be used to assess its existence in non-human animals. Many animal species, such as vervet monkeys, honey bees, and birds exhibit **some** of these features. However, it is debatable whether any non-human species satisfy them all.
- **Chimpanzees** use varied facial expressions, sounds and gestures to communicate, but none seems complex or varied enough to constitute language. However, chimpanzees appear to possess certain aspects of language, such as **cultural transmission**, **displacement**, and **conversation**. These animals can also appreciate the **symbolic** nature of language, its **displacement** quality, and that it can convey information from one individual to another.
- Attempts have been made to **teach** language to a variety of non-human species, including **birds**, **cetaceans** and **primates**. Several species appear to be capable of grasping some of the rudiments of language, but it is only in **chimpanzees** that more sophisticated aspects of language are exhibited. Nevertheless, language remains a special feature of humans because no single species possesses all of the characteristics together, or to the same phenomenal extent, as human beings.
- It appears that humans possess a **language instinct** that evolved by natural selection. Dunbar suggested that language is **an efficient method for cementing social relationships** and its evolution is closely linked to that of the evolution of **intelligence**.
- Variation exists in grammatical ability and evidence suggests that better grammar **can** provide reproductive advantages. For example, it is possible that language may have been used to enhance **resource holding power** or to promote **cooperation** in a hunter-gatherer community. The selective advantages may have been small, but there is more than enough time for language to have evolved.
- Some psychologists have doubted that an evolutionary sequence of increasingly complex universal grammars is possible; that the intermediate links would not have been viable communication systems. However, **comprehension** abilities do not have to be in perfect synchrony with **production** abilities and ungrammatical strings can still

be understandable. Furthermore, if a single mental database is used in production and comprehension, evolutionary changes in response to pressure on one performance would automatically transfer to the other.

- The **biological approach** to language development argues that whilst the environment may supply the **content** of language (such as vocabulary), the **structure** of language (its **grammar**) is an innate, biologically determined capacity of human beings. Therefore the process of language development is essentially one of **acquisition** rather than learning.
- Chomsky proposed the existence of an innate **language acquisition device (LAD)**, which enables us to transform the meaning of a sentence into the words that make it up (and vice versa). This enables children to formulate and understand all types of sentences, even if they have never previously heard them. There is a wealth of evidence supporting the biological approach, suggesting that the ability to learn a language is an **instinct for learning**.
- Skinner argued that language development can be explained by **operant conditioning** and **imitation**. However, there is little evidence to support this approach. It seems that learning may account for the content of language, but it cannot explain the universal structure of language.

PART 5
Darwinian Medicine

13

INFECTIOUS DISEASES

Introduction and overview

Darwinian medicine is an evolutionary explanation of host-parasite relationships in disease states. It attempts to explain why humans are generally susceptible to certain diseases and not others. As such, it does not replace conventional medicine (which tends to ask 'what' and 'how' questions about disease), but complements it (by also asking 'why' questions about disease).

The principles of host-parasite relationships are very similar to the arms races observed between predators and prey (Clamp, 1998). However, bacteria can evolve as much in one day as humans can in 1000 years. This puts us at a significant disadvantage in the arms race, which is only partly compensated for by our large and diverse immune system (see page 120). Of course, we do have the advantage of medicine on our side. However, the rapid mutation rates of many viruses, together with large increases in bacterial resistance to antibiotics, may limit the effectiveness of the medicine weapon in the arms race. Furthermore, underexposure to pathogens (disease-causing organisms), coupled with an over-reliance on medicine, reduces the selection pressure on our immune system. This may result in weakened natural defences. According to Jones (1994), the evolution of mechanisms for resisting disease represents the best example of evolution in action, and most human variation is the remnant of past battles against infection.

The final part of this book (Chapters 13 to 15) considers Darwinian explanations of infectious disease and mental disorders. In the present chapter, I examine the nature of a variety of pathogens and assess the ways in which humans respond to infection.

Viral infections

AIDS

Acquired Immune Deficiency Syndrome (AIDS) is an umbrella term for a variety of life-threatening diseases associated with the decimation of the immune system

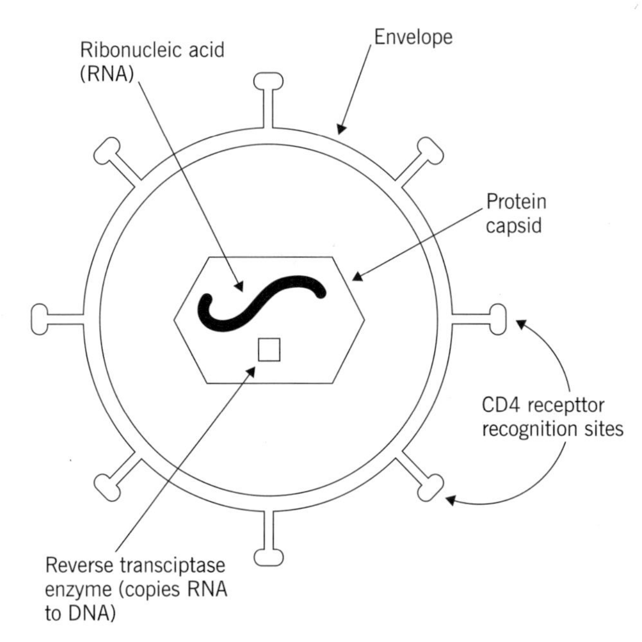

Figure 13.1 Human Immunodeficiency Virus (HIV).

Box 13.1 AIDS and tuberculosis: a dangerous interaction

HIV and *Mycobacterium tuberculosis* enhance each other's virulence. *M. tuberculosis* tends to accelerate the progression of HIV infection to AIDS (Hill *et al*, 1991), and the damage to the immune system caused by HIV promotes the development and contagiousness of tuberculosis (TB) (Stead and Lofgren, 1991). The spread of TB in concert with AIDS is particularly ominous in Africa, where one out of three people is infected with *M. tuberculosis*. In 1990, for example, there were over 250,000 cases of HIV-associated TB (Sudre *et al*, 1992). Furthermore, because *M. tuberculosis* can cause infection even among people with intact immune systems, the amplification of this disease by the AIDS pandemic may also have a serious impact on people with a very low risk of HIV infection. The danger is particularly great in hospitals serving AIDS epicentres like New York City. Highly contagious TB patients often remain in crowded hospital settings for prolonged periods before appropriate infection control procedures can be instituted (Ewald, 1994).

by Human Immunodeficiency Virus (HIV) (Figure 13.1). Following infection, HIV binds to a CD4 receptor on the surface of a helper T cell (normally involved in coordinating the activities of the rest of the cellular immune system), gains entrance, and eventually kills the cell. This causes the person to become more vulnerable to other infections, such as tuberculosis (see Box 13.1), and to cancer. It is these diseases that are eventually responsible for death by AIDS.

Over ten million people are now infected with HIV, and over one million have AIDS or have died from AIDS. These numbers are still small relative to the tolls imposed by influenza, malaria, or the diarrhoeal diseases. However, there is no end to the AIDS pandemic in sight, nor is there any recognised therapy that can cure AIDS or even postpone death for more than a year or so. An examination of the evolution of AIDS may provide a useful insight into the nature of the disease.

Generally, *within-host* selection favours the increased virulence (damage caused by the disease) of pathogens. This is because the infectious organisms will be selected to out-compete rival pathogens and reproduce as fast as possible. However, *between-host* selection acts to decrease virulence, as pathogens will be selected not to kill the host before they can be transmitted. Likewise, diseases spread by personal contact tend to be less virulent than those spread by insects or other vectors (Figure 13.2). It is in the interest of pathogens spread by contact to keep their host feeling reasonably well (Ewald, 1994). This will lead to greater interaction with other people and a consequent increase in the transmission of the disease-causing organism.

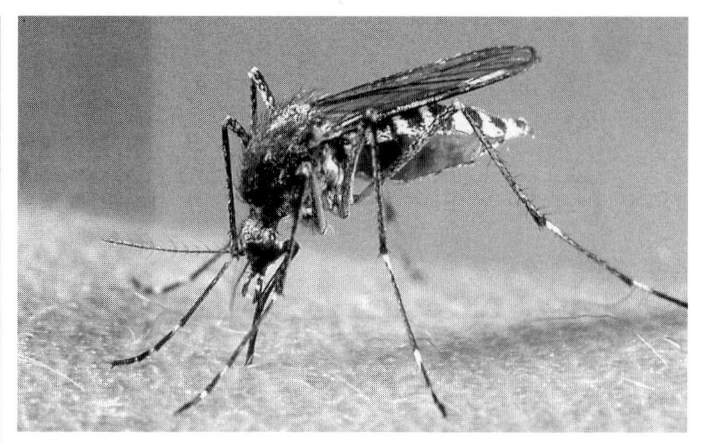

Figure 13.2 Diseases spread by insects tend to be more virulent than those spread by personal contact

AIDS is caused by highly virulent forms of HIV, which appear to have evolved in recent times. It has been suggested that AIDS may have arisen because of changes in social behaviour: increased promiscuity, prostitution and intravenous drug use may have lead to the rapid transmission of HIV. When this occurs, host survival becomes less important to the survival of the virus, favouring the evolution of more virulent forms. Under these conditions, even highly virulent forms of HIV may have the opportunity to disperse to new hosts before the original host dies. An interesting point about this disease is that the use of clean needles and condoms would not only reduce the transmission of HIV, it would also cause the evolution of lower virulence (as hosts would need to be kept alive longer to increase the probability of transmission). This may prove particularly important, as resistance of HIV to anti-AIDS drugs (such as AZT) appears to be on the increase, as described in Box 13.2.

In conclusion, an evolutionary approach to AIDS suggests that it would be advantageous to invest more heavily in programmes that reduce sexual and needle-borne transmission of HIV. Apart from the direct benefit of such a policy (reduced transmission of HIV), there may also be an indirect benefit of the evolution of a more benign form of the virus.

Box 13.2 HIV resistance to AZT

Azidodideoxythymidine (AZT) interferes with the replication of HIV, slowing the progression to AIDS and prolonging the survival of AIDS patients by a year or so (Swanson and Cooper, 1990). Unfortunately AZT, like antibiotics, is not as reliable as it once was, because some HIV strains are now resistant to the drug.

HIV is a *retrovirus*, using ribonucleic acid (RNA) as the genetic material, rather than the more common deoxyribonucleic acid (DNA). One of the features of a retrovirus is its low level of reproductive precision, which means that it produces a significant number of defective copies of itself. Some of these copies may be better at evading the host's immune system, or antiviral drugs like AZT, giving them an evolutionary advantage.

In general, it takes much longer for HIV to evolve resistance to AZT than it does for bacteria to evolve resistance to antibiotics. However, HIV has time on its hands. A single infection can undergo years of replication, mutation and selection within a single host. The unfortunate end-result of this 'interstrain competition' is that the dominant forms of the virus will be the most virulent. Therefore the use of AZT, like that of antibiotics, needs to be carefully monitored and controlled.

COUGHS AND COLDS

A cough is not an illness, it represents a *defence* against disease. Coughing results from a complex mechanism designed specifically to expel foreign material in the respiratory tract. When we cough, mucus and foreign matter are propelled up the trachea and into the back of the throat. Here it may be expelled from the body, or swallowed to the stomach, where acid destroys most bacteria. Therefore, coughing is a coordinated defence mechanism, shaped by natural selection, which is activated in the presence of a specific threat.

Although coughing is obviously a defensive adaptation to deal with infection, it also aids dispersion of the pathogen. The host benefits by having fewer microbes attacking its tissues, the pathogen by an increased chance of finding other hosts. The optimal strategy for a virus would be to invade, reproduce, induce coughing (or sneezing) in the host to promote dispersal, and so on. The true losers in this game are currently healthy but vulnerable individuals.

Given the defensive function of coughing, it seems strange that we try to suppress it with medicines. Blocking a cough excessively could be lethal. For example, patients treated with barbiturates (which suppress coughing) develop pneumonia more frequently and more rapidly than those not given the drugs (Eberhardt *et al*, 1992). Similarly, colds bring many symptoms that we dislike, such as a runny nose, headache, fever and malaise. Nevertheless, these symptoms represent adaptations shaped by natural selection specifically to fight infection (see Box 13.3). Drugs, such as Acetaminophen, can reduce or eliminate some of these symptoms, but may simply exacerbate the condition. However, symptomatic treatment of colds probably has relatively minor consequences because the common cold virus is inherently benign.

Box 13.3 Fever: friend or foe?

Darwinian medicine suggests that, far from being part of the illness, many symptoms such as fever may form a vital part of the body's adaptive response towards parasitic infection (Davies, 1996). Evidence that fever is an adaptive response to infection comes from a range of studies. For example, children infected with chicken pox who were given a fever-lowering drug (acetaminophen) took longer to recover than an untreated control group. In another study, fifty-six volunteers got colds on purpose, from an infectious nasal spray. Some then took acetaminophen, others a placebo. The placebo group had a significantly higher antibody response and less nasal stuffiness. They also had a slightly shorter period of infectious dispersal of viruses. Kluger (1990) believes that using drugs to suppress fever may even kill some patients. So why do we not have more regular and severe fevers? It is important to remember that both pathogens and hosts have to devote their energies to basic needs as well as their arms race. Higher and more frequent fevers would make us less vulnerable to pathogens (as they are killed by the higher body temperature), but would be more than counterbalanced by the costs of tissue damage and nutrient depletion.

A related defence mechanism in humans is *iron withholding*. Iron is a crucial and scarce resource for bacteria, and we have evolved a wide variety of mechanisms to prevent them from getting it. Following infection, the body releases a chemical called leucocyte endogenous mediator (LEM), which both raises body temperature (see above) and greatly decreases the availability of iron in the blood. Iron absorption by the gut is also reduced during infection. Despite these observations, it appears that very few doctors or pharmacists are currently aware that fever suppression or iron supplementation may harm patients with infectious diseases (Nesse and Williams, 1996).

The common cold is caused by a rhinovirus, which reproduces inside the cells that line our nasal passages. The viruses are shed from these cells into nasal secretions (the production of which are stimulated by the virus), which trickle out through a runny nose or blast out in droplets during a sneeze (Figure 13.3). The viruses may then be inhaled by an uninfected person and the cycle continues. In order to ascertain which symptoms are defensive, and which represent pathogenic manipulation of the host's physiology to aid dispersal, it is vital to examine the effects of blocking the symptoms. For example, the prevention of mucus discharge by nasal sprays does not appear to delay recovery. This supports the notion that a runny nose is a transmission strategy by the virus, and not an important defence mechanism (unlike sneezing).

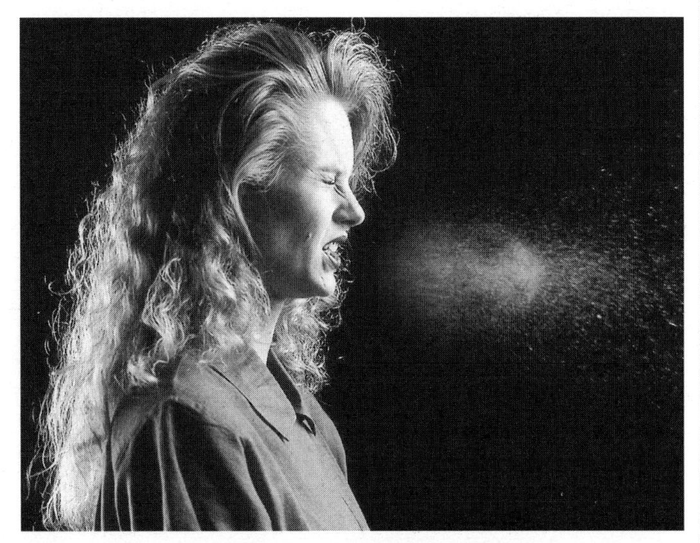

Figure 13.3 Sneezing is an important defence mechanism, designed to expel pathogens from the nasal tract

Bacterial infections

CHOLERA

Cholera is caused by the bacterium *Vibrio cholerae*, transmitted via infected food and water. Those bacteria which survive the stomach acid, and competition with indigenous gut flora, adhere to the lining of the small intestine. Here they release a toxin that causes biochemical changes in the intestinal cells, causing a massive flux of water and solutes into the intestinal cavity (Miller *et al*, 1989). This favours the growth of *V. cholerae* over competing bacteria and washes the competitors out of the intestines. Within hours of the onset of severe cholera, vast quantities of watery faeces are produced, each litre of which may contain over 100 billion *V. cholerae* (Gorbach *et al*, 1970).

The diarrhoea caused by *V. cholerae* does not appear to be defensive. Infected people are harmed because too much of their body fluids are lost, and compensating for this loss by drinking a rehydration solution does eliminate nearly all death from cholera (Hirschhorn and Greenough, 1991). The diarrhoea is best explained as a manipulation of the host to facilitate transmission of the bacteria. Therefore symptomatic treatment that reduces diarrhoea should help the infected person and help control the spread of *V. cholerae*. Similarly, cholera is often associated with anorexia, a loss of appetite. This probably represents a manipulation of the host food intake to reduce the host's ability to muster an immunological or physiological defence against the pathogen.

Box 13.3 suggested that we should reduce iron intake when ill, as this mineral is vital for bacterial survival. However, toxin production by *V. cholerae* is actually *stimulated* by iron-deprivation. In addition, fever often further reduces iron availability, with a consequent increase in the release of toxin. Therefore, the host responses (fever and a reduction in iron-intake) may be maladaptive, resulting in increased damage by the infection, and treatment in this case may be beneficial.

TUBERCULOSIS (TB)

Mycobacterium tuberculosis now ends more human life than any other species of pathogen, and the annual death toll of 3 million is expected to rise (World Health Organisation, 1992). TB is an airborne disease

Figure 13.4 Tuberculosis (TB) is spread much more quickly in large crowded cities

and originally became epidemic in Europe with the rise of large, crowded cities (Figure 13.4). Widespread use of antibiotics, together with improved standards of nutrition and housing, saw a steady decline in the disease during the latter half of this century. This progress has recently been reversed by two factors: the AIDS pandemic (see Box 13.1) and resistance of the bacteria to antibiotics.

Antibiotic-resistance in *M. tuberculosis* reduces the chances for recovery, and thereby increases the extent to which infected people may act as sources of infection for others (Beck-Sague *et al*, 1992). Resistant bacteria are particularly widespread in some urban areas like New York City and in developing countries, and there is no immediate prospect of effective replacement drugs (Edlin *et al*, 1992). One third of all cases of TB in New York City are caused by bacteria resistant to one antibiotic, while 5% of cases are resistant to two or more antibiotics (Nesse and Williams, 1996). People with tuberculosis resistant to multiple drugs have about a 50% chance of survival (the same as before antibiotics were discovered!). This effect is further exacerbated by the relative hardiness of *M. tuberculosis* outside the body. The bacteria can survive for months in the absence of a host, whereas many other pathogens are only viable for hours or days. This increases chances of transmission and, using the argument outlined on page 114, leads to enhanced virulence. *M. tuberculosis* is known as a 'sit-and-wait' pathogen, and gains the benefit of rapid multiplication inside of hosts while paying little cost through immobilisation of the host.

MALARIA: A PROTOZOAN INFECTION

Malaria is caused by *Plasmodium*, a protozoan (single-celled organism) that is transmitted from one person to another by certain species of mosquito. The life-cycle of this micro-organism is summarised in Figure 13.5. Typically, an infected person will have about ten malarial parasites in each milligram of blood during the dispersal stage (*gametocytes*). A standard mosquito 'meal' is around 3 milligrams, containing approximately thirty gametocytes. While inside the mosquito (known as a secondary host), the mature plasmodia migrate to the salivary glands and inject the saliva used to inhibit clotting when the mosquito next feeds. The mosquito then acts as a vector by unwittingly injecting the plasmodia into the next victim (a primary host). An interesting observation is that the parasites frequently alter the mosquito's salivary glands, reducing the amount of blood that can be withdrawn from victims (Conway and McBride, 1991). This results in mosquitos requiring several 'feeds' during each session, increasing the probability of multiple transmission.

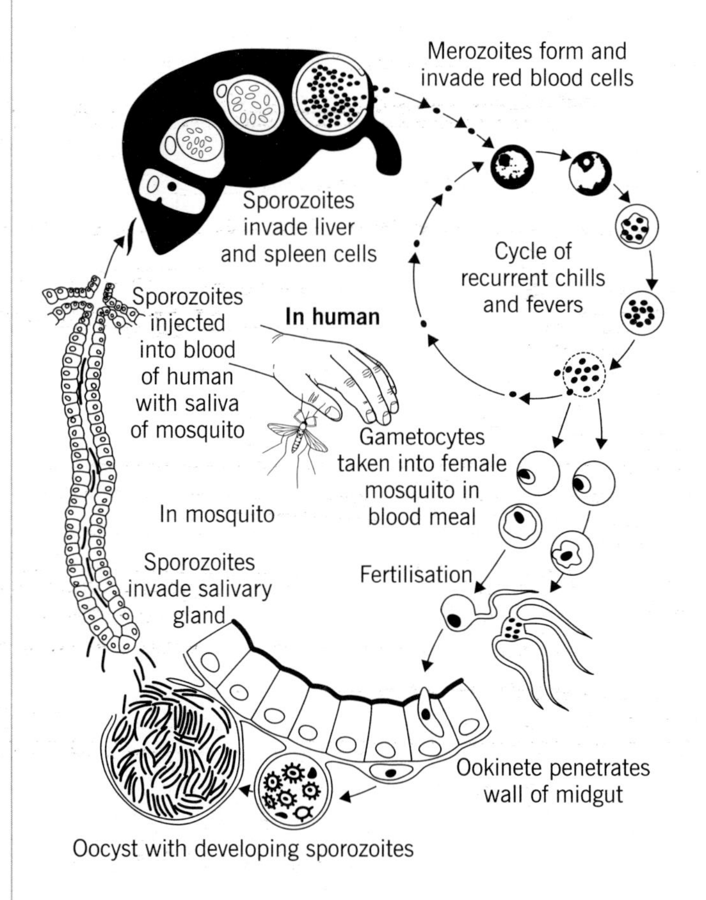

Figure 13.5 The life-cycle of *Plasmodium*

As a vector-borne pathogen, we would expect malaria to be relatively virulent (see page 114). In contrast to the viruses causing coughs and colds, *Plasmodium* gets no benefit from the host's feeling well. In fact, experiments with rabbits and mice have shown that a prostrate host is more vulnerable to mosquitos, and it is unlikely that people suffering from the disease will expend much energy warding off the insects. Extensive multiplication and spread within a human host (characteristic of high virulence) should also increase the probability that a mosquito will become infected. In summary, the strategies employed by *Plasmodium* should reap great fitness benefits with few fitness costs.

It is interesting to note that individuals carrying a single gene for *sickle-cell anaemia* gain substantial protection from malaria, accounting for the widespread incidence of sickle-cell in parts of Africa where malaria is prevalent. This is discussed further in Box 13.4.

Box 13.4 Sickle-cell anaemia: protection against malaria

Sickle-cell anaemia is the classic example of a disease caused by a gene that is also useful. A person who has *one* copy of this gene gets substantial protection from malaria. This is because the gene changes the structure of haemoglobin in such a way that affected red blood cells (which may contain malarial parasites) are rapidly removed from the circulation. However, people with *two* copies of the gene develop sickle-cell anaemia. Their red blood cells twist into a sickle-shape that cannot circulate normally, thus causing bleeding, shortness of breath and sometimes death. Therefore, having *no* copies of the gene increases vulnerability to malaria, whereas having *two* copies reduces fitness due to sickle-cell disease. In other words, individuals with *no* copies of the gene, or those with *two* copies will be selected against. The relative strength of these two selective forces determines the frequency of the gene for sickle-cell anaemia, and explains why sickle-cell disease is widespread in parts of Africa where malaria is prevalent (and so individuals with a single copy of the gene are favoured by natural selection). The sickle-cell gene is probably only one simple example of many similar genes, providing an advantage in small quantities, but a disadvantage as genetic loading increases. The same may be true of the genes involved in the development of schizophrenia, as discussed in Chapter 15.

One strategy currently being employed to reduce the incidence of malaria is the generation of mosquito populations that are genetically resistant to *Plasmodium* (Miller and Mitchell, 1991). However, the success of such a project is likely to be short-lived. There will be strong selection pressure on the protozoa to overcome any resistance mechanism in the mosquitos, especially as the population of resistant insects increases. Simultaneous decimation of the natural mosquito population would reduce the number of pathogens, but this would probably only delay the inevitable evolutionary breakthrough. Similar problems exist for the chemical control of malaria. Traditionally, quinine or quinine-type drugs were used to control the disease. However, resistance to these drugs first arose in the 1960s, and is now widespread. Furthermore, new anti-malarial compounds appear to be following the same course. It looks as if the future will offer an ongoing succession of new anti-malarial drugs and new resistance to the drugs (Peters, 1987). From an evolutionary viewpoint, the optimal strategy would be to attempt to reduce transmission from immobilised hosts. The most feasible way to accomplish this goal would be to make houses and hospitals mosquito-proof. This would be expected to cause a strong evolutionary shift towards benignness. In general, raising the fitness costs that pathogens incur from harming the host should eventually lead to a reduction in virulence, as explained on page 114.

The response to infection

AVOIDANCE AND EXPULSION

Humans have evolved a range of strategies to reduce their susceptibility to pathogens (see Box 13.5). For example, we generally defecate in private and find the sight or smell of others' faeces unpleasant. This means we are unlikely to come into contact with the waste of others, avoiding infection. We generally avoid eating foods which smell unpleasant, taking this to be a sign of bacterial decomposition or fungal contamination. If something already in the mouth tastes bad (bitter substances are more likely to be poisonous), we spit it out. These adaptations help to prevent the ingestion of potentially dangerous microbes or chemicals. Similarly, it was suggested in Chapter 5 that 'morning sickness' in pregnant women may be due to the foetus attempting to avoid certain food-based toxins (see page 42).

Box 13.5 A summary of the major defences against disease

Defence	*Action*
• Skin	Physical barrier with toxic oily secretions
• Lysozyme in tears, nasal passages and urine	Lyses (destroys) bacteria
• Mucus and cilia in respiratory tract	Traps pathogens and transports them to throat (coughed or swallowed)
• Commensal (harmless) bacteria on skin and in gut	Competitively exclude pathogenic bacteria
• Acid and proteolytic enzymes in stomach	Destroy pathogens
• Vomiting and diarrhoea	Expulsion of pathogens
• Immune system	Identification and removal of specific pathogens

Another mechanism to deter invasion is the constant regeneration of human skin. The surface layers of dead cells (containing many millions of bacteria) are lost each day, removing a potential source of infection. Likewise, scratching and other grooming behaviours remove external parasites (Hart, 1990). Pain may also be seen as an adaptation that can lead to escape and avoidance of danger. Occasionally, people are born who cannot feel pain. They are nearly all dead by the age of thirty (Melzack, 1973). Generalised aches and pains are also adaptive. They encourage inactivity, which favours the effectiveness of immunological defences (see page 120) and repair of damaged tissues. Any medication that simply makes an ill person feel less sick may interfere with these benefits.

Many of the body's defences are based on expulsion, such as sneezing and coughing. If we swallow something poisonous, toxins are absorbed into the blood. When the brain detects these toxins, a nauseous response is triggered, followed by vomiting (this is why so many drugs are nauseating, especially the toxic ones used for cancer chemotherapy). It seems that nausea discourages us from eating more of the noxious substance, and its memory prevents future sampling of the food thought to be responsible. The function of vomiting is more obvious: it ejects the toxin before more is absorbed. Similarly, diarrhoea is a defensive mechanism which occurs at the other end of the digestive tract. Blocking this mechanism with drugs, although initially appealing, simply extends the period of suffering (DuPont and Hornick, 1973). Finally, it appears that menstruation in women functions as an effective defence against uterine infection. The same anti-infection benefits that come from sloughing off skin cells are achieved by the periodic shedding of the uterus lining (Profet, 1993). This is supported by evidence that menstrual blood differs from circulating blood in ways that make it more efficient at destroying pathogens while minimising losses of nutrients. However, this hypothesis has been criticised by clinicians who maintain that the pathogen load in the reproductive tract is the same before and after menstruation, and that menstruation does not increase during infection. One other aspect of the menstrual cycle in human females is its apparent connection with the incidence of breast cancer, as discussed in Box 13.6.

Box 13.6 Breast cancer: an evolutionary viewpoint

Darwinian medicine suggests that the relatively high incidence of breast cancer in developed countries is caused in part by changes in the reproductive patterns of many women in these societies. There is no doubt that some of the increase in the frequency of breast cancer is simply due to the fact that cancer is more likely in older people, and women are now living longer. However, the probability of breast cancer *at any age* increases directly in relation to the number of menstrual cycles a woman has experienced. The menstrual cycle is characterised by wide swings in hormone concentrations, accompanied by cellular changes in breast tissue. This may cause cumulative damage and increase the likelihood of developing cancer. The most likely victim of breast cancer is an elderly woman who had an early menarche, a late menopause, and never had her cycling interrupted by pregnancy and lactation. From a historical perspective, this represents a very abnormal reproductive pattern. Women during the environment of evolutionary adaptedness (EEA) would have had much later maturation, earlier menopause, several pregnancies and relatively long periods of lactation. This probably resulted in a maximum of around 150 menstrual cycles in a lifetime. A modern woman, even if she has two or three children, might easily experience two or three times this number of cycles.

Future therapies, based on Darwinian medicine, point to the use of hormones to mimic the beneficial effects of Pleistocene life histories. In the meantime, women at risk from breast cancer should generally avoid environmental hazards, such as nicotine, radiation and diets abnormally high in fat.

In general, expulsion mechanisms are defensive adaptations, not part of the disease. However, there are exceptions. As mentioned earlier, a runny nose may be an adaptation that cold viruses use to disperse themselves. We could speculate that similar mechanisms may be used by organisms that cause sexually transmitted diseases. These organisms may influence the sexual behaviour of their host (perhaps making them more promiscuous or raising their libido) in order to increase the rate and effectiveness of transmission.

THE IMMUNE RESPONSE

The human immune system has been selected over a hundred million years to counteract the effects of pathogens, and it is generally very effective. 'Foreign' proteins (*antigens*) in the body, such as those found on a bacterium or cancer cell, are detected by cells called macrophages and transferred to helper T cells (see page 114). These T cells stimulate white blood cells to produce protective proteins (*antibodies*) that bind specifically to the antigens. This may destroy the foreign material directly, or simply label it for destruction by other cells of the immune system.

The immune system can make two kinds of mistakes: failing to attack when it should, and attacking something when it should not. The first kind of mistake results from an inadequate response, so that a disease escalates instead of being rapidly quelled. This may occur if the infectious agent (which generally evolve very quickly), become better adapted at avoiding recognition by the immune system. For example, malaria parasites have specific surface proteins that allow them to bind to the walls of blood vessels. This prevents them from being carried to the spleen, where they would be filtered out and killed. The genes that code for these binding proteins mutate at a rate of 2% per generation, just enough so that the immune system cannot 'lock in' on the organism. Another strategy is to assume the appearance of host cells. This is the technique used by many species of *Streptococcus* bacteria, which may avoid the immune system completely, or result in antibody production against the host tissues

Box 13.7 Allergy: an excessive response

Allergies can be provoked by inhaling antigens such as pollen or mite faeces, skin contact with a variety of substances, eating certain foods, and injections of toxins such as bee venom. We may develop allergies to random substances (*useless allergies*) or to specific toxins to which we are especially vulnerable (*useful allergies*). The mechanism underlying the allergic response is the immunoglobulin E (IgE) system, which works on the 'smoke-detector' principle. By reacting to a large number of factors, it stimulates an immune response to many 'false alarms'. However, the IgE system is still considered an adaptation, as the one 'real' alarm to which we respond will normally more than compensate for all the mistakes. Nevertheless, it is not totally clear what this real alarm should be, although protection against macroparasites is a currently popular idea. Given that these infections are relatively rare in modern society, this might account for the increasing incidence of allergies as an excessive response to an innocuous stimulus.

According to Buss (1999), three factors may be responsible for the prevalence of allergies in modern societies.

1 Among hunter-gatherer societies the substances that produced an allergic response could usually be identified and then avoided. Modern diets contain many hidden ingredients which are not as easily identifiable, and hence not as easily avoided.

2 Modern humans are exposed to detergents, soaps and shampoos, all containing mixtures of substances not found in hunter-gatherer societies.

3 Breastfeeding is much less common in modern societies. Several studies have shown that infants who are breastfed (usually for at least six months) develop far fewer allergies in adulthood than those who are not (Profet, 1991).

Suppressing the symptoms of allergy may be disadvantageous if it is a useful response, and because some data suggest that allergy may protect against cancer. In truth, little is known about the true purpose of the IgE system, and further studies are required if we are to understand the nature of the allergic response.

(as occurs in rheumatic fever). Alternatively, the pathogen could directly attack the immune system, as seen in AIDS (see page 113).

The second kind of mistake by the immune system results from mounting too aggressive a response to a relatively innocuous pathogenic stimulus. This could result in autoimmune diseases, such as lupus erythematosus or rheumatoid arthritis, or allergy (see Box 13.7). The average person's degree of sensitivity and responsiveness is probably close to what was optimal in the EEA: enough to counter pathogens, but not so great as to attack and damage the host tissues (Nesse and Williams, 1996).

Conclusions

Host adaptions for resisting disease, and pathogenic counteradaptations, represent one of the best examples of evolution in action. Darwinian medicine attempts to explain why we are susceptible to certain infectious diseases and not others. This approach helps us to distinguish between disease symptoms and host defences, resulting in more efficient treatment. Furthermore, it may provide important strategies for the future reduction of transmission and virulence of pathogens.

SUMMARY

- **Darwinian medicine is an evolutionary explanation of host-parasite relationships in disease states**. It attempts to explain why humans are generally susceptible to certain diseases and not others. The evolution of mechanisms for resisting disease represents the best example of evolution in action, and most human variation is the remnant of past battles against infection.
- **Acquired Immune Deficiency Syndrome (AIDS)** is caused by highly virulent forms of **Human Immunodeficiency Virus (HIV)**, which appear to have evolved in recent times. It has been suggested that AIDS may have arisen because of changes in social behaviour, leading to the rapid transmission of HIV and a consequent increase in virulence.
- An evolutionary approach to AIDS suggests that it would be advantageous to invest more heavily in programs that reduce sexual and needleborne transmission of HIV. Apart from the direct benefit of such a policy (reduced transmission of the virus), there may also be an indirect benefit of the evolution of a more benign form of HIV.
- **Coughing** and **sneezing** are not illnesses, they are **defences** against disease. They result from complex mechanisms designed specifically to expel foreign material in the respiratory tract. Blocking these defensive adaptations with drugs may, therefore, exacerbate the disease. It should also be noted that both coughing and sneezing **aid dispersion of the pathogen to new hosts**.
- **Cholera** is a bacterial disease which causes the production of vast quantities of watery diarrhoea, and subsequent life-threatening dehydration. However, in this case the diarrhoea does not appear to be defensive, and is best explained as a **manipulation of the host to facilitate transmission of the bacteria**.
- **Tuberculosis (TB)** is an airborne bacterial disease, which now ends more human life than any other species of pathogen. Widespread use of antibiotics, together with improved standards of nutrition and housing, saw a steady decline in the disease during the latter half of this century. This progress has recently been reversed by two factors: **the AIDS pandemic** and **resistance of the bacteria to antibiotics**.
- **Malaria** is caused by a protozoan (single-celled organism) that is transmitted from one person to another by certain species of mosquito. As a **vector-borne** pathogen, we would expect malaria to be relatively virulent. The protozoan gets no benefit from the host's feeling well, and high virulence increases the probability of further transmission. From an evolutionary viewpoint, the best way to reduce the incidence of malaria would be to reduce transmission from infected hosts. This would be expected to cause a strong evolutionary shift towards benignness.
- Humans have evolved a range of strategies to reduce their susceptibility to pathogens. We **avoid** possible sources of infection, such as

faeces and **contaminated food**, and use the sensation of **pain** to avoid serious injury. In addition, many of the body's defences are based on **expulsion**, such as **coughing**, **sneezing**, **vomiting**, **diarrhoea** and **menstruation**.

- The human **immune system** has been selected over a hundred million years to counteract the effects of pathogens, and it is generally very effective. However, the immune system can make two kinds of mistakes: failing to attack when it should (resulting in disease), and attacking something when it should not (causing an **autoimmune disease** or **allergy**). The average person's degree of sensitivity and responsiveness is probably close to what was optimal in the environment of evolutionary adaptedness.

14

ANXIETY AND EATING DISORDERS

Introduction and overview

When examined in an evolutionary framework, mental disorders (such as anxiety and schizophrenia) are essentially the same as the physical diseases discussed in Chapter 13. In certain cases, there may even be a direct link between physical and mental condition. For example, Sydenham's chorea is an auto-immune disease (characterised by uncontrollable muscle twitches) caused by antibody attack on nerve cells in the basal ganglia of the brain. Many individuals who suffer from Sydenham's chorea in childhood develop obsessive-compulsive disorder later in life (see page 126). It appears that the brain areas involved in obsessive-compulsive disorder are very close to those damaged by Sydenham's chorea, and that some cases of this mental disturbance may result from a malfunctioning of the immune system.

Many psychiatric symptoms are not diseases in themselves, but defences akin to fever and sneezing. According to Nesse and Williams (1996), many of the genes that predispose to mental disorders are likely to have fitness benefits, many of the environmental factors that cause mental disorders are likely to be novel aspects of modern life, and many of the more unfortunate aspects of human psychology are not flaws but design compromises. The present chapter considers the nature of anxiety and eating disorders from an evolutionary viewpoint. This theme is then continued in Chapter 15, which examines two further disorders: affective disorders and schizophrenia.

It should be noted that, although evolutionary explanations are suggested in Chapters 14 and 15 for a number of mental disorders, these explanations represent alternatives to other proposed causes of psychopathology. Evolutionary psychology does not have to explain everything. The number of people in the population who suffer from mental disorders may be considered as quite small, and they may simply represent the extremes of the normal range. Similarly, many disorders are organic in nature and do not necessarily require an evolutionary explanation. Nevertheless, the aim of this part of the book is to encourage the use of an evolutionary approach to generate testable hypotheses about the aetiology of a wide range of diseases.There is little doubt that evolutionary psychology is a useful tool that can significantly improve our understanding of mental disorders.

Anxiety

Anxiety can be described as a general feeling of dread or apprehensiveness, which is typically accompanied by a variety of physiological reactions. These include increased heart rate, rapid and shallow breathing, sweating and muscle tension (Gross and McIlveen, 1996). The capacity to experience anxiety is vital to survival. It has been said that an animal incapable of fear is a dead animal. Anxiety may be thought of as a form of vigilance, which enables an animal to be alert and prepared to act. In many ways, anxiety may be considered as synonymous with arousal. Both states prepare the body for appropriate action, such as fighting, fleeing, freezing or submitting. There are also many parallels between anxiety and the immune system, as described in Box 14.1.

It seems clear that anxiety works on the 'smoke-detector' principle. The cost of getting killed even once is enormously higher than the cost of responding to a hundred false alarms. This was demonstrated by an experiment in which guppies were separated into timid, ordinary, and bold groups on the basis of their reactions when confronted by a larger predatory fish: hiding, swimming away, or facing up to the intruder. Each group of guppies was then left in a tank with a predatory fish. After sixty hours, 40% of the timid guppies and 15% of the ordinary guppies were still alive, but none of the bold guppies had survived.

Box 14.1 Anxiety and the immune system

Nesse (1987) suggested that there are many parallels between anxiety and the immune system. The immune system has a *general response* (such as fever and inflammation), and a *specific response* (including the production of antibodies and natural killer cells). So it is with anxiety. General threats release general anxiety, promoting physiological arousal in preparation for fight or flight, and specific objects or situations can cause phobic anxiety. On certain occasions, anxiety promotes *avoidance* or *escape*. This results in removal of the individual from a source of threat, just as disgust, vomiting and sneezing are designed to separate us from pathogens. On other occasions, anxiety promotes *aggressive defence*, motivating the individual to attack the source of danger. This may be considered synonymous with the attacking of pathogens by the immune system.

Both systems are designed to protect an animal from harm, but both can have deleterious effects in certain circumstances. The immune system can over-react (anaphylaxis), under-react (immune deficiency), or respond to the wrong cue (allergy or autoimmune disease). Similarly, anxiety can be excessive (panic), deficient (hypophobia), or a response to a harmless situation. Only in these cases should anxiety truly be considered as a psychological disorder.

Box 14.2 Is there an optimal level of anxiety?

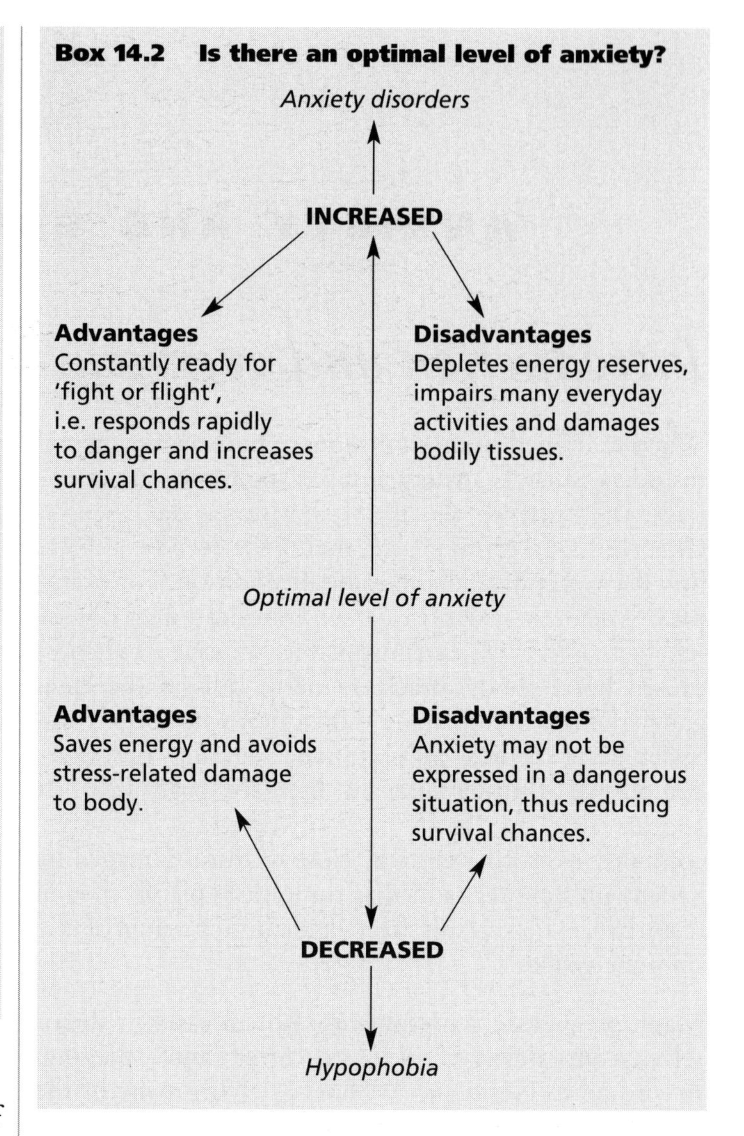

Marks (1987) described the evolutionary function of fear as follows:

> 'Fear is a vital evolutionary legacy that leads an organism to avoid threat, and has obvious survival value. It is an emotion produced by the perception of present or impending danger and is normal in appropriate situations. Without fear few would survive long under natural conditions.'

However, while anxiety can be useful, it usually seems excessive and unnecessary. I worried that I would break a leg during a parachute jump (I didn't), and that something would go wrong on my wedding day (it didn't). Fifteen percent of the US population has had a clinical anxiety disorder (Nesse and Williams, 1996). In order to explain this apparent excess of anxiety, we need to ask how the mechanisms that regulate anxiety were shaped by the forces of natural selection. The concept of an *optimal* level of anxiety is described in Box 14.2. It is important to note at this point that mild anxiety is often associated with increased sexual drive (Hamer and Copeland, 1999), and this observation alone could account for an optimal level of anxiety.

In order to assess whether anxiety relating to a particular stimulus is appropriate in a given situation, we need to know four things:

1 The relative likelihood that a given stimulus signals a danger (as opposed to something harmless).
2 The relative frequency of dangerous and non-dangerous stimuli in this location.
3 The cost of responding to a false alarm.
4 The cost of not responding to a true emergency.

It seems likely that those individuals whose anxiety level is adjusted by rapid and accurate analysis of the

Figure 14.1 An excessive fear of public speaking is a common form of social phobia

above factors will have a survival advantage. However, in general it pays to err on the side of caution, even if it sometimes results in mistakenly avoiding objects or situations that are harmless.

PHOBIAS

A phobia is a type of anxiety disorder in which there is a persistent and unreasonable fear of an object or situation. The three main types of phobia are *agoraphobia* (fear of open spaces), *social phobia* (fear of social situations, as shown in Fig 14.1) and *specific phobias* (fear of a specific object or situation). Some examples of specific phobias are given in Box 14.3.

Box 14.3 Some examples of specific phobias

Phobia	Specific fear
Acrophobia	High places
Algophobia	Pain
Arachnophobia	Spiders
Astraphobia	Storms
Claustrophobia	Enclosed spaces
Cynophobia	Dogs
Haematophobia	Blood
Mysophobia	Contamination
Nycotophobia	Darkness
Ophidiophobia	Snakes
Pathophobia	Disease
Pyrophobia	Fire
Thanatophobia	Death
Xenophobia	Strangers

It has been suggested that the acquisition of many phobias may occur through classical or operant conditioning (Watson and Raynor, 1920). This idea is supported by the effectiveness of behavioural therapies in the treatment of phobic disorders. It is also possible that genetic factors may play a role in the development of phobias (Torgersen, 1983). However, many of the studies implicating genetic involvement have been criticised, and this area remains unclear.

One interesting observation about the development of phobic disorders is that people appear to be more likely to become phobic about some things rather than others. Many more people have phobias about spiders and snakes than about cars, in spite of their greater exposure to cars (making an association with a fearful stimulus more likely). According to Seligman (1971), the objects or situations forming the basis of most phobias were real sources of danger hundreds or thousands of years ago, and those individuals who were sensitive to these stimuli were favoured by natural selection. Darwin himself declared:

> 'May we not suspect that the ... fears of children, which are quite independent of experience, are the inherited effects of real dangers ... during ancient savage time?' (Darwin, 1877)

Seligman argued that some associations are more biologically useful than others, such as taste aversion or predator avoidance. These associations are therefore learned more quickly and are more resistant to extinction. In other words, we have a psychological predisposition or 'preparedness' to be sensitive to, and become phobic about, certain (potentially dangerous) stimuli rather than others. Certain phobias, such as a fear of heights or the dark, are consistent with Seligman's theory.

The preparedness theory has been the subject of much debate in evolutionary psychology. McNally and Steketee (1985) studied snake and spider phobias and found that in 91% of cases the cause for concern was not a fear of being harmed, but rather a fear of having a panic attack. It has also been suggested that these phobias may be explained by social learning theory (Bandura, 1977). Other studies have supported the preparedness theory (Hunt, 1995). Monkeys raised in the laboratory have no fear of snakes and will reach over a snake to get a banana. However, after watching a single video that shows another monkey reacting with alarm to a snake, the monkeys develop a lasting phobia of snakes. This observation could be explained by a preparedness argument (snakes are dangerous animals) or social learning theory (monkeys learn the fear by copying the behaviour of others). However, if the video shows another monkey demonstrating a fear reaction to a flower, no phobia to flowers is created. Monkeys readily learn a fear of snakes, but not a fear of flowers (Nesse and Williams, 1996). Similar findings have been reported for humans (Tomarken *et al*, 1989).

It has been suggested that phobias may result from novel stimuli not found in the Pleistocene era (see Chapter 1, page 1). But new dangers such as guns, drugs, radioactivity, and high-fat meals cause too little fear, not too much (in certain cases, we should be seeking psychiatric help to *increase* our fear). In any case, these evolutionarily novel hazards are far too recent for selection to have established specific fears. It should be noted that some novel situations, such as flying, *do* often cause phobias. However, a fear of flying has probably been prepared by the dangers associated with heights and being trapped in a small, enclosed space (Figure 14.2).

In conclusion, Seligman's preparedness theory provides a very plausible account of the development of some phobias. There is much evidence that the patterning of fears appears to correspond fairly precisely to specific adaptive problems of ancestral environments and displays some evidence of cross-cultural generality (Buss, 1999). Nevertheless, the status of fears and phobias as evolved adaptations remains controversial. It is difficult to see, for example, how this approach could explain certain simple phobias and most social phobias, such as public speaking (see Chapter 15, page 134 for a suggested explanation of social phobias).

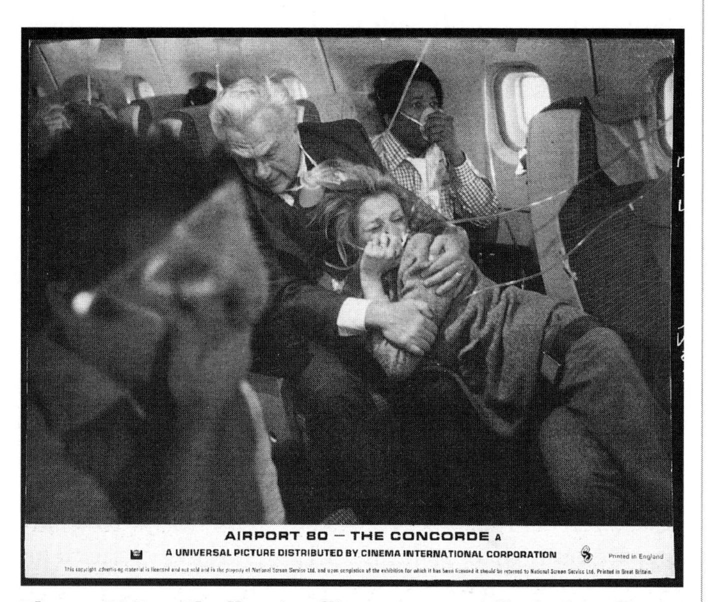

Figure 14.2 Air disaster films may contribute to a fear of flying.

Copyright: Ronald Grant Archive.

OBSESSIVE-COMPULSIVE DISORDER

It has been estimated that one and a half million people in Britain suffer from obsessive-compulsive disorder (OCD). *Obsessions* are involuntary thoughts or images that are recurrent and generally unpleasant. The four most common obsessional characteristics are described in Box 14.4. *Compulsions* are irresistible urges to engage in ritualistic behaviours. These behaviours are aimed at reducing or preventing the discomfort associated with some future undesirable event. Compulsives usually recognise that their behaviours are senseless, yet if prevented from engaging in them, they experience intense anxiety which is reduced when the compulsive ritual is performed (Gross and McIlveen, 1996).

An evolutionary consideration of OCD has lead to much conjecture as to the function of checking and cleaning behaviours. It appears that checking may have arisen in relation to the defence of resources, such as food supplies, territories and mates. When human communities began to store valuable possessions, these had to be protected against thieves. Security arrangements had to be frequently and thoroughly checked to ensure they were effective. A genetic disposition for *excessive* checking (obsessive-compulsive behaviour)

Box 14.4 The four most common obsessional characteristics (Sanavio, 1988)

Obsessional characteristic	Example
Impaired control over mental processes	Repetitive thoughts of death of a loved one
Concern of losing control over motor behaviours	Killing someone
Contamination	Being contaminated by germs
Checking behaviours	Concern over whether a door has been locked

Figure 14.3 Washing and cleaning behaviour may have evolved as a defence against 'contamination'

may have negative fitness benefits in terms of reproductive success. Likewise, those individuals with no genetic disposition for checking may die before reproducing, due to an inability to protect resources. It seems likely that there is an optimal level of checking, and those at the upper end of the continuum are diagnosed as suffering from OCD. (Similarly, there may be an optimal level of jealousy [see Chapter 6, page 51], with those at the top end of the normal distribution being described as suffering from *morbid jealousy*).

Washing and cleaning behaviour may have evolved as a defence against micro-organisms (Figure 14.3). Since pathogens cannot easily be seen or conceptualised, the notion of 'contamination' is common among sufferers of OCD. Those who clean excessively are diagnosed as obsessional, but those who clean too little may suffer increased mortality from infection (Stevens and Price, 1996). In conclusion, it appears that OCD may simply represent an exaggerated form of behaviours which, at a more moderate level, have (or had) significant fitness benefits.

Eating disorders

ANOREXIA NERVOSA

It has been estimated that one in every hundred females in Britain, and one in every thousand males, will suffer from anorexia nervosa. The disorder is characterised by a prolonged refusal to eat adequate amounts of food, resulting in deliberate weight loss (to less than 85% of normal or expected weight). Anorectics also show a decline in their general health, accompanied by physical problems such as low blood pressure, dehydration, and the cessation of menstruation (Gross and McIlveen, 1996). In 5-15% of cases, anorexia nervosa is fatal (Hsu, 1990). Box 14.5 describes a typical case of anorexia nervosa.

Box 14.5 A typical case of anorexia nervosa

Frieda had always been a shy, sensitive girl who gave little cause for concern at home or in school. She was bright and did well academically, although she had few friends. In early adolescence, she had been somewhat overweight and had been teased by her family that she would never get a boyfriend unless she lost some weight. She reacted to this teasing by withdrawing and becoming very touchy. Her parents had to be careful about what they said. If offended, Frieda would throw a tantrum and march off to her room – hardly the behaviour they expected from their bright and sensitive 15-year-old.

Frieda began dieting. Initially her family was pleased, but gradually her parents sensed that all was not well. Meal times became battle times. Frieda hardly ate at all. Under pressure, she would take her meals to her room and later, having said that she had eaten everything, her mother would find food hidden away untouched. When her mother caught her deliberately inducing vomiting after a meal, she insisted they go to the family doctor. He found that Frieda had stopped menstruating a few months earlier. Not fooled by the loose, floppy clothes that Frieda was wearing, he insisted on carrying out a full physical examination. Her emaciated body told him as much as he needed to know, and he arranged for Frieda's immediate hospitalisation.

(adapted from Rosenhan and Seligman, 1984)

Anorectics can generally be categorised into one of two types. The *restricting type* loses weight through constant fasting and engaging in excessive physical activity. The *binge eating/purging type* alternates between periods of fasting and 'binge eating', in which food that is normally avoided (such as that rich in carbohydrates) is

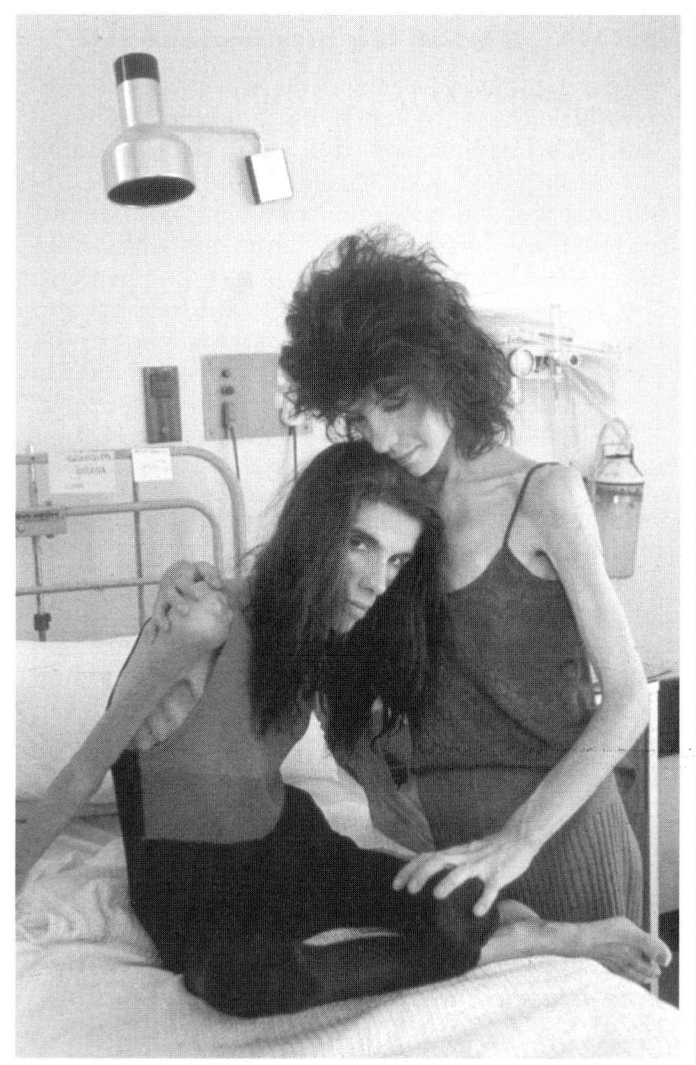

Figure 14.4 The English anorectic twins, Samantha and Michaela Kendall.

Copyright: Rex Features.

Box 14.6 A typical case of bulimia nervosa

Miss A. was a 22-year-old single clerk, who was referred by her doctor for treatment of 'psychiatric problems'. She had a three-year history of uncontrolled overeating. Although she was not originally obese, she disliked her 'square face' and developed a sensitive personality. After failing an examination and being unable to study in further education, she started to relieve her boredom and comfort herself by overeating. Her binges occurred four times per week and lasted one to three hours each. Triggers included feelings of emptiness and critical remarks from others. On average, she secretly consumed 800g of bread and biscuits. Such episodes were followed by abdominal bloating, guilt and dysphoria (inappropriate emotional feelings). There was nausea, but no vomiting. She took excessive laxatives (usually prune juice) to purge and 'calm' herself, restricted food intake and exercised excessively in the next 1-2 days. Her body weight fluctuated by up to 4 kg per week, but her menstrual cycle was normal.

Examination revealed a fully conscious girl who felt helpless over the 'attacks of overeating'. She desired a body weight of 45 kg and disparaged her waistline and square face, which made her 'look like a pig'. She found food dominated her life, and likened her problem to heroin addiction. There was a persistent request for laxatives.

(adapted from Lee *et al*, 1992)

consumed in large quantities. This is often followed by purging, in which anorectics use laxatives or self-induced vomiting to remove the ingested food from the body. Two further characteristics of anorexia nervosa are an intense fear of being overweight and a distorted body image, in which the individual does not appear to recognise the thinness of the body (Figure 14.4).

BULIMIA NERVOSA

Instead of starving, bulimia nervosa is characterised by periodic episodes of binge eating (averaging at least two or three times a week, and sometimes as often as 30 times a week). This is typically followed by purging or strict dieting and vigorous exercise. Box 14.6 describes a case which is typical of bulimia nervosa.

Bulimia nervosa appears to be more common than anorexia nervosa, affecting as much as 5% of the population (95% of which are female). Unlike anorectics, most bulimics maintain a normal body weight. However, they do tend to fluctuate considerably between weight gain and weight loss. Bulimia nervosa is also characterised by damage to the digestive tract, dehydration and depression.

AN EVOLUTIONARY PERSPECTIVE

Certain studies have suggested that both anorexia nervosa and bulimia nervosa may have a genetic basis. There is a tendency for anorexia nervosa to run in families (Strober and Katz, 1987), and there is a reasonably high (55%) concordance rate for identical twins raised in the same environment, compared to only 7% for fraternal twins (Holland *et al*, 1984). Nevertheless, the genetic role is probably not a large one, and probably even less significant in bulimia nervosa. Studies on the incidence of this latter disorder have suggested a concordance rate of only 23% for identical twins and 9% for fraternal twins (Kendler *et al*, 1991).

During the Environment of Evolutionary Adaptedness (EEA), it is unlikely that food supplies would have been constant, regular, and adequate for the daily needs of a hunter-gatherer population throughout the year (Stevens & Price, 1996). Therefore our ancestors probably evolved to conserve resources in their adipose tissues when food was plentiful and to metabolise them sparingly during periods of famine. Binge eating would, therefore, have been adaptive in the EEA, particularly in relation to sweet, fatty or salty foods. These substances were in short supply through nearly all of our evolutionary history. Almost everyone would have been better off with more fat, sugar and salt, and it was consistently adaptive to crave more of them (Box 14.7 shows a plausible relationship between intake and benefit of fat, for both ourselves and our Stone Age ancestors). Similarly, when food supplies were short, it would be advantageous to control appetite and ignore hunger pangs. Today these adaptive strategies are largely obsolete, except among the very poor and those with eating disorders.

Box 14.7 The health implications of an adaptive craving for fatty foods

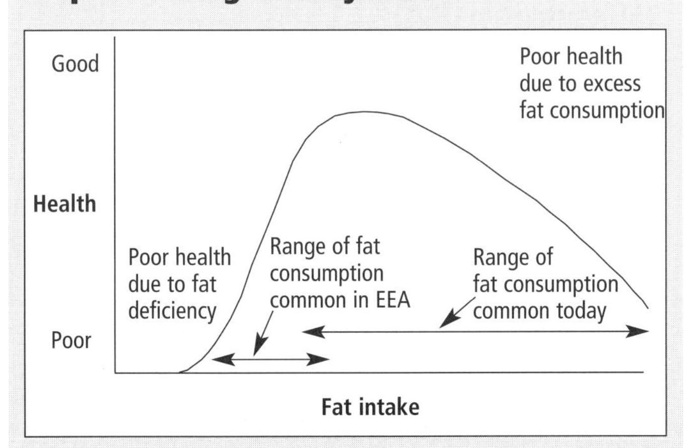

The availability of fatty foods in the EEA was probably significantly less than it is today. A craving for fat was therefore adaptive – the healthiest people were those who ate most fat. We are now in a position to consume much greater quantities of dietary fat, with the result that our craving is now maladaptive (Nesse and Williams, 1996).

An adaption for eating regularly and well when resources are available is particularly important for the female, who requires an adequate diet in order to conceive, nourish the developing fetus and feed the newborn child. This idea is supported by the finding that 79% of female American college students admitted to episodes of 'uncontrolled excessive eating', compared to 49% of males.

A second evolutionary perspective has been suggested by Surbey (1987), who argues that anorexia nervosa may represent a female strategy to suppress reproductive functions at times of environmental stress. This idea is based on the 'reproductive suppression model' of Wasser and Barash (1983), which states that females can optimise their fitness by delaying or suppressing reproduction at times of stress or when they are in poor physical condition. The ability to delay reproduction is adaptive because it enables a female to avoid giving birth when conditions are unfavourable to her offspring's survival. In anorectic females, the pattern of hormone levels remains pre-pubertal in nature, amenorrhoea (cessation of menstruation) occurs, and reproduction is effectively suspended. However, when normal weight is restored, reproductive function appears to be normal and there are no long-term negative effects on fitness.

A final evolutionary explanation of eating disorders relates to social status, and is described in detail in Box 14.8.

Box 14.8 Eating disorders and social status

The symbolic significance of obesity is determined by cultural attitudes and by the availability of food. For example, when food is scarce, obesity symbolises high social status. In certain cultures, 'thinness' equates to a lack of resources and, therefore, low social standing. In these cultures, thin people are generally not desirable.

In societies where food is constantly abundant, low ranking individuals can also acquire the resources required to become fat, and obesity loses its status appeal. As a result, it becomes a symbol of high status to be thin, indicating a great deal of self-control. Those suffering from bulimia nervosa attempt to achieve this high status by cheating. They try to maintain thinness while secretly over-indulging and then purging themselves of their excesses.

It is the high social-desirability of thinness which makes anorexics in particular difficult to treat. The typical anorectic patient is proud of her ability to conquer her appetite and stay thin, and she will naturally resist a therapist's attempt to remove this sense of achievement.

Conclusions

Most phobias appear to be associated with objects or situations which were real sources of danger in the Environment of Evolutionary Adaptedness. Similarly, the checking and cleaning behaviours characteristic of OCD may have been useful for guarding resources or protecting individuals against disease. It appears that there is probably an optimal level of anxiety, which has been shaped by natural selection, and it should only be considered as a mental disorder if it exceeds the requirements of the situation in question.

Modern eating disorders may have been adaptive in the Pleistocene era, when food supplies were very variable. Individuals would benefit from binge eating during times of plenty, and from controlling appetite during lean spells. This is particularly true for females. It has also been suggested that eating disorders may be related to female strategies for controlling reproduction, and to displays of social status.

SUMMARY

- **Anxiety** can be described as **a general feeling of dread or apprehensiveness**, which is typically accompanied by a variety of physiological reactions. **The capacity to experience anxiety is vital to survival**, and it may be thought of as a form of vigilance which enables an animal to be alert and prepared to act.
- While anxiety can be useful, it usually seems excessive and unnecessary. In general, it seems likely that there is an **optimal level of anxiety**, which has been shaped by natural selection. This enables an individual to react rapidly to a dangerous situation, without depleting energy reserves or damaging bodily tissues by constantly being ready for action.
- **A phobia is a type of anxiety disorder in which there is a persistent and unreasonable fear of an object or situation**. The objects or situations forming the basis of most phobias were real sources of danger hundreds or thousands of years ago, and those individuals who were sensitive to these stimuli were favoured by evolution. In other words, we have a **psychological predisposition** or **preparedness** to become phobic about certain (potentially dangerous) stimuli. The preparedness theory provides a very plausible account of the development of some phobias, but it does not seen capable of explaining certain simple phobias and most social phobias.
- **Obsessive-compulsive disorder** (OCD) is one of the most common types of anxiety disorder, characterised by such behaviours as **checking** and **cleaning**. Checking may have arisen in relation to the defence of resources, such as food supplies, territories and mates. Security arrangements for the defence of these resources had to be frequently and thoroughly checked to ensure they were effective. It seems likely that there is an **optimal level of checking**, and those at the upper end of the continuum are diagnosed as suffering from OCD.
- **Washing** and **cleaning** behaviour may have evolved as a defence against micro-organisms. Since pathogens cannot easily be seen or conceptualised, the notion of **contamination** is common among suffers of OCD. Those who clean excessively are diagnosed as obsessional, but those who clean too little may suffer increased mortality from infection.
- The two main types of **eating disorder** are **anorexia nervosa** and **bulimia nervosa**. Anorexia nervosa is characterised by a prolonged refusal to eat adequate amounts of food, resulting in deliberate weight loss. This behaviour is usually accompanied by **a decline in general health**, **an intense fear of being overweight** and **a distorted body image**. Instead of starving, bulimia typically consists of periodic episodes of **binge eating**, followed by **purging** or **strict dieting** and **vigorous exercise**. Unlike anorectics, most bulimics maintain a normal body weight.

- Binge eating would have been adaptive in the EEA, particularly in relation to **sweet**, **fatty** or **salty** foods. These substances were in short supply through nearly all of our evolutionary history, and it was advantageous to crave more of them. Similarly, when food supplies were short, it would be adaptive to control appetite and ignore hunger pangs.
- Anorexia nervosa may represent **a female strategy to suppress reproduction during times of environmental stress**. The ability to delay reproduction is adaptive because it enables a female to avoid giving birth when conditions are unfavourable to her offspring's survival. It has also been suggested that eating disorders are related to asserting the **social status** of an individual.

15

AFFECTIVE DISORDERS AND SCHIZOPHRENIA

Introduction and overview

This final chapter in Part 5 (Darwinian medicine) follows on from Chapter 14 and considers the nature of two further psychological disorders from an evolutionary viewpoint. In this case, I examine Darwinian explanations of affective (mood) disorders and, perhaps the most serious of psychological disturbances, schizophrenia.

Affective disorders

Affective disorders are the most common mental illnesses, with a lifetime risk of around 12% for men and 20% for women. Essentially, they are exaggerations of the universal human capacity to experience sadness and euphoria (Figure 15.1). However, they are classified as illnesses when these moods are judged to be extreme (*depression* or *mania*), incapacitating, chronic, or unresponsive to outside influences.

Figure 15.1 Euphoria – a natural human emotion?

DEPRESSION AND MANIA

The characteristic features of depression are low mood, reduced energy, pessimistic thinking, and disturbances of sleep and appetite. The depressed mood is more intense and sustained than ordinary sadness, and is associated with gloomy thoughts of worthlessness, guilt and hopelessness. Depressed people exhibit a general inhibition of activity and feel unable to cope with the future. Other biological symptoms include constipation, amenorrhoea, and the loss of sexual libido.

Mania may be thought of as a mirror image of depression (see Box 15.1). The mood is elated, self-esteem inflated, and energy levels are high. The future is viewed with extreme optimism, and individuals suffering from mania often maintain a constant flow of confident speech. Sleep patterns are disturbed by hyperactivity (but this is not seen as a problem), and appetite and sexual libido are increased. Eventually, physical exhaustion intervenes and the euphoric mood may be interrupted by bursts of irritability, and sometimes by moments of depression.

15.1 Contrasting features of depression and mania

	Depression	*Mania*
Mood	Depressed	Elated
Self-esteem	Low	High
Energy	Low	High
Social manner	Submissive	Domineering
Speech	Slow	Rapid
Appetite	Reduced	Increased
Sexual libido	Reduced	Increased
View of the future	Pessimistic	Optimistic

THE EVOLUTIONARY PERSPECTIVE

Genetic factors appear to be important determinants of manic-depression, which occurs in one out of every 200 people. For example, Allen (1976) reported a higher concordance rate for this disorder in identical twins (72%) than in non-identical twins (14%). These genes presumably offer some advantage, either in certain circumstances or in combination with certain other genes. Consistent with this idea was Jamison's (1989) study, which reported a disproportionately higher incidence of affective disorders among creative people. For example, among 47 award-winning British writers and artists, 38% had been treated for manic-depression (compared to about 1% in the general population). Interestingly, the genetic co-variance between depression and anxiety (see Chapter 14) is very close to 100% (Kendler *et al*, 1992). This means that the genes associated with anxiety are also responsible for depression. The genes differ in their effects according to environmental factors, such as life events. In general, it seems that anxiety results from the *anticipation* of loss, whereas depression comes from the *experience* of loss (Hamer and Copeland, 1999). The role of genetic and environmental factors in the development of affective disorders is summarised in Box 15.2.

Box 15.2 The role of genetic and environmental factors in the development of affective disorders

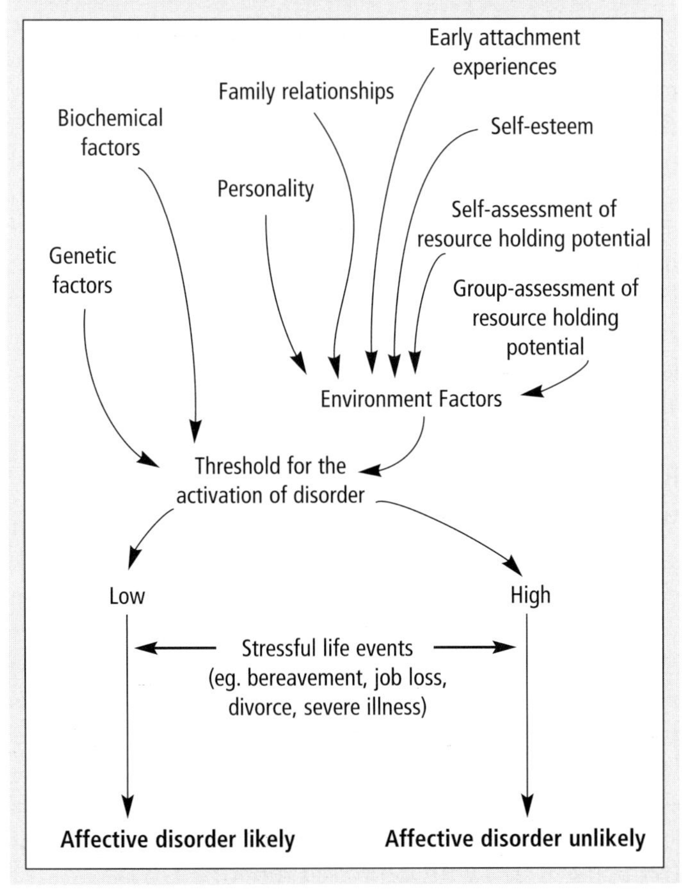

The neurotransmitter *serotonin* appears to play a significant role in affective disorders (Gross and McIlveen, 1996). Interestingly, studies of vervet monkeys have found that the highest-ranking (alpha) male in each group had levels of serotonin that were twice as high as those of other males (Raleigh and McGuire, 1991). When alpha males lose their position, their serotonin levels fall and they begin to show signs of 'depression', such as isolation and lack of appetite. These behaviours can be prevented by administering anti-depressants, such as Prozac, that raise serotonin levels. Furthermore, if the alpha male is removed from a group and Prozac given to another randomly chosen male, that individual always becomes the new alpha male. These studies suggest that the serotonin system may function, at least in part, to mediate status hierarchies and that some low mood may be a normal part of status competition (Nesse and Williams, 1996). Nevertheless, it is unclear as to *how* serotonin achieves its effects in this context, and whether elevated serotonin levels lead to high status, or *vice-versa*.

It has been suggested that there are novel aspects of our modern environment that increase the incidence of affective disorders. This issue is discussed in detail in Box 15.3.

15.3 Depression: a response to modern life?

Some recent evidence suggests that we may actually be in an epidemic of depression. One large-scale study examined data from 39,000 people in five different parts of the world and found that young people are far more likely than their elders to have experienced an episode of major depression (Nesse and Williams, 1996). Furthermore, the rates were higher in societies with greater degrees of economic development. One particular aspect of modern life that may be implicated in the aetiology of depression is *mass communication*.

Mass communication, especially via television and films, effectively makes us one enormous competitive group. In the ancestral environment, a person would have a good chance of being the best at an activity. Even if someone were not the best, the group would probably value their skills. Today, everyone competes with the best in the world. None of us can achieve the fantasy lives we see on television, and our friends and relations may seem inadequate by comparison. Therefore we are dissatisfied with them and even more dissatisfied with ourselves. Studies have shown that after being exposed to photographs or stories about desirable potential mates, people decrease their ratings of commitment to their current partners.

There are several reasons to think that the capacity for sadness is an adaptive trait. Sadness is universal, has relatively consistent characteristics across diverse cultures, and is reliably elicited by certain cues, notably those that indicate a *loss*. The losses in question are often of reproductive resources, such as money, a mate, health, or relatives. It could be that a loss signals maladaptive behaviour. The adaptive nature of sadness may be that it changes our behaviour such that future losses are prevented. What are the features of sadness that increase fitness? First, it may motivate us to stop activities that may be causing losses. Second, it may prevent the usual human tendency of optimism and enable us to assess our lives more objectively (recent studies have found that most of us tend to consistently overestimate our abilities and our effectiveness. This is normally adaptive in that it helps us to succeed in social competition and keeps us pursuing important strategies and relationships even at times when they are not paying off).

Similarly, a manic reaction may be triggered by the perception of a *gain* in reproductive resources (or *resource holding potential, RHP*). Gilbert (1990) would describe this as a gain in *social attention-holding potential (SAHP)*. SAHP refers to the quality and quantity of attention others pay to a particular person. According to this view, humans compete with each other to be attended to, and valued by, others in the group. When group members bestow a lot of quality attention on an individual, that individual rises in status. Ignored individuals are banished to low status. Extreme rises or falls in status may lead to mania or depression respectively. SAHP may also help to explain the *social anxiety* described in Chapter 14 (page 125). Certain social situations, such as public speaking, may have significant consequences for status (SAHP). The greater the potential consequences, the greater we would expect the accompanying social anxiety to be. Social anxiety presumably functions to motivate efforts to avoid status loss (Buss, 1999).

Overall, we can probably say that the human capacity to experiences sadness and joy functions as a punishment and reward system to discourage or encourage behaviour that will decrease or increase the chances of reproductive success. Depression and mania represent the extremes of this system, promoting adjustment to the altered circumstances. Only if these new circumstances are totally accepted will the affective disorder be resolved.

ATTACHMENT THEORY

According to Stevens and Price (1996), 'the formation of a warm, intimate, and lasting relationship with a dependable attachment figure is the basis of human happiness and security'. Threats to this relationship can cause anxiety (see Chapter 14); the loss of an attachment figure may result in depression; and joy comes from the restoration of an attachment thought to have been lost.

Depression as a pathological state is particularly likely to occur in individuals who, because of ineffective attachment in childhood, have failed to develop a mature capacity to deal with loss. Evidence supporting this view comes from studies showing that patients prone to depression commonly recall lack of parental affection (Parker, 1984). However, a problem with attachment theory is that it underestimates the role of individual differences in overcoming childhood trauma. Furthermore, many cases of depression are not readily attributable to the loss of an attachment figure. If there is any loss at all, it may commonly be some other valuable asset, such as a job, status, or financial security.

RANK THEORY

Whereas attachment theory argues that depression is an adaptive response to losing an attachment figure, rank theory proposes that depression is an adaptive response to a loss of status. The function of depression is therefore to promote the acceptance of a subordinate role and the reduction in resources that accompanies this role. This has the dual advantage of preventing further losses, and maintaining the advantages of living in a social group. Gaining rank (thus increasing RHP) is associated with elevated mood, and losing rank (reducing RHP) with depressed mood.

15.4 Self-assessment of resource holding potential (RHP)

Assessment is an algorithmic capacity that enables an individual to weigh-up whether a rival is stronger or weaker, and to produce the appropriate response (fight, submission, or flight). It is on the basis of this algorithm that humans form their internal working models of self in relation to others.

Mental well-being depends on forming estimates of one's own power and attractiveness which are accurate and stable. Good social adjustment results from accurate self-appraisal which indicates that we appear strong and attractive to ourselves and others. An inflated self-perception can lead to mania, a devalued self-perception to depression. Mania or depression are more common in people who are relatively insensitive to external social cues. However, people suffering from manic-depression often have no firm concept of their RHP and are heavily dependent on outside events, such as the comments of others, and internal physiological factors, such as fluctuations in serotonin and noradrenaline levels.

According to rank theory, depression originally arose as a *submitting* component of ritual conflict. Likewise, mania evolved as the *winning* component of such conflict. An important part of this conflict is *self-assessment*, as described in Box 15.4. Both depression and mania reinforce the result of ritual conflict, and establish the respective ranks of the competitors. This idea may also help to explain why the incidence of depression is greater than that of mania; in most human societies there are potentially more losers than winners.

Despite the arguments above, it is still important to point out that both depression and mania are considered maladaptive in modern society. An evolutionary explanation of these disorders is that they are pathological conditions based on the (inappropriate) activation of an evolved means of adaptation (Stevens and Price, 1996). However, non-evolutionary explanations of affective disorders do not have to explain their maladaptive nature, and may be just as valid.

THE INCIDENCE OF AFFECTIVE DISORDERS

Depression occurs when self-assessment of RHP falls to a critically low level. At this point, the individual in question sees themselves as a liability to the social group and is in danger of being rejected. In the ancestral environment this would have very serious consequences, with only a slim chance of survival or reproductive success. However, the act of becoming depressed may elicit nurturance by the rest of the group. This would be expected to enhance perceived RHP, leading to recovery and cohesion of the social group. In modern societies, people can become isolated without risk to their chances of survival. In these circumstances, the isolated depressive cannot gain RHP in the same manner as our ancestors in the EEA. This idea might explain the apparent increase in the incidence of depression over the past century (Seligman, 1975).

Given that rank is more important to the reproductive success of males than females (see Chapter 6), we might expect affective disorders to be more common in men. However, these disorders are twice as common in females (during the reproductive years) than in males. This could be explained relatively simply if depression reduced reproductive success in males more than it did in females. This would result in genes predisposing to depression being selected against more strongly in men, leading to a lower incidence of the disorder.

An alternative explanation of sex-differences in affective disorders is that ritual conflicts between men and women (as opposed to inter-male territorial disputes) often result in *winning* for the male, and *submitting* for the female (leading to depression). This may have been particularly true for the polygynous societies common in the EEA (see Chapter 4). There is some evidence that when women are given equal opportunities, the incidence of depression among them ceases to be greater than for men (Wilhelm and Parker, 1989). However, these findings may reflect a trend towards an increasing incidence of depression for males aged 20-40 years. This could be related to the greater competition men are experiencing from women in the employment market.

A final problem for females is the burden of motherhood (see Chapter 5), including *post-natal depression*. The basis of this condition is unclear, but it is associated with fears of being a bad mother and feeling dominated by the child. This may then invoke a maladaptive submissive routine, which is diagnosed as post-natal depression.

Evolutionary explanations for these gender differences would be strengthened if the differences were universal.

However, cross-cultural comparisons on the incidence of affective disorders are inconclusive in this respect. As mentioned in Chapter 14 (page 123), evolutionary psychology does not have to explain everything. For example, Cochrane (1995) has suggested a number of non-biological explanations of women's greater susceptibility to depression. These include the effects of sexual abuse in childhood (much more common for females), the use of depression as a coping stategy and the acceptance of a traditional female gender role leading to learned helplessness. It seems clear that the evolutionary approach to psychopathology may be useful, but it is only one of many approaches, and an eclectic approach is the best way forward.

SUMMARY

The main factor determining mood is self-assessment of relative RHP (sometimes referred to as social attention holding power, SAHP). Lowered relative RHP will result in negative self-perception and depression; raised relative RHP will invoke joy. According to Stevens and Price (1996), the reason why depression is adaptive is because it promotes adjustment to attachment loss and loss of rank both at the same time.

Schizophrenia

Schizophrenia refers to a *splitting* of the various functions of the mind (such as thoughts and feelings), leading to the personality losing its unity (Gross and McIlveen, 1996). The major symptoms of schizophrenia are thought disturbances, hallucinations and delusions. These symptoms, unlike those of anxiety, are not part of normal functioning. Schizophrenia disrupts the perceptual-cognitive-emotional-motivational system, causing the bizarre and maladaptive behaviour associated with this disorder (see Box 15.5). These factors may make it more difficult to produce a convincing explanation of schizophrenia in evolutionary terms.

THE ROLE OF GENETICS

The likelihood of a person developing schizophrenia is about 1 in 100. However, if a person has one schizophrenic parent, this increases to 1 in 5. If both parents are schizophrenic, the likelihood of developing the disorder becomes 1 in 2 or 1 in 3. This suggests that genetic factors play a significant role in the aetiology of schizophrenia.

15.5 A case study of paranoid schizophrenia

Esther is an unmarried woman who lives with her elderly mother. She is 31 years-old and is afraid to leave the house. This fear is based on the belief that the outside world is filled with radio waves that will insert evil thoughts into her head. The windows in her room are covered with aluminium foil to 'deflect the radio waves'. Esther often hears voices related to the radio signals. For example, one comment appeared to come from an angry old man saying, 'We're going to get these thoughts into your head. Give up the fight!'.

Esther is considered to have paranoid schizophrenia as her life has become totally constrained by her irrational beliefs that she is being persecuted and infiltrated by external forces beyond her control (Halgin and Whitbourne, 1993).

A large number of psychological studies have shown that the concordance rate for schizophrenia is consistently higher for identical than for non-identical twins. This is also true for twins that have been reared apart, supporting the idea of a genetic basis to the disorder (Figure 15.2). Further support comes from studies comparing the incidence of schizophrenia in the biological and adoptive parents of adopted children with the disorder (or the incidence in adopted children of schizophrenic and non-schizophrenic biological mothers). Heston (1966) found that 10% of adopted

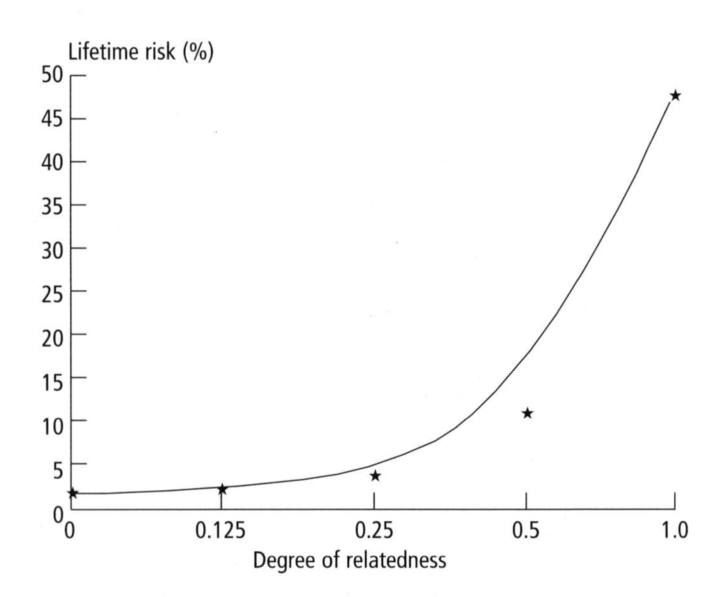

Figure 15.2 The lifetime risk (%) for schizophrenia is closely related to the degree of relatedness to a person suffering from the condition

15.6 The diathesis-stress model for schizophrenia

PREDISPOSING FACTORS	+ *TRIGGER* ⟶	*OUTCOME*
Genetic and/or biochemical predisposition and/or an increased sensitivity to psychosocial factors, i.e. biological vulnerability (**diathesis**)	Environmental **stress**, such as family problems, major life events and/or traumatic experiences	Schizophrenia

children with schizophrenic biological mothers were diagnosed with the disorder, compared to none of the adopted children with non-schizophrenic biological mothers.

However, environmental factors also play a role in the development of schizophrenia, as shown in Box 15.6.

THE EVOLUTIONARY PERSPECTIVE

Schizophrenia occurs in 1% of the general population, and there appears to be strong support for the involvement of genetic factors in the development of the disorder. However, there is also evidence that schizophrenia significantly decreases reproductive success, especially in men. How can we account for the high incidence of genes which appear to reduce fitness?

The most likely explanation is that these genes are advantageous in combination with other genes, or in certain environments, in a similar manner to the gene for sickle-cell anaemia described in Chapter 13 (page 118). Alternatively, the genes that predispose to schizophrenia may have other advantageous effects, even though a small proportion of people with these genes will develop the disease (see Box 15.7). It is not clear what these advantages may be, although many suggestions have been made, such as the positive effect of being suspicious. Although a little vague, this idea is supported by evidence of high levels of accomplishment in relatives of schizophrenics who are not affected by the disease (Nesse and Williams, 1996).

In their 'group-splitting hypothesis', Stevens and Price (1996) argue that, where personal details exist, many charismatic leaders throughout history would have been diagnosed schizophrenic. This has been coupled with social conditions causing the rise of disaffected groups, who would be very susceptible to the ideas of charismatic leaders. For example, Adolf Hitler came to power in Germany on the back of social fragmentation and internal hostility following the defeat in the First World War, high inflation and unemployment, poverty and a feeling of isolation from the rest of Europe (Figure 15.3). These conditions lead to the construction of a new group (the Nazis), as similar conditions had throughout history. According to Stevens and Price, this process may have been vital in producing what we now see as modern society. Therefore, schizophrenia may be associated with leadership (and so greater RHP), as well as being important in the formation of our social world.

Schizophrenic symptoms are often first identified at about the time when young people are attempting to achieve independence and are concerned with

15.7 Schizophrenia: adaptation or disease?

It seems likely that the genetic material associated with schizophrenia is present in a much larger proportion of the population than the 1% who express the disease. How is it that the genetic predisposition which results in schizophrenia in some people can result in adaptive traits in others?

In a sense, the genetic predisposition for schizophrenia may be similar to that responsible for sickle-cell anaemia, which enhances the well-being of carriers by protecting them from malaria, while impairing those with greater genetic loading by afflicting them with anaemia. Therefore, schizophrenia is probably inherited in a graded form (see below). Similarly, other adaptive traits in humans, such as anxiety, depression and jealousy, may become maladaptive in certain individuals.

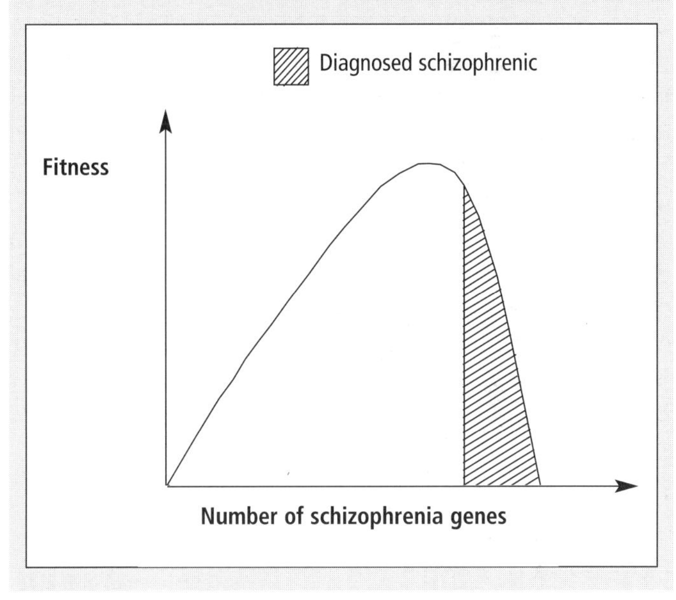

Figure 15.3 Adolf Hitler: a charismatic schizophrenic?

acceptance by, and membership of, their peer group. During the EEA, the difference between family and social environments was less great than it is now. Young people in the modern world who combine a predisposition to schizophrenia with low self-esteem, and a lack of emotional support, are more likely to develop the disorder. This idea is supported by the observation of a slightly lower incidence of schizophrenia in the pre-industrial societies of today. Therefore *rank* and *social context* are important factors in the aetiology of schizophrenia, just as they are for affective disorders (see page 132). Nevertheless, it is difficult to see how schizophrenia promotes adjustment to low RHP in the way that depression might. This is despite the assertion of Laing (1965) that schizophrenia represents 'a sane response to an insane world'.

SUMMARY

Schizophrenic behaviour is, for the most part, maladaptive. However, the disorder is universal and has a significant genetic component. The most likely evolutionary explanation for schizophrenia is that genes predisposing to the condition are advantageous. This will be true unless genetic loading is particularly high and/or the social context is inappropriate. Nevertheless, evolutionary explanations of schizophrenia are not entirely convincing.

Conclusions

This chapter has considered the nature of affective (mood) disorders and schizophrenia from an evolutionary viewpoint. The main factors governing mood are the gain or loss of attachment figures and social rank (measured as *resource holding potential*, RHP). Schizophrenia is more difficult to account for in evolutionary terms. However, its strong genetic basis suggests that genes predisposing to the disorder are advantageous in limited quantities, or in certain social environments.

SUMMARY

- **Affective disorders** are the most common mental illnesses. Essentially, they are exaggerations of the universal human capacity to experience sadness and euphoria.They are classified as illnesses when these moods are judged to be extreme (**depression** or **mania**), incapacitating, chronic, or unresponsive to outside influences.
- **Depression** is characterised by **low mood, reduced energy, pessimistic thinking,** and **disturbances of sleep and appetite**. **Mania** may be thought of as a mirror image of depression. **Mood is elated, self-esteem inflated** and **energy levels are high**.
- **Genetic factors** appear to be important determinants of manic-depression. These genes presumably offer some advantage, either in certain circumstances or in combination with certain other genes. The neurotransmitter **serotonin** also appears to play a significant role in affective disorders. Studies with vervet monkeys suggest that the serotonin system may function, at least in part, to mediate **status hierarchies** and that **some low mood may be a normal part of status competition**.
- There are many reasons to think that the capacity for sadness is an adaptive trait. Sadness is universal, has relatively consistent characteristics across diverse cultures, and is reliably elicited by certain

cues, notably those that indicate a **loss**. The losses in question are often of **reproductive resources**. The adaptive nature of sadness may be that it changes our behaviour such that future losses are prevented.

- Depression as a pathological state is particularly likely to occur in individuals who, because of **ineffective attachment** in childhood, have failed to develop a mature capacity to deal with loss. However, there are two problems with attachment theory: it underestimates the role of individual differences in overcoming childhood trauma; and many cases of the disorder are not readily attributable to the loss of an attachment figure.
- **Rank theory** proposes that depression is **an adaptive response to a loss of status**. Gaining rank (increasing **resource holding potential, RHP**) is associated with elevated mood, and losing rank (reducing RHP) with depressed mood. However, affective disorders are still maladaptive in modern society. Depression and mania are **pathological conditions based on the (inappropriate) activation of an evolved means of adaptation**.
- **Schizophrenia** refers to a splitting of the various functions of the mind, leading to the personality losing its unity. The major symptoms of schizophrenia are **thought disturbances, hallucinations** and **delusions**. These symptoms, unlike those of anxiety, are not part of normal functioning. This makes it more difficult to produce a convincing explanation of schizophrenia in evolutionary terms.
- There appears to be strong support for the involvement of genetic factors in the development of schizophrenia. These genes are probably advantageous in combination with certain other genes, or in certain environments. Alternatively, the genes that predispose to schizophrenia may have other directly advantageous affects, even though a small proportion of people with these genes will develop the disease.
- **Rank** and **social context** are important factors in the aetiology of schizophrenia, just as they are for affective disorders. Nevertheless, it is difficult to see how schizophrenia promotes adjustment to low RHP in the way that depression might. This is despite the assertion that schizophrenia represents **'a sane response to an insane world'**.

REFERENCES

ALCOCK, J. (1993) *Animal behaviour* (5th edition). Sunderland, MA: Sinauer.

ALEXANDER, R.D. (1974) The evolution of social behaviour. *Annual Review of Ecology and Systematics,* 5, 325-383.

ALEXANDER, R.D. (1975) The search for a general theory of behaviour. *Behavioural Science*, 20, 77-100.

ALLEN, M. (1976) Twin studies of affective illness. *Archives of General Psychiatry*, 33, 1476-1478.

ANDERSON, J.R. (1995) *Learning and Memory: An Integrated Approach.* Chichester: Wiley.

ARCHER, J. (1995) Evolutionary social psychology. In: M. Hewstone, W. Stroebe & G. Stephenson (eds) *Introduction to social psychology (2nd edition).* Oxford: Blackwell.

BADCOCK, C. (1994) *PsychoDarwinism.* London: HarperCollins.

BAKER, R.R. & BELLIS, M.A. (1989) Number of sperm in human ejaculates varies in accordance with sperm competition theory. *Animal Behaviour*, 37, 867-869.

BAKER, R.R. & BELLIS, M.A. (1995) *Human sperm competition.* London: Chapman & Hall.

BANDURA, A. (1974) Behaviour theory and models of man. *American Psychologist,* 29, 859-869.

BANDURA, A. (1977) Self-efficacy: Toward a unifying theory of behaviour change. *Psychological Review*, 84, 191-215.

BANDURA, A., ROSS, D. & ROSS, S.A. (1963) Imitation of film-mediated aggressive models. *Journal of Abnormal and Social Psychology,* 66, 3-11.

BARKER, R., DEMBO, T. & LEWIN, K. (1941) Frustration and regression: An experiment with young children. *University of Iowa Studies in Child Welfare,* 18, 1-314.

BARKOW, J. (1989) *Darwin, sex and status: biological approaches to mind and culture.* Toronto: Toronto University Press.

BARKOW, J. (1992) *The adapted mind.* Oxford: Oxford University Press.

BARON, R.A.& BYRNE, D.S. (1994) *Social Psychology: Understanding Human Interaction* (7th edition). London: Allyn & Bacon.

BATESON, P.P.G. (1973) Internal influences on early learning in birds. In: R.A. Hinde & J. Stevenson-Hinde (eds.) *Constraints on learning.* London: Academic Press.

BATESON, P.P.G. (1979) How do sensitive periods arise and what are they for? *Animal Behaviour,* 27, 470-486.

BAYLIS, J.R. (1981) The evolution of parental care in fishes, with reference to Darwin's rule of male sexual selection. *Environmental Fish Biology*, 6, 223-251.

BECK-SAGUE, C., DOOLEY, S.W., HUTTON, M.D., OTTEN, J., BREEDEN, A., CRAWFORD, J.T., PITCHENIK, A.E., WOODLEY, C., CAUTHEN, G. & JARVIS, W.R. (1992) Hospital outbreak of multidrug-resistant *Mycobacterium tuberculosis* infections. Factors in transmission to staff and HIV-infected patients. *JAMA*, 268, 1280-1286.

BENZER, S. (1973) Genetic dissection of behaviour. *Scientific American*, 229, 24-37.

BERKOWITZ, L. (1968) Impulse, aggression and the gun. *Psychology Today,* September, 18-22.

BERKOWITZ, L. (1989) The frustration-aggression hypothesis: an examination and reformation. *Psychological Bulletin,* 106, 59-73.

BERKOWITZ, L. (1993) *Aggression: Its Causes, Consequences and Control.* New York: McGraw-Hill.

BERKOWITZ, L. & LEPAGE, A. (1967) Weapons as aggression-eliciting stimuli. *Journal of Personality and Social Psychology,* 7, 202-207.

BERREMAN, G.D. (1962) Pahari polyandry: a comparison. *American Anthropologist*, 64, 60-75.

BETZIG, L. (1986) *Despotism and differential reproduction: A Darwinian view of history.* New York: Aldine de Gruyter.

BEVER, T.G., CARRITHERS, C., COWART, W. & TOWNSEND, D.J. (1989) Language processing and familial handedness. In: A.M. Galaburda (ed.) *From reading to neurons.* Cambridge, MA: MIT Press.

BINET, A. & SIMON, T.H. (1915) *Method of measuring the development of the intelligence of young children.* Chicago: Chicago Medical Book Company.

BLACKMORE, S. (1999) *The meme machine.* Oxford: Oxford University Press.

BOESCH, C. (1991) Teaching among wild chimpanzees. *Animal Behaviour*, 41, 530-532.

BOESCH, C. & BOESCH, H. (1984) Mental map in wild chimpanzees: an analysis of hammer transports for nut cracking. *Primates*, 25, 160-170.

BOLLES, R.C. (1980) Ethological learning theory. In G.M. Gazda & R.J. Corsini (Eds) *Theories of Learning: A Comparative Approach.* Itaska, IL: Free Press.

BOUCHARD, T.J. & McGUE, M. (1981) Familial studies of intelligence: A review. *Science*, 212, 1055-1059.

BOUCHARD, T.J. & SEGAL, N.L. (1988) Heredity, environment and IQ. In: Instructor's Resource Manual to accompany G. Lindzay, R. Thompson & B. Spring *Psychology* (3rd edition). New York: Worth Publishers.

BOWLBY, J. (1951) *Maternal Care and Mental Health.* Geneva: World Health Organisation.

BOYD, R. & RICHERSON, P. (1985) *Culture and the evolutionary process*. Chicago: University of Chicago Press.

BRESNAN, J. & KAPLAN, R.M. (1982) Grammars as mental representations of language. In: J. Bresnan (ed.) *The mental representation of grammatical relations*. Cambridge, MA: MIT Press.

BROWN, R. (1965) *Social Psychology.* New York: The Free Press.

BROWN, R., CAZDEN, C.B. & BELLUGI, U. (1969) The child's grammar from one to three. In J.P. Hill (Ed.) *Minnesota Symposium on Child Psychology,* Volume 2. Minneapolis: University of Minnesota Press.

BROWN , R. (1986) *Social psychology: The second edition.* New York: The Free Press.

BUGOS, P.E. & McCARTHY, L.M. (1984) Ayoreo infanticide: A case study. In: G. Hausfater & S.B. Hrdy (eds.) *Infanticide: Comparative and evolutionary perspectives.* New York: Aldine de Gruyter.

BURNSTEIN, E., CRANDALL, C. & KITAYAMA, S. (1994) Some neo-Darwin decision rules for altruism: weighing clues for inclusive fitness as a function of the biological importance of the decision. *Journal of Personality and Social Psychology*, 67, 773-789.

BUSS, D.M. (1987) Sex differences in human mate selection criteria: An evolutionary perspective. In C. Crawford, D. Krebs & M. Smith (Eds.). *Sociobiology and psychology: Ideas, issues and applications*. Hillside, NJ: Erlbaum.

BUSS, D.M. (1989) Sex differences in human mate preferences. *Behavioural and Brain Sciences*, 12, 1-49.

BUSS, D.M. (1995) Evolutionary psychology: A new paradigm for psychological science. *Psychological Inquiry*, 6, 1-49.

BUSS, D.M. (1999) *Evolutionary psychology*. Boston, MA: Allyn & Bacon.

BUSS, D.M. & DEDDEN, L.A. (1990) Derogation of competitors. *Journal of Social and Personal Relationships*, 7, 395-422.

BUSS, D.M., LARSEN, R., WESTEN, D. & SEMMELROTH, J. (1992) Sex differences in jealousy: Evolution, physiology and psychology. *Psychological Science*, 3, 251-255.

BYRNE, R.W. (1995) *The thinking ape*. Oxford: Oxford University Press.

BYRNE, R.W. & WHITEN, A. (1988) *Machiavellian intelligence: Social expertise and the evolution of intellect in monkeys, apes and humans*. Oxford: Clarendon Press.

CADE, W.H. (1981) Alternative mating strategies: Genetic differences in crickets. *Science*, 212, 563-564.

CARLSON, N.R. (1988) *Foundations of physiological psychology*. Boston: Allyn & Bacon.

CARROL, D,W. (1986) *Psychology of Language.* Monterey, CA: Brooks/Cole Publishing Co.

CARTWRIGHT, J. (2000) *Evolution and human behaviour.* London: Macmillan.

CAVALLI-SFORZA, L.L. & FELDMAN, M.W. (1981) *Cultural transmission and evolution: A quantitative approach*. Princeton, NJ: Princeton University Press.

CHOMSKY, N. (1957) *Syntactic Structures.* The Hague: Mouton.

CHOMSKY, N. (1959) A review of B.F. Skinner's "Verbal behaviour". *Language*, 35, 26-58.

CHOMSKY, N. (1975) *Reflections on language*. New York: Pantheon.

CLAMP, A.G. (1998) Predator-prey relationships. *Biological Sciences Review*, 10 (5), 31-35.

CLAMP, A.G. & RUSSELL, J. (1998) *Comparative psychology*. London: Hodder & Stoughton.

CLARKE-STEWART, A. (1973) Interactions between mothers and their young children: Characteristics and consequences. *Monographs for the Society of Research in Child Development*, 38.

CLUTTON-BROCK, T.H., HIRAIWA-HASEGAWA, M. & ROBERTSON, A. (1989) Mate choice on fallow deer leks. *Nature*, 340, 463-465.

COCHRANE, R. (1995) Women and depression. *Psychology Review*, 2, 20-24.

CONWAY, D.J. & McBRIDE, J.S. (1991) Genetic evidence for the importance of interrupted feeding by mosquitos in the transmission of malaria. *Transactions of The Royal Society of Tropical Medicine and Hygiene*.

COSMIDES, L. (1989) The logic of social exchange: Has natural selection shaped how humans reason? Studies with the Wason selection task. *Cognition*, 31, 187-276.

COSMIDES, L. & TOOBY, J. (1995) Cognitive adaptations for social exchange. In J. Barkow, L. Cosmides & J. Tooby (Eds.) *The adapted mind*. New York: Oxford University Press.

CRICK, F. (1994) *The Astonishing Hypothesis: The Scientific Search for the Soul.* London: Simon & Schuster.

CRONIN, H. (1991) *The ant and the peacock*. Cambridge: Cambridge University Press.

CROOK, J.H. (1972) Sexual selection, dimorphism and social organisation in the primates. In B. Campbell (Ed.) *Sexual selection and the descent of man*, 1871-1971. Chicago: Aldine.

CROOK, J.H. (1980) *The evolution of human consciousness.* Oxford: Clarendon Press.

DALY, M. & WILSON, M. (1978) *Sex, evolution and behaviour*. North Scituate, MA: Duxbury Press.

DALY, M. & WILSON, M. (1988) *Homicide*. New York: Aldine de Gruyter.
DALY, M. & WILSON, M. (1994) Evolutionary psychology of male violence. In: J. Archer (ed.) *Male violence*. London: Routledge.
DALY, M. & WILSON, M. (1997) Kinship: the conceptual hole in psychological studies of social cognition and close relationships. In: J.A. Simpson & D.T. Kenrick (eds.) *Evolutionary social psychology*. Mahwah, NJ: Erlbaum.
DALY, M., SINGH, L.S. & WILSON, M. (1993) Children fathered by previous fathers: A risk factor for violence against women. *Canadian Journal of Public Health*, 84, 209-210.
DARWIN, C. (1859) *The origin of species by means of natural selection*. London: Penguin.
DARWIN, C. (1871) *The descent of man and selection in relation to sex*. London: John Murray.
DARWIN, C. (1872) *The expression of emotion in man and animals*. London: John Murray.
DARWIN, C. (1877) A biographical sketch of an infant. *Mind*, 2, 285-294.
DAVIES, R. (1995) Selfish altruism. *Psychology Review*, 1, 2-9
DAVIES, R. (1996) *Evolutionary determinants of behaviour*. In M. Cardwell, L. Clark & C. Meldrum (Eds.) *Psychology for A level*. London: HarperCollins.
DAVISON, G. & NEALE, J. (1990) *Abnormal Psychology* (5th edition). New York: Wiley.
DAWKINS, R. (1976) *The selfish gene*. Oxford: OUP.
DAWKINS, R. (1982) *The extended phenotype*. Oxford: W.H. Freeman.
DAWKINS, R. (1989) *The selfish gene* (2nd edition). Oxford: Oxford University Press.
DENNETT, D.C. (1996) *Darwin's dangerous idea: Evolution and the meanings of life*. London: Penguin.
DERSHOWITZ, A.M. (1994) *The abuse excuse*. Boston, MA: Little, Brown.
DIAMOND, J. (1991) *The rise and fall of the third chimpanzee*. London: Vintage.
DICKINSON, A. (1980) *Contemporary animal learning theory*. Cambridge: Cambridge University Press.
DOLLARD, J., DOOB, L.W., MOWRER, O.H. & SEARS, R.R. (1939) *Frustration and aggression*. New Haven, CT: Harvard University Press.
DUDAI, Y. (1989) *The neurobiology of memory*. Oxford: Oxford University Press.
DUNBAR, R. (1988) *Primate social systems*. London: Croom Helm.
DUNBAR, R. (1995) Are you lonesome tonight? *New Scientist*, 145, 26-31.
DUPONT, H.L. & HORNICK, R.B. (1973) Adverse effect of Lomotil therapy in shigellosis. *Journal of the American Medical Association*, 226, 1525-1528.
DURHAM, W. (1991) *Coevolution: Genes, culture and human diversity*. Stanford: Stanford University Press.
EBERHARD, W.G. (1985) *Sexual selection and animal genitalia*. Cambridge, MA: Harvard University Press.
EBERHARD, W.G. (1991) Copulatory courtship and cryptic female choice in insects. *Biological Reviews*, 66, 1-31.
EBERHARDT, K.E.W., THIMM, B.N. SPRING, A. & MASKOS, W.R. (1992) Dose dependent rate of nosocomial pulmonary infection in mechanically ventilated patients with brain oedema receiving barbiturates: A prospective case study. *Infection*, 20, 12-18.
EDLEY, N. & WETHERELL, M. (995) *Men in Perspective: Practice, Power and Identity*. Hemel Hempstead: Harvester Wheatsheaf.
EDLIN, B.R., TOKARS, J.I., GRIECO, M.H., CRAWFORD, J.T., WILLIAMS, J., SORDILLO, E.M., ONG, K.R., KILBURN, J.O., DOOLEY, S.W., CASTRO, K.G., JARVIS, W.R. & HOLMBERG, S.D. (1992) An outbreak of multidrug-resistant tuberculosis among hospitalised patients with the acquired immunodeficiency syndrome. *New England Journal of Medicine*, 326, 1514-1521.
EGELAND, J., GE RHARD, D., PAULS, D., SUSSEX, J., KIDD, K., ALLEN, C., HOSTETTER, A. & HOUSEMAN, D. (1987) Bipolar affective disorder linked to DNA markers on chromosome 11. *Nature*, 325, 783-787.
EIMAS, P.D. (1975) Speech perception in early infancy. In L.B. Cohen and P. Salapatek (Eds) *Infant Perception: From Sensation to Cognition*, Volume 2. New York: Academic Press.
ETCOFF, N.L. (1986) The neuropsychology of emotional expression. In: G. Goldstein & R.E. Taylor (eds.) *Advances in clinical neuropsychology*. New York: Plenum.
EWALD, P.W. (1994) *The Evolution of Infectious Diseases*. New York: Oxford University Press.
EYSENCK, M.W. & KEANE, M.J. (1995) *Cognitive Psychology: A Student's Handbook* (3rd edition). Hove: Erlbaum.
FRANEY, D.F. (1986) *The titler*. Cambridge: Cambridge University Press.
FREUD, S. (1920) *Beyond the Pleasure Principle*. Pelican Freud Library (11). Harmondsworth; Penguin.
GAGNE, E.D. (1985) *The Cognitive Psychology of School Learning*. Boston: Little, Brown and Company.
GARCIA, J. & KOELLING, R.A. (1966) Relation of cue to consequence in avoidance learning. *Psychonomic Science*, 4, 123-124.
GESCHWIND, N. (1979) *The Brain*. San Francisco: Freeman.
GILBERT, P. (1990) Changes: Rank, status and mood. In S. Fischer & C.L. Cooper (Eds.) *On the move: The psychology of change and transition*. New York: John Wiley.

GOOODALL, J. (1965) Chimpanzees of the Gombe Stream Reserve. In I. DeVore (Ed.) *Primate Behavior: Field Studies of Monkeys and Apes.* New York: Holt, Rinehart & Winston.
GOPNICK, M., DALAKIS, J., FUKUDA, S.E., FUKUDA, S. & KEHAYRA, E. (1996) Genetic language impairment: Unruly grammars. *Proceedings of the British Academy*, 88, 223-249.
GORBACH, S.L., BANWELL, J.G., JACOBS, B., CHATTERJEE, B.D., MITRA, R., BRIGHAM, K.L. & NEOGY, K.N. (1970) Intestinal microflora in Asiatic cholera I. "Rice-water" stool. *Journal of Infectious Disease*, 121, 32.
GOULD, S.J. (1990) *An urchin in the storm.* London: Penguin.
GOULD, S.J. & LEWONTIN, R.C. (1979) The spandrels of San Marco and the Panglossian paradigm: A critique of the adaptionist programme. *Proceedings of The Royal Society of London*, 205, 581-598.
GRIER, J.W. & BURK, T. (1992) *Biology of animal behaviour.* Dubuque, IA: WCB Communications.
GROSS, R.D. (1996) *Psychology: The Science of Mind and Behaviour* (3rd edition). London: Hodder & Stoughton.
GROSS, R.D. & McILVEEN, R.J. (1996) *Abnormal psychology.* London: Hodder & Stoughton.
GROSS, R. & McILVEEN, R. (1997) *Cognitive Psychology.* London: Hodder & Stoughton.
GROSS, R.D. & McILVEEN, R.J. (1998) *Social psychology.* London: Hodder & Stoughton.
HALDANE, J.B.S. (1927) A mathematical theory of natural and artificial selection. Part V. Selection and mutation. *Proceedings of the Cambridge Philosophical Society*, 23, 838-844.
HAMER, D. & COPELAND, P. (1999) *Living with our genes.* London: Macmillan.
HAMILTON, W.D. (1964) The genetical evolution of social behaviour I, II. *Journal of Theoretical Biology*, 7, 1-52.
HAMILTON, W.D. (1975) Innate social aptitudes of man: An approach from evolutionary genetics. In: R. Fox (ed.) *Biosocial anthropology.* London: Malaby Press.
HAMPSON, P.J. & MORRIS, P.E. (1996) *Understanding Cognition.* Oxford: Blackwell.
HARLOW, H.F. (1949) Formation of learning sets. *Psychological Review*, 56, 51-65.
HART, B.L. (1990) Behavioural defences against parasites. *Neuroscience and Biobehavioural Reviews,* 14, 273-294.
HAYES, N. (1994) *Principles of Comparative Psychology.* Hove: Lawrence Erlbaum Associates.
HESTON, L.L. (1966) Psychiatric disorders in foster-home-reared children of schizophrenic mothers. *British Journal of Psychiatry,* 122, 819-825.
HILL, A.R., PREMKUMAR, S., BRUSTEIN, S., VAIDYA, K., POWELL, S. LI, P.W. & SUSTER, B. (1991) Disseminated tuberculosis in the acquired immunodeficiency syndrome era. *American Review of Respiratory Diseases*, 144, 1164-1170.
HINDE, R.A. (1974) *Biological Bases of Human Social Behaviour.* New York: McGraw-Hill.
HINDE, R. (1982) *Ethology*. Oxford: Oxford University Press.
HIRSCHHORN, N. & GREENOUGH, W.B.III (1991) Progress in oral rehydration therapy. *Scientific American*, 264 (5), 50-56.
HOLLAND, A.J., HALL, A., MURRAY, R., RUSSELL, G.F.M. & CRISP, A.H. (1984) Anorexia nervosa: A study of 34 twin pairs and one set of triplets. *British Journal of Psychiatry,* 145, 414-418.
HRDY, S.B. (1981) *The woman that never evolved.* Cambridge, MA: Harvard University Press.
HRDY, S.B. (1990) Sex bias in nature and in history: A late 1980s examination of the 'Biological Origins' argument. *Yearbook of Physical Anthropology,* 33, 25-37.
HRDY, S.B. (1999) *Mother nature.* London: Chatto & Windus.
HSU, L.K. (1990) *Eating Disorders.* New York: Guilford.
HUMPHREY, N.K. (1976) The social function of the intellect. In P. Bateson & R. Hinde (Eds.) *Growing points in ethology.* Cambridge: Cambridge University Press.
HUNT, L. (1995) Why a fear of spiders is all in the genes. *The Independent*, 20 December, 17.
JAFFE, Y. & YINON, Y. (1983) Collective aggression: the group-individual paradigm in the study of collective antisocial behaviour. In H.H. Blumberg, A.P. Hare, V. Kent & M. Davies (eds.) *Small groups and social interaction.* New York: Wiley.
JAHODA, G. (1978) Cross-cultural perspectives. In H. Tajfel & C. Fraser (Eds) *Introducing Social Psychology.* Harmondsworth: Penguin.
JAMES, W. (1892) *Psychology: Briefer course.* New York: Henry Holt.
JAMISON, K. (1989) Mood disorders and patterns of creativity in British writers and artists. *Psychiatry*, 52, 125-134.
JONES, S. (1994) *The Language of the Genes.* London: Flamingo.
KADUSHIN, A. & SEIDL, F.W. (1971) Adoption failure: A social work postmortem. *Social Work*, 16, 32-38.
KAPLAN, H. & HILL, K. (1985) Hunting ability and reproductive success among male Ache foragers. *Current Anthropology*, 26, 131-133.
KENDLER, K.S., McLEAN, C., NEALE, M., KESSLER, R., HEATH, A. & EAVES, L. (1991) The genetic epidemiology of bulimia nervosa. *American Journal of Psychiatry,* 148, 1627-1637.
KENDLER, K.S., NEALE, M.C., KESSLER, R.C., HEATH, A.C. & EAVES, L.J. (1992) Major depression and generalised anxiety disorder: Same genes (partly)

different environments? *Archives of General Psychiatry*, 49, 716-722.

KETTLEWELL, H.B.D. (1955) Selection experiments on industrial melanism in the Lepidoptera. *Heredity*, 9, 323-342.

KIRN, J.R. & DEVOOGD, T.J. (1989) The genesis and death of vocal control neurons during sexual differentiation in the zebra finch. *Journal of Neuroscience*, 9, 3176-3187.

KLUGER, M.J. (1990) The adaptive value of fever. In P.A. Mackowiac (Ed.) *Fever: Basic Measurement and Management*. New York: Raven Press.

KOESTLER, A. (1970) *The ghost in the machine*. London: Pan books.

KULIK, J.A. & BROWN, R. (1979) Frustration, attribution of blame and aggression. *Journal of Experimental Social Psychology*, 15, 183-194.

LAING, R.D. (1965) *The divided self.* London: Penguin.

LALUMIERE, M.L., CHAMBERS, L.J., QUINSEY, V.L. & SET, M.C. (1996) A test of the mate deprivation hypothesis of sexual coercion. *Ethology & Sociobiology*, 17, 299-318.

LEA, S.E.G. (1984) *Instinct, Environment and Behaviour.* London: Methuen.

LeBON, G. (1897) *The Crowd: A study of the Popular Mind.* London: Unwin.

LEE, S., HSU, L.K.G. & WING, Y.K. (1992) Bulimia nervosa in Hong Kong Chinese patients. *British Journal of Psychiatry*, 161, 545-551.

LESLIE, A.M. (1987) Pretence and representation: The origins of 'theory of mind'. *Psychological Review*, 94, 412-426.

LEWIS, R.A. (1975) Social influences on marital choice. In S.E. Dragastin & G.H. Elder (Eds) *Adolescence in the Life Cycle.* New York: John Wiley.

LIGHTCAP, J., KURLAND, J. & BURGESS, R. (1982) Child abuse: A test of some predictions from evolutionary theory. *Ethology & Sociobiology*, 3, 61-67.

LORENZ, K. (1935) The companion in the bird's world. *Auk*, 54, 245-273.

LORENZ, K. (1958) The evolution of behaviour. *Scientific American*, 199, 67-78.

LORENZ, K. (1966) *On Aggression.* London: Methuen.

LOVEJOY, C.O. (1981) The origin of man. *Science*, 211, 341-350.

LOW, B.S. (1979) Sexual selection and human orientation. In: N.A. Chagnon & W. Irons (eds.) *Evolutionary biology and human social behaviour: An anthropological perspective.* North Scituate, MA: Duxbury Press.

LUMSDEN, C.J. & WILSON, E.O. (1981) *Genes, mind and culture.* Cambridge, MA: Harvard University Press.

MACE, R. & PAGEL, M. (1994) The comparative method in anthropology. *Current Anthropology*, 35, 549-564.

MACKINTOSH, N.J. (1978) Cognitive or associative theories of conditioning: Implications of an analysis of blocking. In S.H. Hulse, M.Fowler & W.K. Honig (Eds) *Cognitive Processes in Animal Behavior.* Hillsdale, NJ: Lawrence Erlbaum.

MARKS, I. (1987) *Fears, phobias and rituals: Panic, anxiety and their disorders.* New York: Oxford University Press.

MATHES, E.W. (1986) Jealousy and romantic love: A longitudinal study. *Psychological Reports*, 58, 885-886.

MAYNARD-SMITH, J. (1964) Group selection and kin selection. *Nature,* 201, 1145-1147.

MAYNARD-SMITH, J. (1993) *Did Darwin Get it Right?* London: Penguin.

McFARLAND, D. (1996) *Animal behaviour* (2nd edition). Harlow: Longman.

McGREW, W.C. & FEISTNER, A.T. (1992) Two nonhuman primate models for the evolution of human food sharing: Chimpanzees and callitrichids. In: J. Barkow, L. Cosmides & J. Tooby (eds.) *The adapted mind.* New York: Oxford University Press.

McILVEEN, R.J. & GROSS, R.D. (1997) *Developmental Psychology.* London: Hodder & Stoughton.

McNALLY, R.J. & STEKETEE, G.S. (1985) The etiology and maintenance of severe animal phobias. *Behaviour Research and Therapy*, 23, 431-435.

MEDNICK, S.A., GABRIELLI, W.F. & HUTCHINGS, B. (1978) Genetic factors in criminal behaviour: Evidence from an adoption cohort. *Science*, 224, 891-893.

MEGARGEE, E.I. (1966) Uncontrolled and overcontrolled personality types in extreme antisocial aggression. *Psychological Monographs: General and Applied* (Whole No. 611).

MELZACK, R. (1973) *The Puzzle of Pain.* New York: Basic Books.

MENZIES, R. (1937) Conditioned vasomotor responses in human subjects. *Journal of Psychology,* 4, 75-120.

MILLER, N.E. (1941) The frustration-aggression hypothesis. *Psychological Review,* 48, 337-342.

MILLER, G.F. (1998) How mate choice shaped human nature: A review of sexual selection and human evolution. In C. Crawford & D. Krebs (Eds.) *Handbook of evolutionary psychology*. Mahwah, NJ: Erlbaum.

MILLER, B.R. & MITCHELL, C.J. (1991) Genetic selection of a flavivirus-refractory strain of the yellow fever mosquito *Aedes aegypti. American Journal of Tropical Medicine & Hygiene*, 45, 399-407.

MILLER, J.F., MELAKANOS, J.J. & FALKOW, S.(1989) Coordinate regulation and sensory transduction in the control of bacterial virulence. *Science*, 243, 916-922.

MOCK, D.W. & PARKER, G.A. (1997) *The evolution of sibling rivalry*. Oxford: Oxford University Press.

MOLNAR, R.E. (1977) Analogies in the evolution of combat and display structures in ornithopods and ungulates. *Evolutionary Theory*, 3, 165-190.

MONTAGUE, A. (1961) Neonatal and infant immaturity in man. *Journal of the American Medical Association*, 178, 56-57.

MULLEN, B. (1986) Atrocity as a function of lynch mob composition: a self-attention perspective. *Personality & Social Psychology Bulletin*, 12, 187-197.

NESSE, R.M. (1987) An evolutionary perspective on panic disorder and agoraphobia. *Ethology and Sociobiology*, 8, 73-84.

NESSE, R.M. & WILLIAMS, G.C. (1996) *Evolution and healing*. London: Phoenix.

ORIANS, G.H. (1969) On the evolution of mating systems in birds and mammals. *American Naturalist*, 103, 589-603.

PACKER, C. (1977) Reciprocal altruism in *Papio anubis. Nature,* 265, 441-443.

PAGEL, M. (1997) Desperately concealing father: A theory of parent-infant resemblance. *Animal Behaviour*, 53, 973-981.

PARKER, G. (1984) The measurement of pathological parental style and its relevance to psychiatric disorder. *Social Psychiatry*, 19, 75-81.

PARKER, G.A. (1985) Models of parent-offspring conflict. V. Effects of the behaviour of two parents. *Animal Behaviour,* 33, 519-533.

PASSINGHAM, R.E. (1982) *The human primate*. New York: W.H. Freeman.

PETERS, W. (1987) *Chemotherapy and drug resistance in malaria*. London: Academic Press.

PINKER, S. (1994) *The language instinct*. London: Penguin.

PINKER, S. (1997) *How the mind works*. New York: Norton.

PLOMIN, R. (1988) The nature and nurture of cognitive abilities. In R.J. Sternberg (Ed.) *Advances in the Psychology of Human Intelligence,* Volume 4. Hillsdale, NJ: Erlbaum.

PLOTKIN, H. (1993) *Darwin machines and the nature of knowledge*. London: Penguin.

PLOTKIN, H. (1995) *The nature of knowledge*. London: Penguin.

POVINELLI, D.J., NELSON, K.E. & BOYSEN, S.T. (1992) Comprehension of role reversal in chimpanzees: evidence of role reversal? *Animal Behaviour,* 43, 633-640.

PROFET, M. (1991) The function of allergy: Immunological defence against toxins. *Quarterly Review of Biology*, 66, 23-62.

PROFET, M. (1992) Pregnancy sickness as adaptation: A deterrent to maternal ingestion of teratogens. In J.H. Barkow, L Cosmides & J. Tooby (Eds) *The Adapted Mind: Evolutionary Psychology and the Generation of Culture.* Oxford: Oxford University Press.

PROFET, M. (1993) Menstruation as a defence against pathogens transported by sperm. *Quarterly Review of Biology*, 68, 335-386.

RALEIGH, M. & McGUIRE, M. (1991) Serotonin in vervet monkeys. *Brain Research*, 559, 181-190.

RIDLEY, M. (1986) *The problems of evolution*. New York: Oxford University Press.

RIDLEY, M. (1993) *The red queen*. London: Penguin.

RIDLEY, M. (1995) *Animal behaviour* (2nd edition). Cambridge, MA: Blackwell.

RIDLEY, M. (1996) *The origins of virtue*. London: Viking.

ROSE, H. & ROSE, S. (2000) *Alas poor Darwin*. London: Penguin.

ROSENHAN, D.L. & SELIGMAN, M.E. (1984) *Abnormal Psychology*. New York: Norton.

RUMBAUGH, D. & SAVAGE-RUMBAUGH, S. (1994) Language and Apes. *APA Psychology Teacher Network,* January, 2-9.

SANAVIO, E. (1988) Obsessions and compulsions: The Padua inventory. *Behaviour Research and Therapy*, 26, 169-177.

SELIGMAN, M.E.P. (1970) On the generality of the laws of learning. *Psychology Review*, 77, 406-418.

SELIGMAN, M.E.P. (1971) Phobias and preparedness, *Behaviour Therapy*, 2, 307-320.

SELIGMAN, M.E.P. (1975) *Helplessness: On depression, development and death*. San Francisco: W.H. Freeman.

SHERRY, D.F. & GALEF, B.G. (1984) Cultural transmission without imitation: Milk bottle opening by birds. *Animal Behaviour*, 32, 937-938.

SHORT, R. (1976) The evolution of human reproduction. *Proceedings of The Royal Society B*, 195, 3-24.

SHOSTAK, M. (1981) *Nisa: The life and words of a !Kung woman*. Cambridge, MA: Harvard University Press.

SIANN, G. (1985) *Accounting for Aggression - Perspectives on Aggression and Violence.* London: Allen & Unwin.

SINGH, D. (1993) Adaptive significance of waist-to-hip ratio and female physical attractiveness. *Journal of Personality and Social Psychology*, 65, 293-307.

SKINNER, B.F. (1957) *Verbal behaviour*. New York: Appleton-Century-Crofts.

SKINNER, B.F. (1981) Selection by consequences. *Science*, 213, 501-504.

SLOBIN, D.I. (1975) On the nature of talk to children. In E.H. Lenneberg & E. Lenneberg (Eds) *Foundations of Language Development,* Volume 1. New York: Academic Press.

SLOBIN, D.I. (1986) *The Cross-Linguistic Study of Language Acquisition*. Hillsdale, NJ: Erlbaum.

SMITH, R.L. (1984) Human sperm competition. In: R.L. Smith (ed.) *Sperm competition and the evolution of animal mating systems*. London: Academic Press.

SPERBER, D. (1994) The modularity of thought and the epidemiology of representation. In: L.Hirschfield and R. Gelman (eds.) *Mapping the mind*. Cambridge: Cambridge University Press.

STEAD, W.W. & LOFGREN, J.P. (1991) Tuberculosis and HIV infection. *New England Journal of Medicine*, 325, 1882.

STERN, D. (1977) *The First Relationship: Infant and Mother.* London: Fontana.
STEVENS, A. & PRICE, J. (1996) *Evolutionary psychiatry.* London: Routledge.
STROBER, M. & KATZ, J.L. (1987) Do eating disorders and affective disorders share a common aetiology? *International Journal of Eating Disorders,* 6, 171-180.
SUDRE, P. TEN DAM, G. & KOCHI, A. (1992) Tuberculosis: A global overview of the situation today. *Bulletin of the World Health Organisation,* 70, 149-159.
SUGIYAMA, Y. (1984) Proximate factors of infanticide among langurs at Dharwar: A reply to Boggess. In G. Hausfater & S.B. Hrdy (Eds) *Infanticide: Comparative and Evolutionary Perspectives.* New York: Aldine.
SURBEY, M.K. (1978) Anorexia nervosa, amenorrhea and adaptation. *Ethology & Sociobiology,* 8, 47-62.
SYMONS, D. (1979) *The evolution of human sexuality.* New York: Oxford University Press.
THORNHILL, R. & GANGESTAD, S.W. (1993) Human facial beauty: Averageness, symmetry and parasite resistance. *Human Nature,* 4, 237-269.
THORNHILL, R. & THORNHILL, N. (1983) Human rape: An evolutionary perspective. *Ethology & Sociobiology,* 4, 137-173.
THORNHILL, R. & THORNHILL, N. (1989) The evolution of psychological pain. In: R. Bell & N. Bell (eds.) *Sociobiology and the social sciences.* Lubbock, TX: Texas University Press.
THORNHILL, N. & THORNHILL, R. (1990) Evolutionary analysis of psychological pain of rape victims I: The effect of victim's age and marital status. *Ethology & Sociobiology,* 11, 155-176.
TIZARD, B., JOSEPH, A., COOPERMAN, O. & TIZARD J. (1972) Environmental effects on language development: A study of young children in long-stay residential nurseries. *Child Development,* 43, 337-358.
TOMARKEN, A.J., MINEKA, S. & COOK, M. (1989) Fear-relevant selective associations and covariation bias. *Journal of Abnormal Psychology,* 98, 381-394.
TOMASELLO, M., KRUGER, A.C. & RATNER, H.H. (1993) Cultural learning. *Behavioural & Brain Sciences,* 16, 495-552.
TOOBY, J. & COSMIDES, L. (1992) *The adapted mind.* New York: Oxford University Press.
TOOBY, J. & COSMIDES, L. (1996) Friendship and the banker's paradox: Other pathways to the evolution of adaptations to altruism. *Proceedings of The British Academy,* 88, 119-143.
TORGERSEN, S. (1983) Genetic factors in anxiety disorders. *Archives of General Psychiatry,* 40, 1085-1089.
TREVATHAN, W. (1987) *Human Birth: An Evolutionary Perspective.* New York: Aldine de Gruyter.
TRIVERS, R.L. (1971) The evolution of reciprocal altruism. *Quarterly Review of Biology,* 46, 35-57.
TRIVERS, R.L. (1972) Parental investment and sexual selection. In B. Campbell (Ed.) *Sexual selection and the descent of man.* Chicago: Aldine.
TRIVERS, R.L. (1974) Parent-offspring conflict. *American Zoologist,* 14, 249-264.
TRIVERS, R.L. (1985) *Social Evolution.* New York: Benjamin Cummings.
WASON, P.C. (1983) Realism and rationality in the selection task. In J. Evans (Ed.) *Thinking and reasoning: Psychological approaches.* London: Routledge & Kegan Paul.
WASSER, S.K. & BARASH, D.P. (1983) Reproductive suppression among female mammals: Implications for biomedicine and sexual selection theory. *Quarterly Review of Biology,* 58, 513-538.
WATSON, J.B. & RAYNER, R. (1920) Conditioned emotioned reactions. *Journal of Experimental Psychology,* 3, 1-14.
WESCHLER, D. (1944) *The measurement of adult intelligence.* Baltimore, MD: Williams & Wilkins.
WICKLER, W. (1967) Socio-sexual signals and their intraspecific imitation among primates. In D. Morris (Ed.) *Primate Ethology.* London: Weidenfeld & Nicolson.
WILHELM, K. & PARKER, G. (1989) Is sex necessarily a risk factor to depression? *Psychological Medicine,* 19, 401-413.
WILKINSON, G. (1984) Reciprocal food-sharing in vampire bats. *Scientific American,* 262, 76-82.
WILLERMAN, L. (1979) *The psychology of individual and group differences.* San Francisco: W.H. Freeman.
WILLIAMS, G.C. (1996) *Plan and purpose in nature.* New York: Basic Books.
WILLS, C. (1993) *The runaway brain: The evolution of human uniqueness.* New York: Basic Books.
WILSON, E.O. (1975) *Sociobiology: The New Synthesis.* Harvard, MA: The Belknap Press.
WILSON, E.O. (1978) *On Human Nature.* Cambridge, MA: Harvard University Press.
WILSON, M. & DALY, M. (1992) The man who mistook his wife for a chattel. In J. Barkow, L. Cosmides & J. Tooby (Eds.) *The adapted mind.* New York: Oxford University Press.
WOLF, A.P. (1970) Childhood association and sexual attraction: A further test of the Westermarck hypothesis. *American Anthropologist,* 72, 503-515.
WOOLFENDEN, G.E. & FITZPATRICK, J.W. (1984) *The Florida Scrub Jay.* Princeton, NJ: Princeton University Press.
WRANGHAM, R. (1999) In military incompetence adaptive? *Evolution & Human Behaviour,* 20, 3-17.
ZAHAVI, A. (1975) Mate selection: A selection for a handicap. *Journal of Theoretical Biology,* 53, 205-214.

INDEX

Page numbers which appear in bold refer to definitions and main explanations of particular concepts:

PICTURE CREDITS

The authors and publishers would like to thank the following copyright holders for their permission to reproduce illustrative materials in this book:

Action Plus for Figure 8.3 (p. 68) © Neil Tingle and Figure 15.1 (p. 132) © Glyn Kirk; **AKG Photo** for Figure 15.3 (p. 138) © Heinrich Hoffman; **Bruce Coleman Collection** for Figure 2.2 (p. 14) © Kim Taylor and Figure 8.2 (p. 67) © Robert Maier; **Cambridge University Press** for Figure 9.1 (p. 78) from H. Cronin, *The ant and the peacock* (1991); **Corbis** for Figure 5.4 (p. 44); **Format Partners** for Figure 7.1 (p. 57) © Judy Harrison; **Format Photographers** for Figure 14.1 (p. 125) © Joanne O'Brien; **Frank Lane Picture Agency** for Figure 6.1 (p. 47) © J. Zimmerman; **Sally and Richard Greenhill** for Figure 5.2 (p. 40) © Sally Greenhill; **Illustrated London News** for Figure 1.3 (p. 2); **Life File** for Figure 1.5 (p. 5) and Figure 14.3 (p. 127) © Emma Lee, Figure 7.2 (p. 59) © Nicola Sutton, Figure 7.4 (p. 63) © Angela Maynard, Figure 10.1 (p. 86) © Terence Waeland and Figure 13.4 (p. 117) © Graham Buchan; **Professor Leanne T Nash**, Arizona State University for Figure 7.3 (p. 60); **Press Associated Photos** for Figure 8.1 (p. 66) and Figure 8.4 (p. 72) © Ron Edmonds Staff; **Rex Features** for Figure 14.4 (p. 128); **Ronald Grant Archive** for Figure 14.2 (p. 126); **Dr Duane Rumbaugh**, Georgia State University for Figure 12.3 (p. 106); **Science Photo Library** for Figure 4.1 (p. 30) © D Phillips, Figure 13.2 (p. 114) © Noah Pritz and Figure 13.3 (p. 116) © Matt Meadows, Peter Arnold Inc.; **Super Stock** for Figure 6.2 (p. 50).

Every effort has been made to obtain the necessary permission with reference to copyright material. The publishers apologise if inadvertently any sources remain unacknowledged and will be glad to make the necessary arrangements at the earliest opportunity.